RENTON'S DICTIONARY OF STOCK EXCHANGE AND INVESTMENT TERMS

An annotated Guide and Almanac for Share and Property Investors at all levels

NE Renton AM

UNICORN BOOKS
BUSINESS

Publishers
UNICORN BOOKS

J-3/16, Daryaganj, New Delhi-110002
☎ 23275434, 23262683/84 • Fax: 011-23257790
E-mail: unicornbooks@vsnl.com • *Website:* www.unicornbooks.in

Distributors

Pustak Mahal®, Delhi

J-3/16, Daryaganj, New Delhi-110002
☎ 23276539, 23272783, 23272784 • *Fax:* 011-23260518
E-mail: info@pustakmahal.com • *Website:* www.pustakmahal.com

Sales Centres

- 10-B, Netaji Subhash Marg, Daryaganj, New Delhi-110002
  ☎ 23268292, 23268293, 23279900 • *Fax:* 011-23280567
  E-mail: salespmahal@airtelmail.in • *E-mail:* rapidexdelhi@indiatimes.com
- 6686, Khari Baoli, Delhi-110006
  ☎ 23944314, 23911979
- **Bengaluru:** ☎ 22234025 • *Telefax:* 22240209
  E-mail: pustak@airtelmail.in • pustak@sancharnet.in
- **Mumbai:** ☎ 22010941
  E-mail: rapidex@bom5.vsnl.net.in
- **Patna:** ☎ 3294193 • *Telefax:* 0612-2302719
  E-mail: rapidexptn@rediffmail.com
- **Hyderabad:** *Telefax:* 040-24737290
  E-mail: pustakmahalhyd@yahoo.co.in

ISBN 978-81-7806-175-7

Edition : 2009

Printed at: *Unique Color Carton, New Delhi-110064*

To those users of my investment books who find themselves confused by the gobbledegook in their wider reading

Introduction

Many ordinary words have specialised meanings on the share or property markets. All the definitions set out in this book relate to such words as used in an investment or business context.

It should, of course, be noted that a dictionary definition designed for popular use and covering only a few lines of text cannot possibly do justice to a highly technical subject.

Readers desiring a fuller discussion of some aspects are therefore referred to other books, such as the present writer's companion volumes, *Understanding the Stock Exchange* and *Understanding Investment Property.*

For the convenience of non-technical readers of this work the explanations of the various terms have usually been deliberately expressed in shortened form and in simplified language rather than by using, say, the more precise words of an Act of Parliament or a formal accounting standard. Naturally, when the need arises, such fuller authorities should be referred to.

It should also be borne in mind that reading a definition of, say, a taxation term is no substitute for getting proper advice from a qualified tax expert.

In order to make the book more useful some philosophical views have in selected cases been added to the purely factual information. The author takes full responsibility for these.

Several important topical subjects seemed to call for treatment in greater depth than was appropriate within the scope of the short main listings - for example, return on equity, guarantees, margin lending, stock exchange indices and derivatives. Accordingly, such themes have been developed into separate mini-essays which are set out in the chapters which follow.

Contents

Assorted Definitions from Hell

actuary: a person who passes as an expert on the basis of a prolific ability to produce an infinite variety of incomprehensible figures calculated with micrometric precision from the vaguest of assumptions based on debatable evidence from inconclusive data derived by persons of questionable reliability for the sole purpose of confusing an already hopelessly befuddled group of persons who never read the statistics anyway (based on a definition by Kathleen Miller).

business plan: a flexible arrangement, put together by a company's management in order to impress lenders and regulatory authorities, and possibly enhanced by carefully worded references to modern digital technology, established games theory, tested interpersonal relationships, stochastic work profiles, time phase communications tools, random economic activities, reciprocal mission statements, purposeful dynamic options, well designed locational incremental functions, third generation style issues, major logistic programs, statistical engineering concepts, prime operational hardware, stable supervisory strategies and the like.

corporate objectives: a company's goals, normally laid down by its board of directors, especially with respect to the various Critical Success Factors (CSFs) usually applicable to it and also to its general risk profile as determined in an independent optimal audit/review approach which has regard to its resource requirements and to the skills needed to ensure that maximum value is realised from the function whether under base conditions or otherwise.

bull market: a random market movement causing an investor to mistake himself for a financial genius.

financial planner: a professional who says to his client: "I've reviewed your financial picture, and if we manage your money properly, there should be plenty for both of us."

satisfactory return (listed company): either a profitable result or a loss resulting from circumstances said to be beyond the company's control, such as government action or inaction, adverse weather conditions, computer problems, trade union intransigence, disloyalty on the part of customers, criticisms by consumer groups, a failure to get or retain required licences, the millennium bug, activity by environmentalists and/or the advent of unexpected competition.

TWO USEFUL RULES OF THUMB

- The period in which money doubles is 70 divided by the rate of interest.
- The period in which money trebles is 115 divided by the rate of interest.

These approximations allow:

- the relevant period to be calculated for a known rate of interest
- the relevant rate of interest to be calculated for a known period.

Thus, for example, at 5 per cent per annum Rs.100 grows to Rs. 200 in about 14 years. Conversely, if the period is 7 years, then the required rate for doubling is 10 per cent per annum.

Note: These rules give acceptable approximations at normal interest rate levels, but, of course, they cannot be used where precision is required.

DID YOU REALISE?

A one per cent differential in the investment returns offered by two alternative investment proposals does not sound very great.

However, in a superannuation context even such a small reduction in the overall earnings rate can make a major difference to the eventual size of someone's ultimate retirement benefits.

To illustrate, Rs. 100,000 would grow to Rs. 4.53 million at ten per cent per annum over 40 years but only to Rs. 3.14 million at nine per cent per annum.

SEVEN REASONS NOT TO INVEST

- I've never done it before.
- It's too radical a change.
- My family will never let me try it.
- My bank won't like it.
- I'm not ready for it.
- You're right, but ...
- Good thought, but impractical.

About the Author

Nick Renton is a consulting actuary, commercial arbitrator, company director and writer. He was born in 1931 and qualified as a Fellow of the Faculty of Actuaries in 1957. He is also a Fellow of the Institute of Actuaries of Australia.

He holds an Investment Adviser's Licence and qualifications as a commercial arbitrator. In 1975 he was elected a Fellow of the Securities Institute of Australia for his services to the industry.

After 15 years as Principal Officer of a life insurance company he became the first Executive Director of the Life Offices' Association of Australia from 1975 to 1979. He was Executive Director of the Life Insurance Federation of Australia from its formation in 1979 until 1986. In those capacities he acted as the official spokesman for the life insurance industry.

He is now an independent business consultant to leading stockbrokers, insurance companies, employer organisations, government agencies and others. He also serves on the boards of several financial institutions and is in great demand as a speaker at seminars and conferences.

He was the founder and first president of the Australian Shareholders' Association and has been Federal president of the Australian Society of Security Analysts and Victorian chairman of the Commercial Law Association of Australia.

Nick Renton has been published by 12 different publishers in Australia and the United States. He has written books about more different topics than any other Australian author.

His *Guide for Meetings and Organisations*, published by the Law Book Company, has been widely used as a reference work on all aspects of chairmanship and the running of voluntary associations since it first appeared in 1961. It deals with many practical aspects of meetings procedure not covered in Joske and is now in a two-volume 8th edition.

He is the author of nearly 70 published books - covering shares, property, managed investments, taxation, wills, good writing, public relations, the Internet and the Australian economy - as well as of numerous papers to professional bodies.

He has published nearly 600 articles in newspapers and financial journals in recent years. He has presented papers to conferences of linguists and contributed to a textbook on journalism.

In 1992 he was awarded the prestigious H M Jackson Memorial Prize for two of his works, *Understanding Dividend Imputation* and the *Retirement Handbook*.

In 1995 he received the Ken Millar Award for his best-selling *Understanding the Stock Exchange* and his highly controversial *Company Directors: Masters or Servants?*

Nick Renton maintains his own web site of over 130 pages at http://users.bigpond.net.au/renton

As a free community service this site also invites questions on meetings procedure, family trusts, style and investment terms.

He was made a Member of the Order of Australia in 2004.

He is married and has three children. He lives in Melbourne, Australia.

Preface

This dictionary of investment terms is designed for ordinary people who are interested in saving and investing. It will help them to get more out of the vast amount of financial and economic literature currently available - the market pages of daily newspapers, brokers' circulars, prospectuses, company reports, property reviews, specialist financial publications, individually-tailored plans by investment advisers, web sites, and so on.

This new edition has been extensively revised and expanded. It includes a selection of about 3300 investment and related terms in common use and presented in alphabetical order. A wide area is covered - everything from arbitrage to money laundering, and from franking accounts to poverty traps. The symbols used to denote currencies and some terms commonly used by overseas stock exchanges have also been included.

The dictionary now contains many terms not found in similar works.

Some expressions are derived from companies and securities law, some from income tax, GST or social security legislation, some from stock exchange rules and practice, some from accounting standards, some from the common law, and so on.

Others come from the usages of accountants, actuaries, auditors, bankers, commodity dealers, computer experts, demographers, economists, financial planners, geologists, institutions, insurers, investment advisers, journalists, lawyers, mathematicians, property investors, real estate agents, security analysts, statisticians and superannuation practitioners.

Other terms again refer to options and futures, to corporate governance issues, to managed funds, to trusts, to meetings procedure and to the Internet.

The adoption of new technologies has been responsible for some entries. A few years ago terms such as *straight through processing* and *program trading* would have been unheard of. As all these verbal developments clearly demonstrate, the pace of change in the investment world continues unabated.

Of course, sometimes clichés are deliberately used in order to sound impressive when nothing much is really being conveyed - as when a broker's circular advises its readers to be "selective"!

Some entries from the previous edition have been removed or rewritten, often in order to reflect legislative changes.

JARGON

The world of finance has its own peculiar jargon. This is understandable - most experts like to save time by employing shorthand expressions for concepts frequently used by them. However, an everyday phrase to a stockbroker, accountant, lawyer or financial planner is not necessarily a term previously encountered by that expert's clients.

The use of jargon is, of course, not confined to stock exchange situations. Even buying a house involves the use of unintelligible abbreviations in estate agents' advertisements.

Again, superannuation literature is full of references to esoteric terms such as *rollovers* and *eligible termination payments*. The tax office loves to use technical expressions such as *reduced cost base* and *tax offsets* (formerly *rebates*).

Recently the accounting profession decided to replace some old and very familiar terms. A *balance sheet* has become a *statement of financial position* and a *profit and loss account* has become a *statement of financial performance*. Such moves seem to be change for the sake of change.

ABBREVIATIONS AND ACRONYMS

A recent phenomenon of great annoyance to many people is the tendency of writers to use abbreviations and acronyms without explaining them on their first appearance.

For this reason a large number of abbreviations and acronyms encountered in financial writings have been included in the listings.

NEW INVESTORS

A combination of factors has brought many first time investors into the stock market. These factors include:

- a number of privatisation megafloats
- their attendant publicity, often giving the impression that it is all too easy to make money on the stock exchange
- a number of spin-off companies
- the "free" shares handed out as part of demutualisation processes
- relatively low interest rates, making growth stocks more appealing than fixed interest investments
- the popularity of the dividend imputation system and its apparent tax-free element
- the emergence of discount brokers and the abolition of stamp duty on share transfers, greatly reducing transaction costs
- the expansion of Internet broking
- the increase in employee share schemes
- the attractions of shareholder discount schemes.

These days many people have large sums of money to invest - from sources such as lump sum superannuation benefits or retrenchment packages, or the proceeds from the sale of a home or a business.

Such people often realise that they know very little about investment matters and accordingly they seek out some competent professional advice.

They then encounter an unexpected problem - namely, the fact that their adviser uses a number of technical terms which they do not understand. For all the use this is the adviser might as well be speaking to them in a foreign language!

Should they stop there and then and thus display their ignorance? People hesitate before doing that.

On the one hand, they naturally enough do not want to look silly. They have probably made it in life, with high qualifications in their own field, leading to a successful career.

On the other hand, and more importantly, they do not want to add to the complications of the interview. They may already have been caught out in not having pat answers to some significant questions being put to them, such as their investment objectives, their attitude to taking a calculated risk, their likely cash flow pattern, and so on.

So they pretend to understand what is being said and they make intelligent noises - but a lot of the advice has probably gone over their heads. This can be highly dangerous when large amounts of money are at stake, particularly if that money has to last them for the rest of their lives.

LANGUAGE DEVELOPMENTS

Newspaper headlines and television bulletins have helped to make names such as the "Sensex" and its movement up or down so many points, as well as concepts such as family trusts, capital gains tax and negative gearing, widely understood.

However, the communications task is not assisted by practices such as the following:

- The use without explanation of slang terms, such as "bull" (an investor who expects the market to rise), "bear" (one who expects the market to fall) and "stag" (an investor who takes up new shares in a float with a view to selling them for an immediate profit).
- The use of several rather different expressions to mean virtually the same thing, such as "imputation credit" and "franking rebate".
- The use of the same technical term in two or more unconnected senses - for example, "call" in relation to contributing shares and call options.
- The use of ordinary words in special senses, such as "rights" or the "writing" of options or the "passing" of a dividend or "Chinese walls".
- The tendency for listed companies to invent their own pet terms for Dividend Election Plans and the like.
- The practice of unit trust managers to employ non-uniform expressions for the entry and exit prices of their units.

- The paradoxical use by life offices of the (normally) fixed interest expression, "bond", to refer to an equity-linked product.
- The occasional use of London terms such as "jobber" or "acceptance house".
- Differences in United States and local terminology - for example, "stockowner" for "shareholder" or "common stock" for "ordinary shares". In some cases the terms used reflect the fact that the United States is really a remarkably backward country, with astonishing inefficiencies in its share registration procedures.
- The gradual change in the meaning of certain terms, such as "warrants" (originally, "bearer shares"; more recently, "options issued by third parties").
- The use of a word which implies the end of the queue, namely, "unsecured", in relation to unsecured notes, when in fact these rank ahead of shares.
- The use of colourful metaphors such as "white knights" or "junk bonds".

Some expressions which it would be useful to have still need to be coined. To illustrate, what should one call the practice of selectively quoting past results in managed fund prospectuses and the like, in order to give the best possible impression of a fund manager's past performance - for example, by carefully choosing the starting and finishing dates of the period for which the returns achieved are being quoted?

Nick Renton AM
http://users.bigpond.net.au/renton
nrenton@bigpond.net.au

CHAPTER 1

The Return On Equity

Investors are no doubt familiar with the concept of "yield" in relation to their own share portfolios. However, they often find some other technical concepts, such as "return on equity" (ROE) and "return on assets" (ROA) slightly confusing. Both are measures of the efficiency of a company.

The return on assets (ROA) is the ratio obtained by dividing a company's earnings before interest and tax (EBIT) by the gross tangible assets, expressed as a percentage. The calculations are best done using weighted average assets figures for the year.

A less commonly encountered variation of this theme is the return on capital employed (ROCE). Instead of using gross tangible assets in the denominator it uses gross tangible assets less current liabilities.

The return on equity (ROE) is the ratio obtained by dividing a company's profit (net of preference dividends, if any) by the shareholders' funds (net of preference capital and intangible assets, if any), expressed as a percentage. The calculations are best done using weighted average shareholders' funds for the year.

The profit after tax is often used for this exercise, but using profit before tax gives more meaningful year-by-year comparisons if the rate of company tax changes.

The consistency in the numerator and denominator in all these ratios should be noted. If the former is "earnings before/after the deduction of interest" then the latter has to be "assets before/after the deduction of liabilities".

If the ROA is less than the company's weighted average cost of capital (WACC) then, unless this is rectified, continued trading will just destroy shareholder value.

If the ROA is less than the risk-free sovereign bond interest rate then the investors would be better off if they put the company into voluntary liquidation and reinvested the proceeds elsewhere.

These ratios can also be used for comparing different companies with each other and for comparing a single company's results from year to year.

However, important as these ratios can be in helping to identify companies which investors should avoid, they are less useful in picking bargains. This is because the ratios are independent of market price. A very efficient company might also constitute a very expensive investment, as when its price earnings ratio is unduly high.

Instinctively many people may feel uncomfortable when a listed company has huge liabilities in relation to its assets - especially if it is geared to the maximum extent possible. Yet in such a case the shareholders' equity against the total assets will be small and thus an impressive-sounding ROE can result.

Of course, the result will be truly impressive only if the company performs well, but there is nothing wrong with that. By definition this particular yardstick takes into account a company's profits from all sources.

To illustrate: If a company borrows money at, say, 9 per cent and then earns 16 per cent on the funds used in its business then those extra 7 percentage points are just as much a legitimate part of its total profits as when it deals in goods which cost it, say, Rs. 1000 to manufacture but which it then sells for Rs. 1500.

However, the instincts of those worried by the arithmetic are also correct. A heavily geared company is more risky than a lightly geared company, other things being equal. If the earnings rate on the borrowed funds which it is using are ever less than the interest rate which it is paying then it will go backwards. If its assets fall in value while its liabilities do not or if it is unable to renew loans when they fall due then it could even become insolvent.

While the return on equity figure is important, a prospective shareholder should never invest on the basis of just a single yardstick without taking other factors into consideration.

Some investors may wish to avoid companies entirely if they regard the level of their borrowings in relation to their assets as too high. Alternatively, they may be willing to accept the additional risk if they feel that the potential benefits in relation to the share price are sufficient to compensate them for this extra hazard.

CHAPTER 2

What Does the Term "Guaranteed" Really Mean?

Most investors know that when they get investment advice from a stockbroker or a financial planner it is based on value judgements and that the advice thus comes without guarantees of any sort.

BANKS

However, the word "guaranteed" is thrown about in many investment contexts and frequently involves misunderstandings. For example, many people mistakenly believe that bank deposits are somehow guaranteed by the central bank of the country.

They are not - they are really just unsecured loans to a private company which could fail in the same way as any other private company could, through fraud or mismanagement, and, indeed, as a major old-established British bank (Barings) did not so long ago. Some overseas banking institutions have also got into trouble in recent years.

The Reserve Bank of India (RBI) supervises the banks and expresses a willingness to help them out if they are solvent but ever have a temporary liquidity crisis.

INVESTMENT BONDS

Then there are the investment bonds which are widely being marketed as "capital guaranteed".

Usually this just means that they are backed by fixed interest securities, the capital value of which is unlikely to fluctuate much.

ADVERTISEMENTS

Investment advertisements should always be read critically. Whenever anything is said to be "guaranteed" several important questions arise:

- Precisely what is being guaranteed? For example, is it capital or income or both? Does the guarantee apply at all times or can it be called upon only once on some defined future day, possibly many years away?
- Just how strong is the guarantor in relation to the sums actually being guaranteed? If a Rs. 5,000 company "guarantees" the repayment of a Rs. 250 million debt then that guarantee is hardly worth having. A guarantee is only as good as its guarantor.

On a slightly different aspect, it is also nonsensical for the contractual obligations of some entity to be "guaranteed" by the entity itself - the word implies a promise by a third party.

SUBSIDIARIES

Subsidiaries and associates of listed companies are sometimes listed companies in their own right and/or engage in borrowing from the general public. The name of the subsidiary or associate company may or may not resemble that of the parent company. It may or may not be using the parent company's logo.

It should be noted that in the absence of specific guarantees or other contractual arrangements there is no legal obligation on a parent company to assist persons who may be investors in, or creditors of, one of its subsidiaries if such an entity ever gets into financial trouble. In fact, the primary obligation on company directors is to look after the interests *of their own shareholders*.

However, depending on the circumstances, a parent company may, of course, regard itself, especially for commercial reasons, as having a *moral* duty to bail out persons who dealt with a subsidiary in the belief that the parent would always stand behind it.

SPECULATIVE INVESTMENTS

Prospectuses and publicity material for futures funds and other highly speculative ventures sometimes feature a guarantee of some sort in order to make the scheme concerned sound more attractive to conservative investors.

Special attention is drawn to one aspect of this theme - a guarantee from, say, a bank or some other highly reputable institution to the effect that the investors will get all of the original invested amounts back at the end of a certain period, say seven years.

This is made possible by placing about half of each investor's stake in relatively safe fixed interest paper (possibly a zero coupon stock) and using only the balance for the speculative purposes featured by the promoter.

At about 10 per cent per annum compound interest, money doubles in seven years, so nothing particularly outstanding is involved in any such arrangements. It is important to note that such guarantees usually operate only at the end of the stipulated term. They thus do little to protect investors wishing to quit before then.

A guarantee on these lines is sound enough - but hardly free of cost. Merely getting one's own money back without return and without adjustment for inflation is no great bargain.

In any case, any investors so minded can replicate such an arrangement themselves. If they are prepared to forego all annual return for some years then they can ensure the preservation of their capital by putting half of the funds into some safe interest-bearing security and exposing only the other half to any investment risk.

While such arrangements may have a certain amount of marketing appeal, there is a distinct lack of logic behind them. Why should an investor who is looking for the excitement and potential gains of some speculative venture and who desires to back the entrepreneurial judgement of the promoter concerned be forced to put about half of the stake into decidedly dull fixed interest securities?

Having to pay relatively high initial and ongoing fees for the privilege of investing in such paper only makes the whole proposition even less attractive. Promoters wishing to offer such a guarantee to their more timid customers would attract more business from others if the guarantee instead of being compulsory were merely an optional extra.

OTHER ASPECTS

Again, some cash management trusts involve a guarantee from a related company in respect of the face value of the units and all previously declared interest. However, unless the shareholders' funds of that company are large in relation to the trust fund then that guarantee may not be particularly meaningful.

Government loans are usually marketed as "guaranteed". They can indeed be regarded as risk-free in the sense that the regular payment of interest on the due dates and the repayment of the capital on the stipulated maturity date are assured.

CHAPTER 3

What Does the Term "Value" Really Mean?

Shareholders do not always appreciate that the valuation of assets in a company's books is an art rather than a science.

There is no unique "true value" for any asset except at the moment of its sale to an arm's length party.

To illustrate:

- The value of a company in a forced fire sale is one thing.
- Its value on a leisurely voluntary winding up is another.
- Its value as a going concern is different again.
- Its value to keen bidders in a takeover duel, especially when these are looking for an alternative to the expense of setting up a fresh organisation, may be considerably higher than this latter figure.

All these values will, except by coincidence, be different from:

- historical cost
- historical cost indexed for inflation.

In the past it was regarded as desirable to be deliberatively conservative in company balance sheets. However, understatements can be as misleading as overstatements. They can, for example, cause investors to sell out too cheaply, either on the market or when a takeover bid is received; they can also lead to unmeritorious cross-generation subsidies.

In particular, the assets held on any particular balance date and shown in the balance sheet at what is referred to as their "book value" may have a very different value to the enterprise while it is a going concern from the value which they might realise in other circumstances.

To illustrate this aspect further, the stock on hand can be valued, inter alia:

- at cost
- at its market selling value
- at its replacement value.

Certain assets, such as plant and machinery, have a limited economic life, after which they are worthless or nearly so (scrap value). In such cases, it is appropriate to write down or "depreciate" the original cost in gradual stages each year over the expected lifetime of the asset and in due course to write off completely any excess of the residual book value over its realisation price at the time of its disposal.

Such charges constitute part of the costs of running a business.

More than one method for depreciating assets is available and the expected lifetime can itself be a matter of debate.

Working in the opposite direction is inflation. For example, land purchased some years ago may now be worth several times its original cost. To leave the book value unaltered in such circumstances would be rather misleading.

The valuation of assets and liabilities in a company balance sheet involve judgement on the part of the directors in the first instance and later on on the part of the company's auditor.

The precise valuation approach adopted by each company has to be spelt out in notes to its accounts.

See also the definitions of "market value" and "mark to market".

CHAPTER 4

What is a Stock Exchange Index?

An Index is an indicator that gives information about the price movements of products in the financial, commodities or any other markets. Stock market indices are meant to capture the overall behaviour of equity markets. They are created by selecting a group of stocks that are representative of the whole market or a specified sector or segment of the market. Financial indices are constructed to measure price movements of stocks, bonds, T-bills and other forms of investments. An Index is calculated with reference to a base period and a base index value.

Stock market indexes are useful for a variety of reasons. Some of them are:

- They provide a historical comparison of returns on money invested in the stock market against other forms of investments such as gold or debt.
- They can be used as a standard against which to compare the performance of an equity fund.
- An index is a lead indicator of the performance of the overall economy or a sector of the economy.
- Stock indexes reflect highly up to date information.

- Modern financial applications such as Index Funds, Index Futures, Index Options play an important role in financial investments and risk management.

A number of different stock exchange indices covering the Indian market are produced each day. Some cover shares in specific industries while others cover various combinations of these.

In each case the index number represents the market capitalisation of all the shares concerned (for each company, the price per share multiplied by the number of shares on issue), expressed as a number relative to a base number.

Thus if an index is 6500.0 on a particular day and the shares concerned in total go up 1 per cent in value (after adjustment for any capital raised or repaid) then the index will be up 65 points at 6565.0.

Listed companies with high market capitalisations have a greater effect on the indices than smaller companies. However, the volume of turnover has no effect.

Indices give a quick picture of the weighted average price movements in the market as a whole or in a particular sector of the market. The *percentage movement* up or down - rather than the precise number of points - gives the message. While such indices have some conceptual limitations they can be used as yardsticks by which the performance of a particular portfolio can be measured objectively.

Movements in indices can also be used to make comparisons between Indian and international markets.

Indian Stock Exchanges are a structured marketplace for the conduct of trading in company stocks and other securities. There are 23 recognized stock exchanges in India to provide nation-wide services to investors and to facilitate the issue and redemption of securities and other financial instruments. The two most important exchange houses are the Bombay Stock Exchange and the National Stock Exchange. The index of the Bombay Stock Exchange, BSE Sensex is a value-weighted index composed of largest 30 companies. Similarly, National Stock Exchange's S&P CNX Nifty 50 is a value-weighted index composed of largest 50 companies. Securities and Exchange Board of India(SEBI) supervises the activities of stock markets, regulates the functioning of stock exchanges and intermediaries and registers foreign investors trading in Indian stocks.

Following are the BSE's Indices:

Major Indices:

BSE Sensex	BSE 100 Index
BSE 200 Index	BSE 500 Index
BSE MIDCAP Index	BSE SMLCAP Index
BSE IPO Index	

BSE Sectoral Indices:

BSE REALTY Index	BSE POWER Index
BSE TECk Index	BSE PSU Index
BSE AUTO Index	BSE BANKEX
BSE CG Index	BSE CD Index
BSE FMCG Index	BSE HC Index
BSE IT Index	BSE METAL Index
BSE OIL & GAS Index	

BSE Dollex Indices:

Dollex-30

Dollex-100

Dollex-200

Following are the National Stock Exchange (NSE) indices:

Major Indices:

S&P CNX Nifty	CNX Nifty Junior
CNX 100	S&P CNX 500
CNX Midcap	Nifty Midcap 50

S&P CNX Defty

(S&P CNX Defty is S&P CNX Nifty, but measured in US dollars.)

Other Indices:

CNX IT Index	CNX Bank Index
CNX FMCG Index	CNX PSE Index
CNX MNC Index	CNX Service Sector Index
S&P CNX Industry Indices	Customised Indices
CNX Energy Index	CNX Pharma Index
CNX Infrastructure Index	CNX PSU BANK Index
CNX Realty Index	S&P ESG India Index

S&P CNX Nifty Shariah / S&P CNX 500 Shariah

In compiling these indices brokerage is ignored. No adjustments are made for either the sudden price drops as particular shares go ex dividend or the gradual build up of prices between successive dividend distributions. Nor are the indices adjusted for inflation.

CHAPTER 5

What Does the Term "Margin Lending" Mean?

The term *margin lending* is used to refer to a special type of interest-bearing loan secured by shares. Such loans are available from banks, but they are also marketed by organisations associated with some stockbrokers. A minimum loan size is usually imposed.

The precise details of margin loans can vary according to the practices of the lender concerned, but the chief characteristics are commonly as follows:

- The loan is secured over one or more specific parcels of shares. These can be shares already held or shares being purchased with the loan funds or a combination of both.
- The maximum loan granted is based on the market value of the shares pledged and the lender's views of their quality and the volatility of their share price. Typically 30 to 70 per cent of the value of a stock can be borrowed.
- The shares will need to be those of companies on the lender's list of approved securities - basically non-speculative situations. Some unit trusts may also be acceptable. Potential borrowers should scrutinise the list of a proposed lender in advance in order to make sure that it is wide enough for their

needs; it is likely to be in practice, because the leading stocks make up the bulk of the total market capitalisation.

- The shares can be held by individuals, companies, partnerships or trusts.
- The loan can, if desired, be in a different name from that used for the shares.
- No other security needs to be provided.
- No credit checks are required.
- The market value of the total portfolio which has been pledged is monitored by the lender every day. If it drops so that the amount of cover falls below a defined ratio then the lender makes a *margin call.* For example, if the original maximum loan was 70 per cent of the value of a parcel of shares then a call might be made if the loan to value ratio goes over, say, 75 per cent.
- The loan is granted on an "interest only" basis.
- The interest rate is likely to be higher than in the case of loans secured by mortgages on property, but because of the simplicity of the transaction the establishment fees are likely to be less.
- A choice of fixed and variable rates may be available. Interest rates except where fixed can move up or down.
- A choice of interest in advance or in arrear would probably also be available.
- The facility can be used as a revolving line of credit, with the outstanding balance moving up or down to suit the investor's convenience. It can be put in place ahead of the initial shares actually being acquired.
- The investor gets all notices issued by the listed companies concerned and retains the voting rights on the shares pledged.
- The investor can buy and sell through any broker of his or her choice. More than one broker can be used if desired.
- A fixed term is not required.
- Negative gearing is permitted.

A margin call is a formal demand for some remedial action. This can take the form of "topping up" (providing more unencumbered shares from the investor's portfolio, if these are available, and/or cash). Alternatively, the problem can be removed by the investor selling some of the shares held by way of security and applying the proceeds towards reducing the loan.

It is usually desirable for an investor who becomes aware that a margin call is likely to discuss the best course of action with the lender.

If the investor does not act appropriately to a margin call within a very short time frame such as 24 hours then the lender will exercise the power of sale granted by the loan agreement. This may have undesired capital gains tax consequences. It may also cause considerable mental anguish if the market fall which triggered the sale in the stock turns out to have been only a short term aberration.

It is therefore most important for investors to make suitable arrangements in advance if they are going to be away from their normal address.

An investor who drew less than the maximum entitlement has an inbuilt buffer which can eliminate or at least delay the making of a margin call.

The investor can also very readily keep an eye on the daily or even hourly or minute-by-minute market value of the shares concerned.

The investor retains the full entitlement to any dividends and their associated franking credits, and to any rights or bonus issues. However, the market value of a share going ex such entitlements may drop as a result. Naturally, in the case of bonus shares these could easily be added to the security, solving the problem.

The investor also retains the right to participate in dividend reinvestment plans, shareholder discount schemes and similar arrangements.

Cash dividends on the shares can, if desired, be used to reduce the loan, reducing the likelihood of future margin calls.

Interest can be allowed to accumulate instead of being paid. This would, of course, serve to increase the likelihood of margin calls. Not paying interest is to some extent equivalent to drawing on capital and would not be healthy if it led to bigger consumption expenditure as distinct from further investment.

It is also desirable to have a spread of stocks rather than just a single stock, so that random fluctuations in price can more readily cancel out.

Depending on the practice of the lender concerned any money paid in response to a margin call can be applied either by way of reduction of the loan or as a credit to some other account controlled by the lender. The latter may be more convenient where the investor wants to retrieve the money if the market picks up again quickly.

CHAPTER 6

A "Plain English" Guide to the Concept of Derivatives

A *derivative* is a product constructed from some existing product - for example:

- an option over a share
- an interest rate swap
- a futures contract (as discussed below).

A derivative is sometimes referred to as a *synthetic instrument*.

The concept of a commodity such as wool being sold for cash will be familiar to everybody. This is called a "spot sale".

However, it is also possible for a farmer to sell a bale of wool for delivery to a wool processor at a defined future time, for settlement on delivery, but at a price agreed to at the time of sale. This is called a "forward sale". It would protect both parties against adverse price movements in the interim, although at the cost of also depriving them of the benefit of favourable price movements.

A futures market takes this simple concept one stage further, by eliminating the one-to-one relationship between a specific buyer and a specific seller and introducing instead a special contract which can be traded through a clearing house.

Each contract of a particular type is identical with every other contract of that type, just as all shares of any one class in any company are completely interchangeable.

Buyers and sellers on a *physical* market normally exchange commodities for cash, with an immediate transfer of ownership taking place.

By way of contrast, trading on a *futures* market involves, not physical commodities, but rather *standardised contracts* for the delivery of a given quantity of a commodity (of a defined quality) at some specified future date, at a price agreed on at the time of the deal. This price can be either higher or lower than the "spot price" (the price for immediate delivery). The buyers undertake to take delivery and to make payment at the settlement date and the sellers undertake to effect delivery at that time.

Originally futures contracts related to rural products, such as wool, live cattle, boneless beef, and so on, or to minerals, especially gold. Both producers and consumers of such commodities often desire to guarantee for themselves a price negotiated long before the intended date of delivery, often before the commodity even comes into existence.

This can be achieved *directly* by entering into "forward contracts" as mentioned above - bilateral arrangements between a specific producer and a specific consumer for the delivery of the commodity concerned at some future date, thus facilitating forward planning and reducing uncertainty for both parties.

However, a similar economic effect can also be achieved *indirectly* by means of "futures contracts", where the use of standardised terms facilitates the matching of demand from buyers and supply from sellers, without the two parties even knowing each other.

In conjunction with cash sales futures contracts can also be used to iron out fluctuations in price. Unlike options - which holders (although not writers) can allow to lapse - futures impose binding obligations on both parties.

The concept can be taken further again by writing contracts involving:

- shares of a particular company instead of commodities
- "baskets" of shares, such as those represented by a share index
- foreign currencies
- financial instruments of various types.

With real commodities settlement can be either in kind or in cash, according to the terms of the particular deal. With artificial "commodities" (financial instruments where physical delivery would not be practicable) cash settlements would always apply.

Futures contracts do not need to be held until the nominated delivery date. The obligations can be "liquidated" (extinguished) by the making of off-setting transactions instead. This is known as "closing out an open position". This process is made possible by the use of standardised terms for the contracts.

When producers and consumers use futures in the way described above they are said to be engaged in *hedging*. Hedging involves taking an opposite position in the futures market to the one already held, so that any loss in the physical market will be offset by a corresponding profit in the futures market, thus providing a form of price insurance.

However, while the hedger has the advantage of being able to budget in the knowledge that a specific price has been locked in regardless of any future fluctuations, any profit in the physical market will now be offset by a corresponding loss in the futures market.

But futures contracts can also be used for *speculating*. Persons who have no involvement in the physical commodity as either buyers or sellers can trade in futures as a convenient way of benefiting from expected price movements.

Futures trading as currently practised involves one feature of great significance. By laying out only a relatively small deposit and transaction charges a speculator can trade a contract many times the value of his or her deposit and make gains as large in dollar terms as if the investor had held a "long" or "short" physical position equivalent to the assets represented by the face value of the contract.

This "leverage" aspect can be very attractive to speculators, although, as always, leverage is a two-edged sword. It can produce large profits if things go well and large losses if they do not. For example, on a five per cent deposit a five per cent rise in the underlying commodity would double an investor's money; a five per cent fall would completely eliminate the stake.

Futures trading is a *zero sum game*. This means that:

- For every buyer of a contract there has to be a corresponding seller and vice versa.
- For every "long" position (a contract promising to take) there must be an equal "short" position (a contract promising to deliver).
- For every rupee of profit made by one player there must be a rupee of loss made by somebody else.

The participation of speculators in the game thus assists both producers and consumers to find matching parties and helps to broaden the market.

Dictionary

101: comprising the introductory material in, or as if in, a formal course of study - for example, "Derivatives 101".

54/11: the practice used by some members of superannuation funds to resign from their jobs at or near the age of 54 years and 11 months, where due to anomalies in the rules and poor fund design this produces a larger benefit than by taking early retirement at or after the age of 55 years.

a priori: from what was before.

A to P: see authority to prospect.

AAA: see ratings agencies.

AAPR: abbreviation for annualised average percentage rate.

AAT: abbreviation for Administrative Appeals Tribunal.

ab initio: from the beginning.

abandon: to cease exploration or activity on a prospect.

abnormal items: items of revenue or expenses which arise in the normal course of business, but which distort the profit because of their unusual size or nature - for example, items really relating to a prior year, costs relating to branch closures or the provisioning of bad debts. The concept is no longer employed.

Abnormal items used to be disclosed separately in the profit and loss account but were included in the operating profit. Contrast extraordinary items.

above par: where a loan issue is priced above its nominal or face value.

above the line: profit or loss items regarded as part of a company's normal operating profit.

ABS: abbreviation for asset backed securities.

absolute majority: the greater part of; that is, more than half.

absolute return funds: high risk unlisted managed funds which aim to deliver positive returns for their investors in both rising and falling markets, by the use of non-traditional techniques and hedging strategies. They may, for example, use derivatives, short positions, arbitrage, leverage and exotic securities. Some such funds set out to exploit market inefficiencies. They all focus on absolute investor returns rather than on returns which merely exceed a particular index. However, they often charge substantial incentive or performance fees, on top of the usual management fees. Some absolute return funds invest in a portfolio of other absolute return funds (this is known as a "fund of funds" approach).

absorption costing: a method of valuing inventory which includes the appropriate share of both variable and fixed costs.

abstention: the refusal to vote "aye" or "no" on a motion or to vote for the candidates in an election.

abyssal: pertaining to deep within the earth. In the case of deep sea exploration this refers to depths of more than 1000 fathoms (about 2000 metres).

AC: abbreviation for air core (a drilling term).

accelerator theory: an economic theory which explains the relationship between changes in consumption and the flow-on effect on investment in capital items.

acceptance fee: a commission charged to the borrower by a bank or merchant bank for drawing or endorsing bills of exchange.

acceptances closing date: see application closing date.

accident and sickness: an insurance contract which provides a benefit in the event of death, total or permanent disability or loss of eye(s) or limb(s) caused by accident, or an income benefit if the life insured is temporarily disabled by sickness or accident.

accident benefit: a benefit payable under an insurance policy if death occurs as the result of an accident.

accountancy: the profession of accounting.

accounting: the recording, classifying, analysing and summarising of quantitative information about a business.

accounting standards: Accounting Standards Board, set up by the Institute of Chartered Accountants of India (a statutory body) formulates accounting policies and practices to be followed in India and the methods of applying these principles in the preparation of financial statements so that they give true and fair view of an enterprise.

accounts payable: amounts owing to trade creditors.

accounts receivable: amounts owing by trade debtors.

accruals: when securities sold cum entitlement are not registered in the name of the buyer on the date of closing of the transfer books, the entitlement to be transferred from the original seller to the unregistered buyer is termed an accrual on the original purchase.##

accruals basis: the method of accounting where revenue and expense items are recognised as they are earned or incurred and not when they are actually received or paid, as distinct from the cash basis of accounting.

accrued dividends: dividends which have notionally accumulated on a security since the last payment date, based on the time since then and the annual rate.

accrued interest: interest which has notionally accumulated on a security since the last payment date, based on the time since then and the annual rate.

accumulate: advice to buy more shares, but with less force than a "strong buy" recommendation.

accumulated depreciation: the aggregate of depreciation over time charged against an asset. It is disclosed in the balance sheet and is subtracted from gross assets to arrive at net assets.

accumulated profits: the balance in the profit and loss account, profits which have not been distributed to shareholders but which are being retained for use in the operations of a business. Also known as unappropriated profits, undistributed profits, retained earnings or plough-back. They form part of the shareholders' funds.

accumulation index: a share price index calculated on the assumption that all dividends are reinvested back into the underlying security. For this purpose the incidence of income tax and the effect of the imputation system are both ignored. This index can be used to judge the performance of funds which do not make income distributions, but the comparison will, of course, not be valid except in the case of tax-free funds. It will, however, be much fairer than using a non-accumulation index.

accumulation of income: the process of retaining income in the trust fund, as distinct from distributing it to beneficiaries - the equivalent in the books of a trust of maintaining a balance in the profit and loss account of a company; undistributed profits are taxed to the trustee at a special rate.

accumulation plan: a superannuation plan involving defined contributions which are invested and accumulated at interest in order to produce a retirement benefit. Contrast defined benefit plan.

ACE: abbreviation for adjusted common equity ratio (banks).

ACE ratio (banking): abbreviation for adjusted common equity ratio.

acid: igneous rocks with over 66% silica ($SiO2$), as distinct from basic or intermediate rocks.

acid test: a measure of liquidity. Basically, it compares the sum of a company's cash and debtors and those securities which are readily convertible into cash with its current liabilities. This ratio differs from the working capital ratio in that it disregards stock (inventories). If the ratio is too high, then this indicates idle funds which could be better employed; if it is too low, then this gives a warning sign as to a potentially dangerous situation. Two alternative approaches are in use:

- ratio = (CA-S)/CL
- ratio = (CA-S)/(CL-OD)

where
CA = current assets
CL = current liabilities
S = stock
OD = bank overdraft

Also known as the liquid ratio, the liquid assets ratio, the quick test, the quick ratio, the quick assets ratio.

acidising: the injection of an acid solution into a well for the purpose of dissolving limestone in the porous area, thereby increasing permeability so that oil will flow more freely through the formation to the well.

acquisitions (GST): goods and services *purchased* or the amounts *payable* for them.

across the board: where there is a broad range of rises or falls in the sharemarket.

active assets: for CGT purposes, assets that are used in the course of carrying on a business (for example, premises), but also including intangible assets such as goodwill (qv) and intellectual property (qv).

active client: a customer of a stockbroker who maintains a sufficient level of trading activity to be considered as "active". The threshold level of activity will vary between firms and from time to time.

actuary: a person professionally trained in the mathematical and technical aspects of life insurance and related fields and responsible for the calculation of premiums, reserves and bonuses; an applied statistician, specialising in probabilities and their financial effects.

ad hoc: for this special purpose.

ad hoc committee: a committee appointed for a specific task and which ceases to exist when that task has been completed.

ad idem: of the same mind.

ad valorem: according to value.

ad valorem duty: a tax based on the dollar value of a transaction as distinct from a tax levied at a flat rate per transaction.

ADI: abbreviation for authorised deposit-taking institution (for example, building societies and credit unions).

adit: a nearly horizontal passage or level driven into the side of a hill to intersect a mineral deposit. Strictly, an adit is open at one end; if open at both ends then the passage is a tunnel.

adjournment (debate): the procedural motion: "That the debate be adjourned."

adjournment (meeting): the procedural motion either to close the meeting and to have a further meeting on a predetermined date or on a date to be fixed in some predetermined manner; or alternatively to have a break in the meeting and to continue the same meeting on a predetermined date or on a date and in a place to be fixed in some predetermined manner.

adjustable rate loan: a loan with the interest rate made subject to periodical changes (up or down) in line with market changes or according to some formula.

adjusted common equity ratio (ACE ratio) (banking): the shareholders' funds less certain deductions (such as those for hybrid equity, intangible assets, investments in insurance, funds management and securitisation entities), divided by the risk-weighted assets (RWA) (qv).

adjustments: retrospective alterations to accounting information. They may be year end or prior period adjustments and are made by an accountant in preparing a set of accounts. Adjustments are also made by a security analyst to a published set of accounts to make it conform to personal analysis techniques. Adjustments are made to a per share series to produce comparable details.

administration (of an estate): the court supervised distribution of the estate of a deceased person by its executor or administrator.

administrator (of an estate): the person charged with winding up a deceased estate when there is no valid will or when there is no executor.

admission of age (life insurance): the confirmation endorsed on a policy that a life insurance company has noted evidence of the date of birth of a life insured.

ADR: abbreviation for alternative dispute resolution.

ADR: abbreviation for American Depositary Receipt.

ADS: abbreviation for American Depositary Share.

advance/decline: the number of companies the share price of which rose to the number the price of which fell. It is an indicator of trading conditions.

adverse possession: the doctrine under which title in land occupied without challenge by a person other than its rightful owner for a statutory period can, after the end of that period, on application to the authorities be transferred without compensation to that person, in extinguishment of the previous owner's rights to and interest in that land.

AEC: abbreviation for Atomic Energy Commission.

aerial map: a geological map of the different types of rocks exposed at the surface.

aerial survey: a survey made from the air, including photographic, magnetometric, radioactive, etc., recording of data.

affiliated company: a company which is associated through an ownership of 50 per cent or less, and/or through common directors.

affiliation: two organisations can be said to be affiliated with each other where they have a close connection or business relationship and/or constitutional links. The term can also refer to the relationship between a parent organisation and its branches.

AG: abbreviation for Aktiengesellschaft.

age structure: the distribution of people in a population by age.

agenda: the list of the items of business before a meeting and the order in which it is proposed that the meeting should deal with them.

agent: a person acting on behalf of another (the principal). A stockbroker is an agent.

aggregation arrangement: an arrangement between a stockbroker, a company and its shareholders whereby shareholders with a small parcel of shares have the opportunity to sell out or buy more shares at a specified price independent of market value.

agitation: mechanical stirring or shaking used to separate minerals.

AGM: abbreviation for annual general meeting.

agreed takeover bid: one supported and agreed to by the board of the target company.

AIMR: abbreviation for Association for Investment Management and Research.

air drill: a drill employing air rather than water to remove cuttings.

Aktiengesellschaft (AG): a limited liability company (German).

alkaline: containing ions of one or more alkaline metals, such as lithium, sodium, potassium, rubidium or caesium.

alkane: a hydrocarbon of the paraffin series.

allfinanz: see convergence (finance sector).

allocated pension: a tax-advantaged superannuation product which only very loosely resembles a true pension. It involves the investment of an initial lump sum, with the investor compulsorily drawing out periodical payments. The taxation legislation specifies the minimum and maximum amounts to be drawn each year, having regard to the attained age of the investor. Depending on the investment performance net of expenses and the longevity of the individual investor it is possible that the funds become exhausted some years before the investor's death.

allotment: the formal allocation of new securities to subscribers. In oversubscribed issues an individual allotment may be less than the number applied for.

allowable deductions (tax): deductions from assessable income for tax purposes. They fall into two main classes - expenses incurred in the earning of assessable income and the so-called "concessional deductions", such as donations to charity.

alloy: a mixture of two or more metals.

alluvial deposit: a deposit spread by flowing water.

alluvial gold: water worn gold.

alpha factor: a coefficient measuring the risk-adjusted performance of a stock, considering the risk due to its specific nature, as distinct from that due to the overall market. A large alpha factor indicates that the stock has performed better than would have been predicted from its beta factor (the measure of its volatility compared with that of the market as a whole). Shares which rise when the market as a whole is falling have a positive alpha factor; those which fall when the market as a whole is rising have a negative alpha factor.

alteration halo: subtle changes in the rocks surrounding an orebody which act as indicators of mineralisation.

alternate director: a person who has approval to sit on a board in lieu of a regular director who is absent.

alternative cost: the cost of producing a good in terms of another.

alternative dispute resolution (ADR): arbitration, conciliation or mediation, as distinct from litigation in the courts.

alternative investments: investments in something other than traditional financial instruments. Depending on the context the term could refer to items such as units in hedge funds, shares in co-operative companies, vacant land, wine, commodities, venture capital situations, infrastructure investments, units in pooled development funds, global macro funds, capital protected products, antiques or works of art. The term can also refer to private equity - unlisted companies, including those proposing to float on the stock exchange later on. Alternative investments are often relatively illiquid and can pose higher than normal risks. They are usually unsuitable investments for superannuation funds. Past performance is best judged against an accumulation index.

alumina (aluminium oxide): the first stage of processing bauxite into aluminium.

aluminium: a primary metal processed from bauxite. Its principal qualities are its light weight and resistance to corrosion. Chemical symbol: Al.

amalgamation: see merger.

amendment (of a constitution): a formal change to the wording of a constitution, made in accordance with its amendments clause.

amendment (of a motion): an alteration or proposed alteration to the terms of a motion, designed to improve the motion but without contradicting it.

amendment (of a trust deed): a formal change to the terms of a trust deed, made in accordance with powers conferred by the deed.

American Depositary Receipt (ADR): a form of shareholding. Shares in some listed Indian companies are traded in the United States, with a special document of title called the American Depository Receipt being used as the trading unit. An ADR may represent, say, two shares or four shares in an Indian company, with the market value in US dollars then being the equivalent of the market value of two or four Indian shares. ADRs are created by certain US banks, which hold the underlying scrip and become the registered shareowners as far as the Indian company is concerned. This device facilitates changes of beneficial ownership when trading occurs on the stock exchange in America. Naturally, all dividends belong to the beneficial owners in the usual way.

American style: options or warrants which are exercisable *at any time* before their expiry date; contrast *European style*.

amicus curiae: friend of the court.

amorphous: relating to rocks or minerals that possess no definite crystal structure or form.

amortisation: the process of writing the initial value of an asset gradually down to zero over a number of years in a systematic fashion, in order to spread the total amount equitably over these years; the charging against revenue of expenditure which has been incurred in a prior accounting period and which has been capitalised. It is a non-cash charge in the profit and loss statement. It is similar to depreciation in its nature but it usually refers to intangible assets such as patents or goodwill or to capitalised mining and oil exploration expenses or to the expenses of a new issue.

analysis: a test usually by chemical means to determine the overall constituents of minerals or rocks, as distinct from an assay.

angel investors: persons who are willing to contribute their capital in order to fund a startup business.

angle of deflection: when a well is drilled at an angle the angle of deflection measures the deflection from the vertical.

angle of repose: the maximum slope at which dumped but loose material will stand without sliding.

annual general meeting: the statutory meeting of shareholders held once a year. It is held after the release of the annual report and is used to gain any necessary shareholder approvals and to discuss the performance and activities of the company.

annual report: the statutory report prepared by companies to inform shareholders and other interested parties of results and operations over a period, which is usually twelve months. It includes the profit and loss account, the balance sheet, and the directors' and auditor's reports to shareholders, as well as other statutory information.

annualised average percentage rate (AAPR): a notional mortgage interest rate which also allows for non-interest charges and which is designed to make different mortgage products comparable.

annuity: a payment of a defined sum of money at regular intervals; the right to a series of periodical payments purchased from a life office by either single or periodical premiums. Effectively, a private pension. See also deferred annuity and immediate annuity.

annulus: the space around a pipe suspended in a wellbore, the outer wall of which may be the wall of either the borehole or the casing. Also known as the annular space.

anomaly: a divergence from background levels of physical or chemical properties of an area that could be an indication of a mineral deposit, which may or may not be an economic discovery.

anthracite: a hard black lustrous coal of low volatility.

anti-trust: referring to legislation aimed at limiting monopolistic or oligopolistic practices. Used particularly in reference to the United States.

anticline: a fold of strata in an arch-like shape. It can form a trap for hydrocarbon accumulations. Opposite of syncline.

antimony: a primary metal, commonly alloyed with lead in batteries. Chemical symbol: Sb.

Anton Pillar order: a legally binding court order which allows an applicant, without prior notice to the respondent, to enter the respondent's premises and to inspect and/or seize documents or other items. It is designed to prevent the destruction of incriminating evidence - for example, in connection with the alleged illegal use of copyrighted software or other material.

application: a request by a subscriber for securities in a new issue.

application closing date: the date by which application money must be received for a new share issue. It is the last day on which rights can be traded, except where a shortened timetable is used. Also called acceptances closing date.

application for listing: a request by a company to have its shares listed on the official list of the Australian Securities Exchange.

application money: money payable in a cash issue of shares or other securities. It represents capital and may by payable in a lump sum or by instalments as nominated by the company.

appointor: the person given the power to remove or appoint the trustees of a trust and the power to nominate the person to be the successor of the appointor.

apportionment: the division of a sum of money into income and capital components; or the division of an interest in an asset into a life interest and a remainder interest.

appreciate: to increase in value.

appropriation: the allocation of resources for a special purpose. In accounting it refers to the Profit and Loss Appropriation Account which specifies how profits are to be apportioned - for example, to dividends, to unappropriated profits, to reserves, and so on.

APR: abbreviation for annual percentage rate.

APRA-regulated entity: a bank or other authorised deposit-taking institution (ADI), a life or general insurance company, a superannuation fund or a non-operating holding company (NOHC) for any of these which is regulated by the Australian Prudential Regulation Authority (APRA) in order to minimise losses to depositors, policyholders and members of superannuation funds.

aqueous: formed by water.

arbitrage: in relation to many commodity markets (including those dealing in shares, bonds, currencies, metals, and so on) the purchase of an asset in one market and the simultaneous sale of an equivalent asset at a higher price, usually in a different market. Ideally, this produces a risk-free profit for the arbitrageur ("pure arbitrage"). The term "arbitrage" is also used more loosely in situations which only approximate to this ideal, as, for example, when the two legs of the transaction are not quite simultaneous or when the two lots of assets are not quite identical - circumstances in which the arbitrageur is then exposed to some minor risk. Arbitrage activity is useful in that it helps to smooth out anomalies between different markets. A common example available even to small investors occurs in share exchange takeover situations, by switching between shares in the bidder and target companies.

arbitration: the formal determination of a dispute by an independent person, without involving a court of law. Arbitration because of its speed and privacy can be very useful for settling disputes involving leases. The word "arbitration" is also used loosely but inaccurately in relation to the determination of a market rent by an independent expert.

Archaean Period: the older of the two periods in the Precambrian Era.

arenaceous: applies to rocks that have been derived from sand or that contain sand, as distinct from siliceous.

argentite: silver sulphide, an ore of silver.

arithmetic average: see mean.

arm's length transaction: a dealing between parties who are strangers to each other, as distinct from one between parties who know each other and/or who have legal or moral obligations to each other.

arrangement: see Scheme of Arrangement.

arrears: unpaid dividends due on cumulative preference shares or unpaid interest due on fixed interest securities.

artesian basin: a structure which contains water underground.

articles of association: a document detailing how the business of a company shall be carried on. These articles deal only with a company's internal rules. The external activities are subject to the memorandum of association.

as of right: as an entitlement.

ask (stock exchange): a selling quote; an offer to sell.

assay: a test of ore to determine the amount of valuable metals contained, as distinct from analysis.

assessable income (tax): loosely speaking, "gross profit", covering both personal exertion income and the returns on investments - for example, salary, wages, commission, bonuses, professional fees, profits from business operations, pensions, dividends, interest, rent, capital gains and the like, together with the imputation credits attached to franked dividends. The allowable deductions are subtracted from the assessable income to arrive at the taxable income.

asset allocation: the composition of an investment portfolio in the interests of diversifying risk and reducing volatility. The main asset categories for serious investors wishing to be in conventional investment asset classes are ordinary shares, property (real estate) and fixed interest securities. The latter can include long term investments, as well as cash or "near cash" (qv). The fixed interest component of a portfolio can be either positive or negative (as when borrowed funds are used). Asset allocation involves weighing risk and return. To illustrate, a conservative investor might aim at 30 per cent each in shares, property and medium term fixed interest securities, with 10 per cent in "near cash".

asset backing: see net tangible asset backing.

asset lock-up: an arrangement under which the target company in a takeover agrees to sell to the bidder some desirable assets in order to make itself less attractive to potential rival bidders and/or as part of a deal to give the bidder the opportunity to undertake due diligence.

asset revaluation: the recognition in accounting of the appreciation of an asset above its book value. The amount of this revaluation is added to the asset revaluation or similar reserve as well as to the value of the asset.

asset revaluation reserve: see reserves.

asset stripping: selling off assets of a company acquired.

assets: resources owned by a company or person. Assets can be divided into a number of different categories based upon their liquidity, that is, the ease with which they can be converted into cash. These classifications are:

- current assets
- investments
- fixed assets
- intangible assets.

assets test: a criterion, the level of wealth owned, which is applied in order to determine eligibility for social security pensions and benefits.

assignment (insurance): the process by which the legal ownership of a life insurance policy is transferred from one person to another.

assignment (property): the process by which the lessee under a lease (as assignor) with the consent of the lessor transfers the rights and obligations of that lease to another person (the assignee). In the same way the rights and obligations under other contracts can also be transferred with the agreement of all parties.

associate director: a company executive without the full responsibilities and privileges of a director, but awarded this title as a courtesy and as an indication of seniority.

associated company: a company in which a long term investment is held and over which significant influence can be exercised. The investment is between 20 per cent and 50 per cent of the ordinary capital. These companies can be equity accounted. See also holding company.

at arm's length: the relationship between parties who are strangers to each other, as distinct from that between parties who know each other and/or who have legal or moral obligations to each other.

at call: monies on loan which are subject to immediate repayment upon request from the lender.

at limit: a buying or selling order on which a limiting price has been set by the client.

at market: a buying or selling order to be effected at current market prices.

at sight: a bill of exchange payable on demand.

at the opening: a buying or selling order to be effected at the market price at the opening of trading on a particular day.

ATF: abbreviation for as trustee for.

ATP: see authority to prospect.

ATS: symbol for the Austrian schilling.

attitude: direction and degree of dip of a structure such as a vein, a lode, a zone of mineralisation, etc. Attitude may be expressed in terms of dip and strike.

attorney: a person appointed by another person under a power of attorney to act on that person's behalf.

auction: with regard to the stock market, the auction of forfeited shares or shares not subscribed for under the terms of an issue.

AUD: symbol for the Australian dollar.

audit: a formal verification of the accuracy of accounting records and published accounts. An audit can be external or internal and is undertaken both to ensure the correctness of classifications and amounts and to discover fraud. The external auditor has a statutory responsibility to report on the truth and fairness of the accounts.

audit trail: a step-by-step record by which accounting entries can be traced back to their source (usually original documents), thus demonstrating the accuracy of financial data and the quality of internal controls.

auditors' report: a statutory statement by the auditors of a company to its shareholders in the annual report.

auger drilling: shallow exploratory drilling with rotating bits through solid and soft rock. Cuttings are fragmented and therefore core samples are not obtained for analysis.

auriferous: gold bearing.

Australasia: Australia and New Zealand.

authorised dealer: a company with lender of last resort facilities operating in the official short term money market.

authorised investments: securities in which a trustee is permitted to invest by the terms of a trust deed. See also trustee securities.

authorised representative: a person authorised by a financial services licensee to provide certain financial services on behalf of the licensee.

autogenous grinding: a process of grinding using the ore itself rather than conventional steel balls or rods in the rotating mill.

average: see mean, median and mode.

average rate of return: the ratio of the average annual profit after tax to the average investment in a project. It is a measure of profitability.

averaging: the act of buying further parcels of shares at a lower price than previous purchases in order to reduce the average cost price. However, such transactions do nothing to reduce the size of the unrealised capital loss already incurred. See also pyramiding.

ayes: those voting in favour of a particular motion.

b: abbreviation for bonus shares.

baby boomers: the generation of persons in Western countries born between the end of World War II in 1945 and about 1965. This generation is much larger than the preceding and following generations. At the time of their young adulthood its members saw massive changes in attitudes to many social issues, including opposition to the Vietnam War, the sexual revolution and mass political action for causes such as civil rights and feminism. See also generation X.

back door listing: the strategy of merging an unlisted company with a listed company as a quicker and cheaper way for the former to list on the stock exchange. Where the listed company is a shell, the other company's activities are simply injected into its structure.

back off: to unscrew one threaded section of pipe from another.

back office: those parts of a stockbroker's business that do not come to the public's eye - for example, settlement and accounting functions.

back up: to hold one section of pipe while another is being screwed into or out of it.

back-end bookbuild: a bookbuild conducted in respect of the shortfall in a rights issue.

backfill: waste material used to support the walls of a stope and provide a working platform after removal of the ore.

background: in prospecting, the normal range of a given element under investigation. Comparison of survey data with background data determines the existence of an anomaly.

backroom: those parts of a stockbroker's business that do not come to the public's eye - for example, settlement and accounting functions.

backs: mineral between the slope (or level) and the next level.

backwardation: in metals and other commodities trading, a fee paid by a seller of stock deliverable by a specified day for the right to delay delivery till another specified day. See also contago.

bad debt: a debt, the collection of which is believed to be impossible.

bail (mining): to recover bottom-hole fluids, samples, or drill cuttings by lowering a cylindrical vessel, called a bailer, to the bottom of a well, filling it, and retrieving it.

balance date: the date on which the accounts are closed for preparation of the annual report. This may be on any day but is usually 31 March in India.

balance of payments: the money flowing into or out of a country. See capital account (trade), current account (trade), current account deficit.

balance sheet: a table, also called a *statement of financial position*), summarising the financial condition of a company or other enterprise as at a specific point in time (the *balance date*). It sets out, under appropriate headings, brief details of the assets and liabilities and shows their book values. It also shows the net worth of the business (the *shareholders' equity* or *shareholders' funds*), this being the excess of the total assets over the total liabilities. For listed companies balance sheets are usually published in the annual report about three months after the balance date. They complement the profit and loss statements.

balanced gearing: the situation when an investment such as property or shares is purchased with the assistance of borrowed funds and where the rental or dividend income (after the deduction of expenses) is exactly equal to the interest commitment in the course of a financial year.

ball mill: a machine used to grind ore into small particles. It is a cylindrical steel container filled with steel balls or rods into which crushed ore is fed. The ball mill is rotated, causing the balls to roll, thereby grinding the ore.

balloon payment: in a loan arrangement, one big final payment to clear the debt, following regular, smaller payments for a pre-arranged period.

ballot: the voting on a question before the chair or at an election in writing, in a way which allows accurate figures to be ascertained, but without the names of those voting in any particular way becoming available.

bancassurance: see convergence (finance sector).

banded rocks: rocks having thin and almost parallel bands of different textures, minerals or colours.

bank bill: a bill of exchange that has been accepted and/or endorsed (and thus effectively guaranteed) by a bank.

bank line: a line of credit which is flexible and on which the borrower pays interest on only the amount of funds used.

bank reconciliation: the process of comparing the bank balance in the customer's records with that shown in the bank's records and finding a satisfactory explanation for any discrepancies.

barbecue stopper: an unexpected favourable political or economic development.

bare trust: a trust where the sole obligation of the trustee is to convey capital and income to the beneficiaries when they require this.

barge: any one of many types of flat-decked, shallow-draft vessels, usually towed by a boat. A complete drilling rig may be assembled on a drilling barge, which usually is flooded with water at the drilling site. Drilling equipment, crew quarters, and so on,, are mounted on a superstructure above the water level.

barite: the principal ore of barium. Used in paints, drilling muds and medical applications.

barrel (bbl): a measure of volume for petroleum products. One barrel (1 bbl) is the equivalent of about 159 litres or 42 United States gallons or 35 imperial gallons. One cubic metre (1 m3) equals 6.2897 bbl.

barrier options: specialised put and call options, available in a great many varieties - for example, some become activated only if and when the underling security reaches a predetermined price level, known as the barrier, while others become void in similar circumstances.

baryte: the principal ore of barium. Used in paints, drilling muds and medical applications.

BAS: abbreviation for Business Activity Statement.

basalt: an extrusive rock composed primarily of calcic plagioclase and pyroxene.

base metal: generally a metal inferior in value to gold and silver; mainly copper, lead, zinc and nickel.

basic rocks: igneous rocks containing between 45 and 52 per cent silica, as distinct from acid or intermediate rocks.

basin, sedimentary: a segment of the earth's crust which has been downwarped. The sediments in such basins increase in thickness toward the centre of the basin. By their nature hydrocarbon and coal deposits are located in sedimentary basins.

basis points: a means of expressing interest rates. A basis point equals 0.01 per cent per annum. Thus a move from 13.29 per cent to 13.41 per cent can be described as a 12-point increase.

battery: an extraction plant made up of several stamps to crush the ore.

bauxite: aluminium oxide, the principal ore of aluminium.

BDT: symbol for the Bangladeshi taka.

bear: an investor who expects the market to go down, a pessimist. The term is said to come from hunters who sold bear skins which they did not yet own - from bears which they had not so far caught. On the stock exchange bears include short sellers - speculators who sell shares which they do not yet own, in the belief that they will be able to buy them back on the market at a lower price before delivery is required. Opposite of a bull.

bear market: a falling market.

bearish: holding a pessimistic opinion of future performance. Also used to describe a bear market.

beauty parade: a mechanism for a company or a government agency to select a provider of financial and professional services. The company or agency normally draws up a short list of potential providers, who are then invited to make appropriate presentations.

bed: a specific layer of earth or rock, in contrast to other layers of different material lying above, below, or adjacent to it.

bedrock: solid rock, often covered by overburden or alluvial material.

BEF: symbol for the Belgian franc.

below par: where a loan issue is priced below its nominal or face value.

below the line: profit or loss items reported as extraordinary because they are regarded as non-recurring. They are not treated as part of a company's normal operating profit.

bench: a terrace or level layer worked separately in an open-cut mine.

benchmark: (1) the yardstick by which a fund manager can be judged - for example, the target investment return per annum after charges from a particular fund might be defined as the movement in the consumer price index plus three percentage points. Alternatively, it might be defined in terms of a share price index. (2) commonly used yardsticks for specifying interest rates in a variety of commercial situations include the bond rate (qv) for long term rates and the cash rate (qv) for short term rates.

beneficial ownership: the entitlement to the benefits flowing from a particular asset, as distinct from being recorded as the registered proprietor of that asset.

beneficiaries (deceased estates): the persons who collectively are entitled to receive income and capital payments from a deceased estate, in accordance with the terms of the will or the laws relating to intestacy.

beneficiaries (trusts): the persons who collectively are entitled to receive income and capital payments from a trust fund, in accordance with the rules set out in the trust deed; persons can be beneficiaries for income only, for corpus only or for both.

beneficiate: to concentrate or enrich ore. Usually refers to concentrating mineral sands or iron ore.

benefit promise plan: a superannuation plan in which the member's retirement benefits are related to a combination of the salary at or near retirement (or over some other period) and the years of service or membership. Contributions at a level sufficient to purchase these benefits need to be paid. Contrast accumulation plan.

bentonite: a clay which is used in oil drilling because of its water absorption capacity.

bequest: property left to a person by another person's will.

Besloten Vennootschap (BV): a limited liability company (Dutch).

beta factor: a measure of volatility in share and futures trading. It gauges the movement of a commodity's price against a related composite index. The whole market, by definition, has a beta factor of 1.0. If a stock has a beta of less than 1.0 its price is expected to rise or fall proportionately less than the market, while stocks with a beta greater than 1.0 are expected to rise or fall more than the market as a whole. The higher the beta the higher the price volatility. See also alpha factor, capital asset pricing model, systemic risk.

betterment (income tax): the gross increase in a taxpayer's wealth over the course of a financial year, other than from capital appreciation or from certain non-taxable windfall situations such as gambling winnings, gifts or bequests.

betterment (property): the enhanced value of real estate arising from local improvements.

BHD: symbol for the Bahraini dinar.

Bi: chemical symbol for bismuth.

bid (stock exchange): a buying quote; an offer to buy.

bid (takeovers): a formal approach made by a company wishing to buy some or all of another company's shares.

bidder's statement: see takeovers.

"big four" accounting firms: Deloitte Touche Tohmatsu, Ernst & Young, KPMG and PricewaterhouseCoopers.

bigger fool theory: the approach followed although rarely vocalised by investors in speculative stocks. They realise that a stock is not worth the price they are foolishly paying for it, but they expect to be able to sell it profitably to an even bigger fool at a higher price before the stock crashes.

bill market: the market for bills of exchange.

bill of exchange: a negotiable instrument, often used as a method of raising funds by promising to make a payment at a future date. A contingent liability remains with each acceptor until payment. Each acceptor endorses the bill and where a bank has accepted the bill it becomes a "bank accepted bill" and is therefore more secure.

billion: originally a billion was a million million and a trillion was a million million million - a coherent pattern. Unfortunately, a different, quite illogical, usage developed in the United States and France and has now taken over. Under this approach, a billion is 1000 million and a trillion is 1000 billion.

binder: an agreement between an insurer and an insurance broker under which the broker is authorised to act on the insurer's behalf in accepting risks and/or handling claims.

birth rate: the number of births per 1000 population in a given year. Contrast population growth rate.

bismuth: a primary element used as a metallurgical additive and as a pharmaceutical. Chemical symbol: Bi.

bit: the cutting or boring element used in drilling. Made from hard material, frequently tungsten and diamonds.

bituminous: containing a large amount of organic or carbonaceous matter and yielding volatile bituminous matter on heating.

black box: a computer trading programme which is designed to tell investors what shares to buy and sell and when to do so, according to criteria set either by the investor or by the vendor of the software. A moment's thought will show that if someone really had a foolproof way of creating wealth then he would exploit it himself in private rather than make it generally available.

black economy: goods and services which are purchased for cash without any record being made in the usual accounting ledgers, normally in order to evade tax.

Black Monday: 19 October 1987, the day on which Wall Street crashed, the Dow Jones Index falling 508 points in the course of the one day. This was the night of 19-20 October in Australia. The corresponding fall in Australia took place on Black Tuesday, 20 October 1987.

blackhole expenditure: expenses incurred by a company which are not directly related to the earning of assessable income - for example, money spent on raising fresh capital, or the costs associated with a company either making an unsuccessful takeover bid for another company or - in the reverse situation - defending itself against an unwelcome takeover offer received by it.

blast furnace: a metallurgical furnace which combines ores, fluxes, fuels and oxygen blasting for the chemical reduction of metals. Iron ore is most commonly treated this way.

blast hole: a hole drilled for purposes of blasting rather than for exploration purposes.

blind trust: a device sometimes used by politicians and certain other persons with a potential conflict of interest. It involves putting some of their assets and especially their listed and unlisted shares into a special trust, so that an independent trustee can in future make (and be seen to be making) all the required investment decisions.

The beneficial owner of the assets under such an arrangement is then not only precluded from giving any directions to the trustee but is also denied all knowledge of the actual composition of the portfolio for the duration of the blind trust. The theory is that owners in that position can then carry out their official duties without being influenced by the effect on their own pockets.

blister copper: an intermediate stage in the production of copper before refining.

block caving: a cheap method of underground mining whereby large blocks of ore are undercut and their supporting pillars blasted out.

block sale: the sale of a large parcel of shares. Also called a special.

block: a sub-unit of an exploration licence.

blocking: see ore blocking.

blog (or web log): a web site created by a single individual as a form of public diary. Unlike a wiki, it does not allow other users to change the contents, although they can add their own comments.

blowout preventer: equipment installed at the wellhead at surface level on land rigs and on the seafloor of floating offshore rigs to prevent the escape of pressure.

blowout: an uncontrolled flow of gas, oil, or other well fluids into the atmosphere. A blowout, or gusher, can occur when formation fluids enter the wellbore and steps are not taken to stop the entry of fluids. A kick warns of an impending blowout.

blue chip stock: stock in a major company where it is felt that there is little likelihood of that company passing into liquidation. This does not mean that there is no risk to capital from buying such shares. See risk. Originally an American term, from the highest value poker chip.

blue sky element: in a speculative stock, the difference between the market price and the perceived value if the former exceeds the latter.

BND: symbol for the Brunei dollar.

board boy: see chalkie.

board of directors: those people who have been chosen to direct the running of a company. Directors must be re-elected regularly to retain their position. They may be executive or non-executive.

body corporate (generally): an organisation recognised by the law as having standing as a person for legal purposes - for example, a company or a statutory corporation.

body corporate (in relation to strata title complexes): a special sort of company, a non-profit organisation, jointly owned and controlled by and run for the benefit of the property owners concerned. However, it is not subject to the normal companies legislation. It also owns the common property shown on a plan of subdivision. The owners have a number of votes each, as set out in the plan of subdivision. Also known as owners corporation.

boiler plate clauses: standardised text, usable as a template in contracts, annual reports, prospectuses, trust deeds, letters and so on.

Bombay Stock Exchange (BSE): located in Mumbai, it is the oldest stock exchange in Asia and has the greatest number of listed companies in the world, with 4800 listed as of August 2009.

bon: abbreviation for bonus shares.

bona fide: genuinely, sincerely.

bona fides: honest intention.

bond (rental property): the security deposit lodged by a tenant at the start of a lease, to cover the costs of repairing any damage to the premises. Any money not required for this purpose is returned at the end of the tenancy.

bond rate: the yield on long term Commonwealth bonds. It is a proxy for a risk-free rate of return and a yardstick by which the returns from other investments can be judged.

bonds (insurance): life insurance company or friendly society policies, usually subject to single premiums and usually without death benefits, which are backed by professionally managed fixed interest and/or equity portfolios. They can be either capital guaranteed or investment-linked and either superannuation or non-superannuation.

They do not involve cash distributions, but pass on the investment returns either through bonuses added to the nominal sum insured or, in the case of unit-linked contracts, through a rising unit value.

In some ways they resemble unit trusts, but income tax is paid by the institution and not the investor. Withdrawals within the first ten years also attract tax in the policyholder's hands in respect of the net gain, but this is subject to a special rebate. Also called investment bonds.

bonds (stock exchange): a government issued fixed interest security, usually having a fixed date of redemption. See Commonwealth bonds.

bonus (life insurance): the share of the life insurance company surplus which is added to the face value of a participating policy. It is normally payable at the same time and under the same conditions as the basic sum insured.

bonus element: portion of the market value of shares involved in a rights issue which seems to some commentators to be a free handout, resembling a bonus issue. Adjusting earnings per share for the bonus element in a rights issues involves calculating the ratio of the number of shares ex rights to the number of shares cum rights, in the case of a hypothetical investor who sells a sufficient number of rights at their theoretical value in order to enable him to take up exactly the balance of his entitlement - in other words, with no money either put in or taken out.

bonus issue: in the days of par values, so-called free shares issued to shareholders in proportion to their holdings, either in addition to or in place of dividends - effectively a share split. A bonus issue did not affect the proportion of a company held by an investor or the underlying value of any parcel. For capital gains tax purposes the cost base per post bonus share is the total cost base of the original parcel divided by the new total number of shares.

bonus option plan (BOP): a dividend election plan.

bonus share plan (BSP): a dividend election plan.

bonus units: additional units in a unit trust issued without cost to existing unitholders to reflect capital growth.

book value: the original purchase price of an asset which may not be its current market value. In the absence of a revaluation the net book value is the gross book value less the accumulated depreciation.

bookbuild: an offer of securities in a new issue which is made to institutional investors, with these making competitive bids in regard to the price or yield wihin an indicative range at which they are willing to subscribe and as to the number of securities which they are willing to take up. This method is used by companies to establish a fair issue price for new shares. The method is much fairer to the vendors (the company itself and/or its founders), but it increases the risks for investors and reduces the prospect of making large gains immediately on listing.

books close: the date as at which the share register is closed for determining entitlements to a dividend, a vote, a share issue or some other reconstruction. The "ex dividend", etc., date is usually five working days prior to the books closing date. Shares purchased after that time do not participate in the dividend or issue.

books closing date: see ex dividend.

Boolean logic: a field of mathematical analysis particularly useful in regard to computers in which comparisons are made - for example, the Boolean operator AND allows something to happen if, and only if, both of two items are present.

boom: excellent trading conditions generally or in a particular area of activity - for example, mining boom, share boom, retail boom, etc.

BOP: abbreviation for bonus option plan.

bord: an underground passage made in solid coal.

borehole logging: the recording of subsurface geological formations. Logging takes two forms: records of penetration rate and downthrust on the drilling bit to show changes in strata; and specialised geophysical surveying with the small diameter of the borehole.

borehole: the hole made by drilling or boring.

bornite: copper iron sulphide, an ore of copper.

bottom feeder: a person who tries to buy shares from unsophisticated holders at a fraction of their true value. Typically the victims of such an exercise are elderly persons who acquired shares in a demutualisation and who do not even know a stockbroker whom they could consult for advice.

bottom-hole pressure (mining): the pressure in a well at or near the bottom of the hole.

bottom line: the final result, profit or loss, but before extraordinary items are taken into account, in a profit and loss statement. Certain items are treated as being above the line - profit or loss items regarded as part of a company's normal operating profit. Others again are treated as being below the line - profit or loss items reported as extraordinary because they are regarded as non-recurring.

bottom up: an equity management style which places little emphasis on the significance of economic and market cycles and focuses instead on an analysis of individual stocks.

bottoms: see tops and bottoms.

boundary line: a line drawn on a chart to indicate a formation.

bourse: stock exchange (French). The word is also used poetically in English to refer to any stock exchange.

bracket creep: the effect of the sliding scale in use for personal income tax rates; in conjunction with inflation this scale allows governments to lift the proportion of gross incomes absorbed in tax in successive financial years without incurring the political odium which would follow overt increases in the actual tax rates in force. In times of inflation the nominal incomes of employees and many other taxpayers rise (other things being equal), with the extra income becoming subject to a much higher tax rate than the average tax rate which applied to the pre-rise incomes. The problem would disappear if governments were prepared to legislate for the automatic indexation of the tax brackets.

breach of confidence: the disclosure of information to a person not entitled to it by someone who has an obligation to keep it confidential. See also Chinese walls.

breach of trust: action by a trustee outside the trustee's power.

break-even point: that point in the operation of a business at which the gross sales revenue equals all the costs.

break fee: a fee payable by the target company in a takeover to the bidding company (or vice versa) if an agreed bid fails in certain circumstances - for example, because another party makes a higher offer.

breakout: in charting, price movements which do not conform to the existing formation and which are expected to move the shares into a new phase.

breast (mining): a working face, usually restricted to a stope.

breccia: rock consisting of angular fragments in a finer grained matrix, as distinct from conglomerate.

BRIC: Brazil, Russia, India and China - regarded as countries with rapidly developing economies.

bridging finance: a temporary loan, often at a relatively high rate of interest, to enable the settlement of a property purchase to take place pending the grant of a permanent loan or the completion of the sale of another property.

BRL: symbol for the Brazilian real.

broker: an agent who effects buying and selling orders for clients.

brokerage: the commission payable to a broker for effecting a transaction.

browser: a special computer programme which allows a user to read hypertext (see below) and to provide a user interface to the World Wide Web. It enables the contents of pages on an Internet site to be viewed on an ordinary computer. Links on these pages (also called "hyperlinks" or "hot links") enable ready navigation from one page or part of a page to another.

BSE: abbreviation for Bombay Stock Exchange.

BSP: abbreviation for bonus share plan.

BTU: abbreviation for British Thermal Unit, a measure of energy (about 1055 joules).

bubble: the height of a speculative boom. A subsequent crash is referred to as "when the bubble bursts".

bucket wheel excavator: a machine providing continuous mining. A series of buckets with teeth mine a deposit, rotating the ore till it is dumped on a conveyor before the bucket again mines the deposit.

budget deficit: the amount by which government expenditure exceeds government revenue in a financial year.

budget (Union): the annual paper presented to Parliament by the Finance Minister, usually in February, setting out the

Government's proposals for revenue and expenditure, and comparing them with past results. Taxes can be used for economic management and to redistribute wealth as well as to finance government outlays. However, the budget is no longer the "one day of the year" event that it once was, as many fiscal measures are announced at other times.

buffer stock: a large representative sample used to verify assays.

buffer: parcels of stock horded and later sold to influence prices.

bull market: a rising market.

bull: an investor who expects the market to go up, an optimist; one who takes a "long" position in the market, i.e., is a buyer, in the belief that share prices are going to rise. Opposite of a bear.

bullion: precious metal in bars or ingot form. Usually refers to gold.

bullish: holding an optimistic opinion of future performance. Also used to describe a bull market.

burn rate: the rate at which a company is spending its existing cash reserves - in other words, its negative cash flow (usually expressed as a rate per month).

burning cost: a premium in general insurance designed to cover expected claims and expenses plus a profit margin.

burning ratio: the ratio of an insurance company's actual or expected claims to the sums insured in force.

business plan: a document which describes a company's management, business concepts and corporate objectives (both short term and long term). It is a vital tool for any company seeking bank loans or any other type of outside investment funding, but it can also be of great value in clarifying the realities for the owners of the enterprise themselves. A business plan should include details of the finance being injected by the proprietors and the expected internal rate of return; an assessment of the target market and the likely competition; a summary of the board and management team and their experience and expertise; brief job descriptions for the key employees and a summary of their contractual arrangements; details of any keyman insurance; balance sheet, profit and loss and cash flow projections; the attractions of the product or service for potential customers; details of the premises to be used and of any leases; marketing plans; any proposed Internet presence; and so on (as appropriate for the particular case).

butane: a gaseous hydrocarbon of the paraffin series.

butterfly effect: the phenomenon that small variations in the initial condition of a non-linear dynamical system can produce large variations in the long term behavior of the system.

buy and hold: refers to an investment strategy which involves buying a portfolio and thereafter managing but not trading those securities. See efficient capital market theory.

buy on margin: see margin.

buyback: the purchase by a company of its own shares.

buyers' market: the state of a market when supply outstrips demand and buyers rather than sellers can dictate prices.

buying off the plan: acquiring a plot of land plus a contract to erect a building, at an agreed price, from a developer, subject to the payment of a relatively small deposit initially, with the balance not due till completion. This approach can be used for both owner-occupied and investment properties.

In some States this results in a substantial stamp duty saving, as the duty is levied on the value of the land before construction starts, rather than on the much larger value of the land and the completed building.

However, purchasers run the risk that the finished product and its environs will not be quite as they had imagined. They also run the risk that the market can change in the interval between the time funds are committed and the time the building is actually ready for occupation.

Many off the plan residential developments look glamorous, but they can result in an oversupply of a type of property in a given area. Once any pent-up demand for this type of property has been satisfied prices are likely to fall until after a number of years further demand eventually builds up. By that time there could be further supply both from original purchasers who want to sell (or from their estates, similarly) and from competing developers.

Buying residential units off the plan by paying the small deposit using borrowed funds in the expectation of a capital gain based on the much larger total cost is a popular but highly risky strategy for small speculators.

buyout: the acquisition of a company by purchasing a controlling interest in it (often 100 per cent of its capital). See also management buyout.

BV: abbreviation for Besloten Vennootschap.

by-product: a secondary or additional mineral.

CAD: abbreviation for central activities district.

CAD: abbreviation for current account deficit.

CAD: symbol for the Canadian dollar.

cage: transportation device used to transport men and equipment in a shaft.

CAGR: abbreviation for compound annual growth rate.

Cainozoic Era: an era covering from 70 million years ago till the present. Includes the Quaternary and Tertiary Periods.

calcareous: containing calcium carbonate.

call: a demand for a further payment, by a specified date, on contributing shares. If the company is a no liability company then the call is not enforceable and the shareholders are entitled to forfeit their shares as an alternative to meeting the call. If the company has limited liability then the call is enforceable at law.

call: abbreviation for shares trading as call paid.

call in power: the power under planning legislation for the relevant minister in certain circumstances to direct a planning authority to refer a particular application for a permit to the minister for determination.

call option: a contract which entitles (but does not require) its holder to buy a fixed number of shares (usually 1000) in an underlying company at a stated price on or before a specified expiry date. See also option, cash covered option, scrip covered option.

Cambrian Period: a geological period from 500 to 600 million years ago.

cap (finance): the agreed maximum interest rate on a variable rate loan.

cap (mining): the outcrop of a lode (usually altered) or the blue halo of ignited firedamp (methane) which glows above the yellow flame of a safety lamp when exposed to air in coal mines containing small amounts of firedamp.

cap rock: impermeable rock overlaying a hydrocarbon reservoir.

capex: abbreviation for capital expenditure.

capital: wealth; money which is invested; the corpus of a trust estate or of a company or some other enterprise, as distinct from its income; risk capital; cash; productive machinery or the input of resources. The term is used in various senses:

- Colloquially, it can be used by both individuals and corporations to mean just a supply of money, as in the phrase "I have built up some capital".
- It can also be used more technically, for example, to distinguish between "share capital" and "loan capital", or between "capital items" and "revenue items".
- The expression "working capital" is used in accounting to mean "current assets less current liabilities".

capital account (trade): A country's receipts and payments from overseas transactions other than imports and exports, including invisibles - that is from new loans and equity investments either by governments or the private sector or from the repayment of past loans or investments. See also current account deficit.

capital adequacy: the statutory requirement for a financial institution to have sufficient equity.

capital asset pricing model: the model developed by Sharpe which relates the return from an investment to the risk free rate, market return and risk (beta). The formula is:

$$Rp = Rf + (Rm - Rf)\ Bp$$

where:

Rp is the return from the portfolio.
Rf is the risk free rate.
Rm is the return from the market.
Bp is the beta of the portfolio.

capital commitment: contracted obligations to make certain capital expenditure in the future. It does not appear in the balance sheet but is recorded in the notes to the account.

capital expenditure: see capital good.

capital gain or loss: a surplus or deficit resulting from the disposal of an asset which had not been acquired for resale and which therefore is classified as a revenue gain or loss and taxed accordingly.

capital gains tax (CGT): income tax levied on the realised capital gains when assets are sold or otherwise disposed of. Capital losses realised on assets sold or otherwise disposed of are allowed as an offset to the realised capital gains of the same or a future financial year. Disposal of the following does not give rise to any capital gains tax:

- The sole or principal residence (but not a second house, such as a holiday house, or an investment property).
- Motor vehicles.
- Life insurance policies (including investment bonds).
- Superannuation.

Furniture and ordinary household effects are also generally exempt, but works of art, collectible items, and so on, are not. Certain receipts of money are also regarded as not appropriate for taxation - for example, winnings from lotteries and other forms of gambling, and damages and compensation awards.

capital good: a good used to produce other goods and services. The acquisition of a capital good is called capital expenditure.

capital guarantee: the promise in a managed investment that the original capital and the interest which is credited from time to time are firm rather than subject to fluctuations related to market value changes, as in the case of investment-linked products.

capital indexed bonds: Commonwealth treasury bonds involving quarterly interest payments under which the investors get a low coupon, but with the amount of interest paid each three months and the prospective amount of capital at maturity both moving up in line with changes in the Consumer Price Index (CPI) each quarter. Interest payments are based on the written-up capital value at the time.

capital intensive: industries which have a heavier input of assets and machinery than labour.

capital items: items such as the acquisition or disposal of assets, the incurring or discharge of liabilities, and so on, as distinct from revenue items.

capital market: the broad market for financial assets or obligations. In a narrower sense it is the market for longer term funds, as distinct from the short term money market.

capital market line: in portfolio theory, the theoretical line representing all possible combinations of risk and return in a market. It represents the maximum return available for each level of risk.

capital ratio (banking): see minimum capital standards.

capital reserve: those reserves which arise from realised capital gains or asset revaluations and which are not free for distribution as dividends through the profit and loss account. Other capital reserves can be given names such as exchange fluctuation reserve, and so on.

capital, cost of: in relation to equity, the return which could be obtained by investing elsewhere; in relation to debt, the interest rate and associated charges.

capitalisation: the converting of capital reserves into capital which in former times was often distributed to shareholders as a bonus issue. See also market capitalisation.

capitalisation issue: in the days of par values, a bonus issue; so-called free shares issued to shareholders in proportion to their holdings, either in addition to or in place of dividends - effectively a share split. Such issues did not affect the proportion of a company held or the underlying value of the parcel.

capitalisation method: a method of valuing property by discounting actual or notional net rental payments in perpetuity at a suitable market-based interest rate in order to obtain their present value.

capitalisation rate: the rate of interest used for discounting future payments. See capitalisation method.

capitalise: to treat an item of expenditure as the purchase of an asset rather than as an expense. Common examples are holding charges on development properties and exploration and development expenses on mining properties.

capped interest rate: the agreed maximum interest rate on a variable rate loan.

captive (general insurance): an insurance company owned and controlled by its principal customer but having the appearance of independence.

carat: measure of fineness of a gold alloy or weight of gemstone. With gold, one carat is one twenty-fourth part, therefore pure gold is 24 carats. With gemstones, one international metric carat is 200 milligrams.

carbon credit: the right to emit a certain amount of carbon into the atmosphere. Emitting less than an allotted quota allows the remaining credit to be sold to companies desiring to emit more than their quota.

carbonaceous: composed largely of carbon.

Carboniferous Period: a geological period from 280 to 362 million years ago.

carried (of motions): adopted by a meeting following the receipt of the required majority of the votes.

carry trade: a self-financing position involving an investor who borrows in a low interest rate currency and lends or invests the proceeds in a high interest rate currency, in the expectation that the spot currency values will change by less than the net interest differential, thus yielding a profit.

carrying a dividend: the phenomenon of the price of a share ex dividend equalling its previous price cum dividend. Theoretically, the market price immediately after a share goes ex dividend should drop to reflect the amount of the distribution. If it does not, then the shares are said to have "carried" their dividend.

carrying capacity: the maximum sustainable size of a resident population in a given ecosystem.

cartel: a group of interested parties who voluntarily agree to co-ordinate their policies and thus artificially affect the market forces of supply and demand to their own advantage.

carve out: an exception to the general rule requiring listed companies to disclose immediately all material information of relevance to the market. The exception covers information which is regarded as immature or which relates to negotiations which are still confidential for commercial reasons.

cash and carry: an option or futures trading strategy involving the purchase of actual stock or a commodity and the simultaneous writing of an option against the stock or the sale of the commodity forward.

cash and near cash: assets which are readily convertible into cash such as bank accounts, money at call and marketable government securities.

cash basis: the method of accounting where revenue and expense items are recognised as they are actually received or paid and not when they are earned or incurred, as distinct from the accruals basis of accounting.

cash burn rate: the rate at which a company is spending its existing cash reserves - in other words, its negative cash flow (usually expressed as a rate per month).

cash covered option: a call option which is written and covered by cash rather than by the ownership of the underlying security.

cash cow: a company which generates a constant supply of cash from its normal activities.

cash economy: goods and services which are purchased for cash without any record being made in the usual accounting ledgers, normally in order to evade tax.

cash flow: the net funds generated from the operations of a business, as distinct from funds raised by capital subscriptions, borrowing, asset sales, and so on. It is commonly calculated by adding back non-cash items such as depreciation and amortisation charges to the net profit. The amount does not represent the actual cash remaining from operations, as much of this is directed into financing current assets; neither does it equate to profit.

cash flow statement: a statement which details the sources and uses of a company's cash during a reporting period. See also cash flow.

cash issue: see share issue.

cash management trust (CMT): a fixed interest unit trust designed specifically for short term investors. For this reason no front-end or rear-end fees are imposed, the manager's expenses and profits being covered by a periodical charge based on the total value of the fund. Units are normally issued at $1 and redeemed at $1, with interest accruing on a daily basis at a variable rate related to the fund's actual earning rate each day. A particularly valuable feature introduced by some cash management trusts is the ability for unitholders to write cheques drawn on their own accounts, either in favour of themselves or in favour of third parties (although usually not for cash).

cash rate: the interest rate which financial institutions pay when borrowing funds or charge when lending funds in the money market on an overnight basis.

cash reserve ratio: is a bank regulation that sets the minimum reserves each bank must hold with respect to customer deposits and notes. These reserves are designed to satisfy withdrawal demands, and would normally be in the form of currency stored in a bank vault, or with the central bank.

cash settled: settled by handing over cash rather than goods. In contrast, certain financial instruments are said to be "deliverable", meaning that settlement involves the physical transfer of an underlying security as distinct from an equivalent cash payment. See also warrants.

cashbox companies: companies with assets mainly in cash, usually run by entrepreneurs regarded as skilled in making profitable corporate plays.

cashed up: highly liquid, able to take advantage of buying opportunities. This can, however, be an expensive strategy in a rising market.

casing: a steel pipe placed in an oil or gas well to prevent the wall of the hole from caving in during drilling and to provide a means of extracting petroleum if the well is productive.

cassiterite: tin oxide, the most important ore of tin.

casting vote: a second vote sometimes given to the chairman of a meeting by the rules, exercisable only in the event of an equality of voting for and against any proposition, in order to break the tie.

catalyst: an additive used to induce a reaction.

cats and dogs: third grade stocks, usually showing great volatility in price.

caucusing: the system under which all members of a sub-group vote in the main group in accordance with a prior majority decision of that sub-group.

caveat: an entry made in the Court at the instance of a person claiming an unregistered interest in land to ensure that he is notified of any proposed dealings and given the opportunity to take legal steps to protect his position. (Latin, "let him beware".)

caveat emptor: let the buyer beware. The buyer has no redress for faulty goods based on this principle.

caveat venditor: let the seller beware.

CBD: abbreviation for central business district.

CBT: abbreviation for Chicago Board of Trade.

CC: stock exchange quotation symbol for cum capital return.

CCI: abbreviation for Competition Commission of India.

CCIL: abbreviation for Clearing Corporation of India Limited.

CCV: abbreviation for card check value (plastic cards).

cd: stock exchange quotation symbol for cum dividend (see ex dividend).

CDO: abbreviation for collateralised debt obligation.

ce: stock exchange quotation symbol for cum entitlement.

ceiling price: the maximum price at which a share or commodity, and so on, may be purchased by a broker for his client.

cementing: filling the space between the wall of the hole and the casing with cement so that fluids and gas cannot enter through the bottom of the well or work their way up outside the casing. It also strengthens the casing, should very heavy pressure be encountered.

certificate of title: the document which evidences the ownership of land. The "original" certificate is held in the Register Office and the "duplicate" is issued to the owner.

CFD: abbreviation for contract for difference.

CFI: abbreviation for conduit foreign income.

CGI: abbreviation for Corporate Governance International.

CGS: abbreviation for Commonwealth government securities.

CGT: abbreviation for capital gains tax.

chain reaction: a series of events following on quickly from each other, with each event being the cause of the following one.

chairman: the person charged with ensuring the orderly conduct of a meeting and/or to head an organisation and its committee.

chairman: the person elected to head a board of directors.

chalcocite: copper sulphide, an ore of copper.

chalcopyrite: copper and iron sulphide. The most important ore of copper.

chalkie: in the pre-computer era, a youth who recorded, by medium of chalk and blackboard, the buying and selling quotes of operators on the trading floor.

channel: see trend channel.

characteristic line: the regression line showing the relationship between the return from a stock or portfolio and the return from the market portfolio. Its slope is the beta of the stock or portfolio.

charge: a form of security for the payment of a debt and/or the performance of an obligation, such as a mortgage over land. A charge gives lenders prior rights against certain assets owned by a borrower. A charge may be fixed, so that the lender has a claim to a particular asset, or floating, so that the lender has a claim over a group of assets (which the borrower may vary).

charity: a non-profit organisation set up out of love of mankind with aims such as the relief of poverty, the advancement of education or religion or for other like purposes beneficial to the community. Most religious institutions, aged persons' homes, hostels for the homeless, organisations serving the special needs of people with disabilities or promoting the fine arts are charities.

For income tax purposes the essential characteristics of a charity are that it is an entity which is also a trust fund or an institution, that it exists for the public benefit or the relief of poverty, that its purposes are charitable within the legal sense of that term, that it is a non-profit body and that its sole or dominant purpose is charitable.

charting: the process of estimating expected future share prices by reference to historical movements of prices and turnover. Also known as technical analysis. Contrast fundamental analysis.

chartist: a proponent of technical analysis.

chattels: property other than freehold land. Chattels such as light fittings, carpets and partitions leased by an owner to a tenant along with the building are generally specified in the lease. Chattels sold with the building are generally specified in the contract of sale.

CHESS: the Clearing House Electronic Subregister System, a system for recording shareholdings in companies listed on the Australian Securities Exchange without using scrip certificates.

CHF: symbol for the Swiss franc.

Chicago Board of Trade (CBT): the largest commodity exchange in the world, based in the United States.

Chicago Mercantile Exchange (CME): the second largest commodity exchange after the Chicago Board of Trade.

Chinese walls: the invisible barriers which are meant to keep confidential information known to one section of an organisation from other sections and thus to avoid problems relating to breaches of confidence, insider trading, conflicts of interest, and so on. For example, one department of a stockbroker might be advising a corporate client in respect of a planned takeover; Chinese walls then allow other departments to give normal investment advice to clients in respect of shares in the companies concerned while all this is going on.

chip sample: a sample obtained by chipping a rock.

choke: a valve used to control the flow of hydrocarbons from a well. The choke size is important in assessing the significance of a flow.

Christmas tree: the control valves, pressure gauges, and chokes assembled at the top of a well to control the flow of oil and gas after the well has been drilled and completed.

chromite: ferrous chromic oxide, the principal ore of chromium.

chromium: a primary metal, the principal uses of which are as a plating material and as a ferro alloy to produce strengthened steel. Chemical symbol: Cr.

churning: the practice of an investment adviser inducing a client to sell certain securities and to buy others, with the principal aim being the earning of commission by the adviser.

chute: an opening through which ore is sent from a higher level to a lower one.

ci: stock exchange quotation symbol for cum interest.

cif: cost, insurance and freight. Opposite of fob.

circulation: the movement of drilling fluid out of the mud pits, down the drill stem, up the annulus, and back to the mud pits.

CIV: abbreviation for collective investment vehicle.

claim (insurance): a demand on an insurer for the payment of benefits under a policy.

claim (mining): a tract of land over which government approval has been granted for exploration. Approval covers a specified length of time and is subject to certain conditions.

claims ratio (general insurance): incurred claims as a proportion of earned premiums.

class action: a lawsuit brought by a representative member of a large group of people on behalf of all members of that group - for example, an action by shareholders of a failed company against its former directors and auditors, seeking damages.

class of option: option contracts of the same type (puts or calls) and covering the same underlying security.

class ruling: a public ruling issued by Income Tax Commissioner in order to provide certainty about the application of the tax law to a specific class of persons in relation to a particular arrangement not covered by the product rulings system - for example, in regard to the tax consequences for shareholders when the restructure of a company takes place or in regard to the tax consequences for employees when their employer is setting up an employee share acquisition plan.

clean up: to collect periodically all the valuable products from operations in stamp mills, sluice, boxes, etc.

cleanskin: an application form for a managed investment that does not bear the name of an intermediary entitled to commission.

Clearing Corporation of India Limited (CCIL): set up with the initiative of Reserve bank of India, CCIL provides exclusive clearing and settlement for transactions in money, government securities and foreign exchange.

clearing house: an organisation maintained by a common interest group to facilitate the exchange of securities, commodities, options, futures, etc., and the payments for these.

CLERP: abbreviation for Corporate Law Economic Reform Program.

client adviser: a person who advises a stockbroker's clients and takes orders.

close: the closing price of a share, being the last actual sale price of a share on a day, adjusted for any higher buying quote or any lower selling quote.

closed circuit: a loop in a milling process causing the reprocessing of ore.

closed end unit trust: a unit trust under which investors desiring to quit their interests dispose of them to other holders (on the stock exchange or privately), as distinct from having them redeemed by the fund manager.

closing price: the last actual sale price of a share on a day, adjusted for any higher buying quote or any lower selling quote.

closing purchase: a transaction in which an investor who has previously sold (written) an option liquidates his position as a writer by purchasing an option in the same series as the option previously written.

closing sale: the last sale of a stock on the day. In options terminology it is a transaction in which an investor who has previously purchased an option liquidates his position as a taker by selling his option in the secondary market.

closure: the procedural motion: "That the question be now put."

CMBS: abbreviation for commercial mortgage backed securities.

CME: abbreviation for Chicago Mercantile Exchange.

CMT: abbreviation for cash management trust.

cn: abbreviation for convertible notes.

cnt: abbreviation for convertible notes.

CNY: symbol for the Chinese renminbi.

coal: a solid fuel formed from buried vegetation in sedimentary strata or seams.

cobalt: a primary metal the principal use of which is as a ferro alloy. Chemical symbol: Co.

CODB: abbreviation for cost of doing business.

codicil: an addition or alteration to an existing will, executed as a separate document but with the same formalities as a will.

coefficient of variation: the ratio of the standard deviation to the mean. It is a measure of dispersion.

cognate debate: a single debate covering two or more relatively non-contentious motions dealing with the same broad subject, but preceding separate votes on each motion.

COGS: abbreviation for cost of goods sold.

cohort: a group of people sharing observed through time - for example, all those born in a given year.

collar (finance): the agreed maximum and minimum interest rates on a variable rate loan.

collar (mining): the structure at the mouth of a shaft.

collateral security: a security given in addition to the principal security.

collective investment vehicle: a unit trust which meets certain criteria and which because of this is not taxed itself in respect of distributed income; instead, each category of this income "flows through" to the unitholders for income tax purposes.

collusion: the arrangement by persons with seemingly conflicting interests acting together in order to harm another party for their own benefit.

COMEX: abbreviation for Commodities Exchanges in New York, Chicago and Los Angeles, a market place for commodity trading.

commercial property: shops and offices.

commercial residential accommodation (GST): hotels, motels, hostels, boarding houses, caravan parks and the like.

commingle: to combine separately owned assets into common fund, typically to reduce administrative costs.

committee of the whole: a meeting of members able to discuss issues without the normal constraints of standing orders and/or in private.

Committee on Uniform Securities Identification Procedures (CUSIP): a CUSIP number is a unique nine-digit code allotted to shares and bonds in the United States and Canada. The first six digits identify the issuer. The next two digits represent the security that was issued. The final digit is a check digit.

commodity: an article of trade or commerce, especially one traded on commodities or futures exchanges - for example, sugar, wool, wheat, coffee, gold, silver, lead, copper, tin.

common funds: an arrangement, similar to a cash management trust, offered by a trustee company. These funds are made up of a large number of small cash balances, pooled for investment purposes in order to get a higher return at a lower cost, with the net return being distributed pro rata.

common law: the past decisions of the superior courts and the precedents which these create, as distinct from both statute law (Acts of Parliament) and equity.

common stock: ordinary shares (United States).

Commonwealth bonds: bearer securities transferable by mere delivery. Each bond has an identification number and particulars of the interest rate and maturity date. Attached to the bonds are coupons covering each interest payment during the currency of the issue and these may be cashed as they fall due, either with the Commonwealth Registry or any bank. Bonds are freely convertible into inscribed stock which are not bearer securities. The term is also used to cover Commonwealth loans generally.

CFD: abbreviation for contract for difference.

company: a legal entity formed to undertake a business or activity. Most companies fall into one of three major categories, namely, public limited companies, private limited companies and no liability companies. Public companies are usually owned either directly or beneficially by a large number of shareholders. They can issue shares and debentures by way of a public issue and there are usually no limitations on the transfer of shares.

Private or proprietary companies are usually owned by a small number of shareholders and there are restrictions on the ability to transfer shares. In the case of both public and private companies where there is limited liability the shareholder is responsible to the company only to the extent of the fully paid-up value of the capital and any premium stipulated at the time of issue.

On liquidation shareholders are not liable beyond any uncalled capital and premium. With no liability (NL) companies, shareholders are not responsible for any uncalled capital and have the right to forfeit their shares in the event of a call.

Most NL companies are mining and exploration concerns. Other forms of companies also exist, such as companies limited by guarantee and unlimited companies. Only public companies, including NL companies, can be listed on the stock exchange.

company doctor: usually a management expert or consultant brought in to rejuvenate a company.

competent rock: rock which is relatively free of defects and which stands unsupported once openings are established.

Ccompetition Commission of India: Created by statute 'Competition Act 2002', Competition Commission of India (CCI) is empowered with the powers to prohibit anti-competitive agreement so as to prevent abuse of dominant position by any enterprise.

The Competition Act 2002: it refers to the legislation passed aimed at limiting monopolistic practices.

complete a well: to prepare a well for production.

complex ore: ore containing a number of minerals, generally making it expensive to process.

compliance listing: listing on the stock exchange by an existing enterprise which already has a sufficient spread of shareholders. It can seek listing without raising any money and without any offer of shares to the public by either the company or its current shareholders.

compound interest: interest calculated on both the original capital and on the accumulation of past interest amounts, in contradistinction from simple interest; compound interest is the only meaningful way to measure the return on an investment. The period between interest calculations affects the total amount of interest paid, with shorter periods or rests resulting in effectively higher interest payments than longer periods (in respect of any particular nominal rate of interest).

compressor: a machine to compress air which can be used to power machinery.

compulsory acquisition: see takeover.

compulsory liquidation: see liquidation.

con: abbreviation for convertible.

concentrate: milled ore that has been processed to contain a higher metal content.

concentrator: a machine to concentrate ore.

concession capital gains: the portion of capital gains under the discount method which is exempt from income tax (50 per cent for individuals and 33 1/3 per cent for superannuation funds). Receipt of this portion does not attract tax, nor does it reduce the cost base of the asset.

concessional deductions (tax): deductions which may be claimed although unrelated to the earning of assessable income, such as donations to charities and contributions to superannuation funds.

conciliation: the process under which a neutral third person attempts to bring two disputing parties to a situation where they can reach their own agreement.

condensate: the liquid hydrocarbons which condense from a gas to a liquid when the pressure and temperature are lowered during production. Includes pentane, hexane, etc.

conditional: see takeover.

confer (abbreviated *cf*): compare.

confidence interval: a statistical measure expressing the confidence with which a statement is made. Expressed as a percentage.

conflict of interest: the state of affairs when a person in a decision making situation has a duty to others which could be at variance with a benefit to that person - for example, a person negotiating a contract between himself or herself in a personal capacity as one party and himself or herself in the capacity as trustee of a fund as the other party. See also pecuniary interest.

conformable beds: rock strata in which each stratum is superimposed on another. See also unconformity.

conglomerate (business): a large organisation, usually with diversified interests/businesses.

conglomerate (mining): a sedimentary rock formed by the cementing together of rounded water worn particles, as distinct from breccia.

connate water: water trapped in a sedimentary rock at the time of formation and which has not escaped.

consideration: the money value of a stock exchange transaction (the number of shares multiplied by the price per share), before adding or deducting brokerage and stamp duty.

consolidated accounts: statements representing the combined group position of an enterprise, that is, parent and subsidiary companies together, after eliminating inter-company transactions. For investment purposes it is usual to examine the consolidated rather than the parent company accounts. See also equity accounting.

consolidated balance sheet: a balance sheet obtained by combining the separate information for the parent company and for each subsidiary company, after eliminating inter-company transactions.

consolidated profit: the profit of the group, not just of the parent company. See also consolidated accounts, profit.

consolidated profit and loss account: a profit and loss account obtained by combining the separate information for the parent company and for each subsidiary company, after eliminating inter-company transactions.

consolidation (charting): a charting formation which occurs following strong share price movements and prior to further expected movements.

consolidation (company accounting): the act of preparing a consolidated balance sheet and a consolidated profit and loss account for a group of companies.

consolidation (shares): the combining of a company's shares into a smaller number of shares, each with a correspondingly higher market value. The total value of any investor's holdings is not affected by the consolidation. Sometimes consolidations are made to avoid a "penny dreadful" image. The opposite of a share split.

consortium: two or more organisations which combine resources and risks for joint projects.

constant dollars: monetary values which have been expressed in the dollars of some base year. By using constant dollars to express values the effects of inflation are removed.

constitution: the rules governing a company. Under legislative changes which commenced on 1 July 1998 the constitution replaced the memorandum and articles of association.

Consumer Price Index (CPI): an index of price changes based on final consumption goods. It is the most common measure of inflation. It is measured in the March, June, September and December quarters, and compiled from thousands of individual prices.

contact zones: the zones within which rock layers or bodies touch.

contamination: the addition of foreign rock material by a subsequent geological process to an orebody.

contango: a fee paid by a buyer of stock for the right to delay taking delivery. Used in commodities. See also backwardation.

contingent liabilities: uncertain liabilities for which the obligation, if any, has not been determined. Examples are the liabilities which may arise from law suits and guarantees provided to associated companies' creditors. Due to their uncertain nature these items do not form part of the liabilities listed in a company's balance sheet but they are disclosed in the notes to the accounts.

continuous disclosure: the requirement under the SEBI/NIFTY Listing Rules that all listed companies immediately notify the exchange of (and thus effectively publish to the world) any information in their possession *at any time* which is likely to materially affect the price of their securities or which is necessary in order to avoid the establishment or continuation of a false market in those securities. Any information which investors or their professional advisers "would reasonably require" must be disclosed. This very wide general wording would appear to cover just about everything. But in order to make doubly sure that not even inexperienced company directors or managements can possibly misunderstand their obligations the rule also refers specifically to the making of an informed assessment of a company's assets, liabilities, profits and losses, as well as of its current financial position and future prospects.

continuous miner: an underground mining machine.

contract: an agreement between two or more parties which is enforceable at law. Contracts can be written, oral or inferred from conduct, although certain contracts (such as those for the sale of land) need to be in writing. Contracts can be terminated or varied by the mutual consent of all parties. The essentials of a valid contract are:

- offer and acceptance
- form and/or consideration
- legal capacity of all parties to contract
- legality of purpose
- intention to create a legal relationship

- sufficient certainty of the terms
- mutual consent.

See also force majeure.

contract (futures market): the standardised unit of a commodity traded on a futures exchange.

contract depth: the depth of a well at which the drilling contract is fulfilled.

contract drilling: frequently the actual physical drilling is performed by another party under contract. The contractor's remuneration is fixed under the contract and is independent of the results.

contract for difference (CFD): a futures contract involving shares under which the gains and losses are settled in cash.

contract mining: frequently the actual physical mining is performed by another party under contract. The contractor's remuneration is fixed under the contract and is independent of the results.

contract note (property): a simple-looking but important document signed by the vendor and purchaser of land, evidencing the contract of sale binding both parties. Such notes have the same legal effect as the more formal older-style "contract of sale of real estate" documents.

contract note (stock exchange): a same day written confirmation of an order executed on the stock exchange, issued by a stockbroker, which sets out the date of the transaction, the required settlement date, whether the securities were "bought" or "sold", the names of the broker, the client and the company concerned, the quantity, the class of security, the unit price, the total consideration gross, the brokerage, the GST on that brokerage and the balance due to or by the broker. The contract note would also have on it a reference to the fact that the transaction was subject to the rules, customs, and so on, of the Securities and Exchange Board of India (SEBI) and that the Note was subject to the correction of errors. Securities traded near a books closing date would be identified as being either "cum" or "ex" the entitlement concerned.

Changes in the ownership of the securities take place at the moment that the orders placed by the buyer and the seller are matched by the exchange's computer, the subsequent issue of the contract note only *recording* a contract which has already been made.

contrib: abbreviation for contributing shares.

contributing shares: shares on which only part of the capital (and/or, formerly, the share premium) has been paid. The outstanding money is payable in one or more calls at times set out in the terms of the issue or specified by the company. Also called partly paid shares, partly paids, contribs. Abbreviated to ctg.

contributory: a shareholder in a company in liquidation or a former shareholder in such a company who is liable in respect of uncalled capital.

controlled entities: a holding company's subsidiary companies.

controlling interest: technically, a shareholding in a company giving a voting power in excess of 50 per cent; loosely speaking, any shareholding which because of its size and the spread of the other shareholders, is in practice sufficient to pass resolutions at general meetings.

conv nts: abbreviation for convertible notes.

convergence (derivatives): the gradual movement of the price of a futures contract towards the price of the underlying cash commodity as the time value of the contract decreases to zero at its expiry.

convergence (finance sector): the coming together under the one ownership of entities which were formerly regarded as operating in some or all of discrete industries - such as banks, building societies, insurance companies, funds management groups and trustee companies. The phenomenon is sometimes referred to as allfinanz or bancassurance.

convergence (physical equipment): the trend for television, telephones and computers to become a single instrument, as all content is converging into digital streams of information that can represent text, graphics, audio or video, and can be distributed over multiple media such as satellites, CDs, DVDs, cable lines, wireless and land-based telephone connections.

convergence (politics): moves such as those in the European Union (qv) to bring about free trade between member nations, to give its citizens freedom to travel, study and work in the entire area, to have a common currency and a common central bank and to harmonise the laws of the different countries.

conversion ratio: the number of ordinary shares obtainable on the conversion of one convertible preference share or convertible note.

convertible note: a fixed interest security convertible under specified conditions into ordinary shares on the basis of some defined ratio, often one for one.

convertible redeemable preference shares: preference shares, ranking after loan securities but ahead of ordinary shares, which in accordance with their terms of issue can be either converted into ordinary shares on the basis of some defined ratio or redeemed in cash on one or more specified dates.

conveyance: the transfer of an interest in land by sale, mortgage, lease, etc.

conveyors: a form of transporting ore or coal. Material is fed onto the conveyor belt or chain, which is driven by a series of rollers over a continuous path with the material being carried to an appropriate point and then being dumped.

COP: symbol for the Colombian peso.

copper: a primary metal processed from a number of copper ores, including chalcopyrite, chalcocite and bornite. Its principal qualities are its high conductivity and resistance to corrosion. These characteristics make it widely used in electrical and liquid reticulation applications. Chemical symbol: Cu.

copyright: the exclusive but marketable right to publish and distribute original literary, artistic and similar works. Copyright also covers software. Copyright automatically belongs initially to the creator of a work and lasts for his or her lifetime and for a further 60 years. The rights can be assigned to other persons in whole or in part. Many authors grant licences in exchange for royalties.

core: the cylindrical cutting formed within the stems of drill rods during diamond drilling.

core analysis: the laboratory analysis of a core sample to determine its composition.

core inflation: inflation as measured by the Consumer Price Index, but with adjustments to eliminate irregular influences and thus better reflect the trend of price changes on an ongoing basis.

core samples: samples collected inside the stems of drill rods during diamond drilling.

cornering: the practice by an investor or a syndicate of buying all or much of the available stock in a particular security or commodity with a view to forcing the price up and then exiting at a large profit.

corporate action: an event which affects a company's investors - for example, a rights issue or a share split.

corporate horoscope: a horoscope prepared for a company as though it were a human being who was born on the day that the company was incorporated. There is no reason to believe that any such astrological document has any value whatsoever in forecasting performance on the stock exchange. Using a computer to prepare such a horoscope is a great perversion of a marvellous scientific device.

corporate raiders: persons who profit by acquiring control of a listed company at a price below its real value and then selling off its assets.

corporate veil: the protection given to shareholders in companies by the principle of *limited liability.* Under this principle, companies are legal entities separate and distinct from their individual shareholders. Thus liability to a company's creditors is limited to the assets of the company itself and does not extend to the personal assets of its shareholders.

corporation: see company.

Corporatisation: the turning of a semi-governmental authority into a company, with all the discipline which that implies. Initially all the shares are owned by the government concerned, but the process is often the first step to full privatisation.

corpus: the capital of a trust estate, as distinct from its income.

correlation co-efficient: in statistical analyses, the strength of the relationship between two sets of data. Scores can range between -1 and 1. A score of 1.0 indicates a perfect direct relationship. Zero indicates no relationship. Negative scores indicates an inverse relationship.

cost base: the (adjusted) purchase price of an asset, as defined for capital gains tax purposes.

cost of capital: in relation to equity, the return which could be obtained by investing elsewhere; in relation to debt, the interest rate and associated charges.

cost-benefit analysis: an evaluation of a project involving a comparison of the expected outlays and the expected returns.

costean: a trench dug across the surface of a zone with a bulldozer or backhoe.

counterparty risk: the risk that the other party to a financial transaction not involving a standardised contract settled through a clearing house, such as a currency or an interest rate swap, will default.

country rock: the rock surrounding the orebody.

coupon: an attachment to bearer bonds representing interest payments. See also Commonwealth bonds, coupon rate.

coupon rate: the nominal return on a fixed interest security. It is the interest rate applied to the par value of a security. It is not necessarily the effective return on the security to an investor. See redemption yield.

covenant: a legally binding promise or agreement - for example, a clause in a lease; a restrictive covenant endorsed on a title serves to limit the use which any subsequent owner can make of the land.

cover: see dividend cover and interest cover.

cover note (general insurance): a brief interim document which confirms that a proponent is being held covered for a short defined period, pending the issue by the insurer of a formal policy document.

cp: stock exchange quotation symbol for call paid.

CPA: abbreviation for Certified Practising Accountant.

CPI: abbreviation for Consumer Price Index.

cq: stock exchange quotation symbol for cum off-market buy-back.

cr: stock exchange quotation symbol for cum rights.

crab market: a market which is in neither a bull nor a bear phase, with prices relatively steady.

cracking: the breaking down of crude oil into lighter grade crude in refining by the application of high temperatures and pressure.

crash: a significant and sharp decline in share prices.

credit facility: the predetermined right to be able to borrow money.

credit foncier: a loan involving regular periodical instalments comprising both principal and interest.

credit rating: a measure of credit worthiness derived from an analysis of financial statements, business experience, etc.

credit union: a non-bank financial institution the members of which have a common bond. It takes deposits from its members and offers funds for housing and consumer credit finance.

creditable acquisitions (GST): acquisitions which are "taxable supplies" to the other party to the deal.

creditor: a person or corporation to whom money is owed.

Cretaceous Period: a geological period from 65 to 135 million years ago.

CRISIL: an organization earlier known as Credit Rating and Information Services of India Limited but now only by its shortened name CRISIL. It is the premier credit rating, research and policy advisory organization for credit rating, capital market information, industry analysis and detailed reports about companies, industries and economy.

critical mass: the minimum amount of something - for example, funds under management or paid-up customers - for a commercial enterprise to be viable.

crosscut: a level driven across the course of a vein or the direction of the main workings.

crossing: a sale where the broker is acting for both the buyer and the seller. Same as marriage.

crowding out: government borrowings forcing the private sector out of the market.

crude oil: oil as it comes out of the ground. It requires refining before commercial use.

crusher: a machine for crushing ore. Includes a gyratory crusher, jaw crusher, stamp mill, etc.

crystallise a loss: to turn an unrealised capital loss into a realised capital loss by disposing of an asset and, in the process, also establishing the exact amount of that loss (and, in an investment or business context, enabling that loss to become an offset to realised capital gains for capital gains tax purposes).

CSO: Central Statistical Organisation (CSO) is a body responsible for coordinating, evolving and maintaining statistical standards in India. Its activities include national income accounting, industrial surveys, economic censuses, index of industrial production, consumer price indices etc.

CSR: abbreviation for corporate social responsibility.

ct: abbreviation for conditional trading.

ct: stock exchange quotation symbol for conditional trading.

CTA: abbreviation for commodity trading adviser (US).

ctg: abbreviation for contributing shares.

cum: abbreviation for cumulative.

cum: with something - for example, shares bought cum rights or cum dividend entitle a purchaser to those benefits, rather than the seller. Contrast ex. (Latin for "with".)

cum dividend (cd): see ex dividend.

cumulative: a type of preference share. The term means that if any year's preference dividends are not paid out (for example, because of lack of profitability) then all arrears must be paid off before payment of ordinary dividends is permitted. Dividends on non-cumulative preference shares, by way of contrast, are looked at only one financial year at a time and shareholders have no protection against missed declarations.

currency board: a monetary system based on an explicit legislative commitment for a note and coin issuing authority, the currency board, to exchange the domestic currency of a country for a specified foreign currency (for example, the United States dollar) at a fixed exchange rate, with the domestic currency remaining fully backed by appropriate foreign assets.

currency tax: see Tobin tax.

current account (banking): a cheque account.

current account (trade): A country's receipts and payments from imports and exports, including invisibles.

current account deficit: the amount by which the value of a country's imports of goods exceeds the value of its exports of goods in a period, allowing for invisibles. By definition, this equals the capital account surplus for the same period. See also trade deficit.

current assets: assets which in the ordinary course of business would be consumed or turned into cash within 12 months. Examples include cash, deposits, prepayments, stock, trade debtors, etc. See also assets.

current cost accounting: a method of accounting aimed at presenting accounts in terms of current values. It was developed to provide meaningful details in times of inflation. The result for any one period of accounting is determined by matching the revenue for the period with the current cost of producing that revenue. In the balance sheet, items are stated on the basis of their current cost.

current dollars: monetary values which have been expressed in the historical dollars. In contrast, constant dollars are used if it is desired to remove the effects of inflation.

current liabilities: liabilities which in the ordinary course of business would be consumed or turned into cash within 12 months. Examples include overdraft, trade creditors, short term financial debt, and the current provisions for taxation, dividend, leave, etc. See also liabilities.

current ratio: a measure of liquidity, the current assets divided by the current liabilities. Also known as the working capital ratio. Contrast liquid assets ratio.

curvilinear table: a vibrating table used to concentrate heavy minerals.

CUSIP: abbreviation for Committee on Uniform Security Identification Procedures.

cut and fill: a method of mining where ore is removed and the resulting excavation filled with waste to support the stope before the next section is mined.

cutoff grade: the lowest grade of ore used in the calculation of reserves.

cuttings: the broken pieces of rock formed by the bit during drilling. These are removed by accumulating in the drill rod to form a core, or in oil drilling by the circulation of drilling mud.

The analysis of cuttings is an important part of the evaluation of a well.

cvnts: abbreviation for convertible notes.

cyanidation: the process of extracting gold or silver by dissolving the crushed ore in a weak solution of sodium cyanide.

cyclical stocks: shares in companies in industries that are perennially subject to the vagaries of the business cycle - for example: construction, steel, resources, automobiles and chemicals. Contrast defensive stocks.

CYP: symbol for the Cyprus pound.

cz: stock exchange quotation symbol for cum priority.

D&O: abbreviation for directors' and officers' liability insurance.

data: facts.

data mining: the analysis of large groups of data in a database, using tools which look for previously unknown trends or anomalies or hidden patterns, without regard to the meaning of the data.

datum: a fixed point serving as a reference.

day trader: a person who buys shares and then sells them again on the same day.

days of grace (insurance): a period, usually 28 or 30 days, after a premium falls due in which it may be paid without penalty for non-payment and without prejudicing the cover.

days receivable: the number of days that it takes to collect outstanding accounts. It is calculated by dividing 365 by the debtors' turnover.

days stock: see stock turnover ratio.

DBP: abbreviation for dividend bonus plan.

DCT: abbreviation for deferred company tax.

dd: abbreviation for deferred delivery.

de facto: in fact (especially in contradistinction to de jure).

de jure: by right (especially in contradistinction to de facto).

de novo: anew.

dead cat bounce: a quick and moderate rise on the stock exchange following a steep fall, with the likelihood of a further fall.

dealer: a person or company licensed to trade in Securities.

death duties: taxes levied on the net assets of a deceased estate.

death rate: the number of deaths per 1000 population in a given year.

debate: the formal discussion on a question before the chair.

debenture: a medium to long term borrowing by a company at a specified rate of interest, usually maturing on a specified date, and secured on the assets of the company. Debentures are transferable by selling through stockbrokers (or privately). Debentures may have various levels of priority - for example, a first ranking debenture ranks ahead of a second ranking debenture. All rank ahead of unsecured liabilities.

debenture trust deed: see trust deed.

debt to equity ratio (companies): a company's total outside liabilities divided by its shareholders' funds.

debt to equity ratio: a measure of gearing calculated by dividing all financial debt by the shareholders' equity or the investor's own stake in a project.

debtor: a person or corporation that owes money.

debtors' turnover: the number of times in a year that debtors are collected. It is calculated by dividing credit sales per annum by the trade debtors. The ratio is usually divided into 365 to show the average number of days required for clients to pay their accounts.

deceased estate: the assets left behind by a person at the time of death.

decile: every ten per cent of a ranked series of scores.

deductible (general insurance): the amount of loss that is to be borne by the insured when claiming under a policy.

deduction (tax): an amount which may be subtracted from assessable income before income tax is calculated.

deed of settlement: an instrument "signed, sealed and delivered" which sets up a trust and defines its terms.

deed of trust: an instrument "signed, sealed and delivered" which sets up a trust and defines its terms.

deed poll: a deed "signed, sealed and delivered" by a single party (the word "poll" refers to the straight edge of such documents in olden times, in distinction from "indentures" which were instruments created by dividing a single parchment into two duplicate parts by cutting along a wavy line, enabling their genuineness to be demonstrated by the matching teethlike edges).

deeming: a social security concept. In order to counter a perceived abuse of the system a concept known as "deeming" now applies in the case of certain assets called "financial investments". For these the actual investment return is disregarded for the purpose of the income test and a notional or *deemed* rate of return applied to the current value of the asset is used instead.

deep discount stock: a fixed interest security which makes only very small periodical interest payments. It is issued at a price substantially below its redemption or maturity price (usually styled par). Investors get part of their return from the difference between this discounted price and the redemption price. A zero coupon stock is an extreme version of a deep discount stock.

deep leads: a deeply buried alluvial deposit.

defalcation: misappropriation of money.

default: a failure to repay a debt, or to pay interest or rent, or to observe the other covenants, under a loan agreement or a lease.

defd: abbreviation for deferred shares.

defd del: abbreviation for deferred delivery.

defensive stocks: shares in companies which are regarded as relatively immune to adverse changes to the economy - for example, in industries such as food, tobacco and utilities. Contrast cyclical stocks.

deferment period: the period (a week or more at the option of the policyholder) during which no income benefit is paid under accident, sickness or disability policies. Deferment starts on the date of disability.

deferred annuity: an annuity under which the periodical payments commence on some specified future date.

deferred assets: assets which in the ordinary course of business would not be consumed or turned into cash within 12 months. See also assets.

deferred delivery: new shares which are already listed but for which records of title are still being processed. The shares can be traded on the basis of settlement on some specified date later than normal.

deferred liabilities: liabilities which in the ordinary course of business would not be consumed or turned into cash within 12 months. Examples include provision for deferred tax, other non-current provisions, long term financial debt. See also liabilities.

deferred shares: shares which do not currently rank for dividend.

deferred tax: a tax expense which has been charged to the profit and loss account but which is not payable for over twelve months.

deferred tax liability: the estimated amount of future income tax likely to arise from the reversal of timing differences. See also tax effect accounting.

deficit: see budget deficit, trade deficit, current account deficit.

defined benefit plan: a superannuation plan in which the member's retirement benefits are related to a combination of the salary at or near retirement (or over some other period) and the years of service or membership. Contributions at a level sufficient to purchase these benefits need to be paid. Contrast accumulation plan.

defined contribution plan: a superannuation plan involving defined contributions which are invested and accumulated at interest in order to produce a retirement benefit. Contrast defined benefit plan.

del: abbreviation for deferred delivery.

delist: to remove a company's shares from the official lists and boards of quotation at the stock exchange.

deliverable: settled by handing over goods rather than cash. Certain financial instruments are said to be "deliverable", meaning that settlement involves the physical transfer of an underlying security as distinct from an equivalent cash payment. See also warrants.

DEM: symbol for the German mark.

dematerialise: to turn security holdings represented by scrip certificates into uncertificated holdings recorded electronically as book entries.

demerger: the disintegration of a company into separate operations in the expectation that this will enhance performance.

demography: the scientific study of human populations, including their composition, distribution and growth.

density: the weight of a substance per unit of volume.

dependency ratio: the ratio of the economically dependent part of the population to the workforce.

deposit margin: a cash buffer set by the clearing house in the futures market, which is paid by a trader to cover against losses. This is variable daily.

deposition: sedimentation.

depreciation: a non-cash charge against profit representing the theoretical value of a fixed asset used up, or depleted, in a period; the systematic writing down each year of an asset with a limited economic life, especially for balance sheet or income tax purposes; or the amount of this writing down. A number of methods exist for calculating depreciation, the most common of which are:

- prime cost (straight line)
- diminishing value (declining balance)
- sum of the years digits.

depression: a hollow surrounded by high ground.

derivative: a financial instrument or product that *derives* its value from the price of another more basic instrument or product - for example, an option, a swap or a futures contract.

derrick: the tower or framework over a drillhole.

determination: a formal decision - for example, a resolution made by a trustee or a ruling by a tribunal.

devalue: reduce the value of a unit of one country's currency against a unit of another country's currency.

development: the establishment of infrastructure and access to the ore body prior to mining. Normally capitalised in the balance sheet.

development well: a well drilled in proven territory to complete a desired pattern of production.

deviation: see angle of deflection.

Devonian Period: a geological period from 362 to 413 million years ago.

dewater: to pump water out of an abandoned mine.

DFAT: abbreviation for Department of Foreign Affairs and Trade.

DFCS: abbreviation for Department of Family and Community Services (the Commonwealth Government department responsible for social security).

DGR: abbreviation for deductible gift recipient.

DI: abbreviation for depository interest.

diamond: a stone made from pure carbon. It is the hardest naturally occurring substance and is used as a gem and, for industrial purposes, in cutting tools. Found alluvially and in kimberlite pipes.

diamond drill: a rotary type of rock drill in which the cutting is done by abrasion rather than percussion. The cutting bit is set with diamonds and is attached to the end of long hollow tubes through which water is pumped to the cutting face. The drill cuts a core of rock which is recovered in long cylindrical sections of varying diameters.

diamondiferous: (in relation to any rocks, unconsolidated sediment or soil) containing diamonds.

differential flotation: a milling process using the flotation process, by which concentrates are made of each of the various valuable minerals in an ore.

dike: an essentially vertical, tabular body of igneous rock that cuts across the structure of adjacent rocks. Formed by an intrusion.

diluted earnings per share: earnings per share adjusted for the existence of options and convertible securities. Diluted earnings should always be used if these are lower than undiluted earnings.

dilution (companies): issues of new shares made other than on a pro rata basis to existing shareholders and particularly placements offered to outsiders at a price which is less than either the market value or the net tangible asset backing of equivalent existing shares. These have the effect of reducing the equity of the current investors in the company and for this reason are often regarded as immoral.

dilution (mining): the reduction in grade which results from the unavoidable mining of waste rock with the ore.

dilution factor: a decimal fraction which is used to adjust a historical per share series of data in order to make it comparable with current data. The adjustment is made to deflate prior data by the value of the bonus element in any capital change.

diminishing value: see depreciation.

DIP: abbreviation for dividend investment plan.

dip: the angle at which a rock stratum or a vein is inclined from the horizontal.

direct costing: a method of valuing inventory that includes the appropriate share of variable costs only. Sometimes called variable costing or marginal costing.

direct taxation: broadly speaking, taxes levied on money received - for example, income tax on individuals, company tax and the former death duties. Contrast indirect taxation.

directional drilling: intentional deviation of a wellbore from the vertical. Although wellbores are normally drilled as vertically as possible, it is sometimes necessary or advantageous to drill at an angle from the vertical. Controlled directional drilling makes it possible to reach subsurface areas laterally remote from the point where the bit enters the earth.

director: a person chosen by the members of a company to guide the management of a business. See also shadow director.

director's share qualfication: see share qualification.

directors' and officers' liability insurance (D&O): insurance policies giving individual directors and officers of a company the protection they need from personal liabilities and financial losses arising out of wrongful acts or omissions committed (or allegedly committed) by them in their capacity as directors or officers.

directors' report: a statutory statement in a company's annual report containing the replies to certain questions set out in the legislation. Most listed companies also provide non-statutory reviews of the company and its operations and prospects, usually in the form of reports by the chairman and/or the chief executive.

directors' statement: a statutory statement in a company's annual report certifying that the accounts give a "true and fair view".

DIRP: abbreviation for dividend and interest reinvestment plan.

disability benefit: benefit payable under a policy if the life insured becomes disabled, temporarily or permanently.

discount: the excess of the nominal or face or par value of a security over its price. It does not necessarily indicate a bargain. The opposite of premium.

discount method: one of the ways of calculating capital gains tax which can be chosen for the disposal of assets acquired, provided that the assets concerned had been held for at least 12 months.

discount rate: the interest rate used in a discounted cash flow calculation. The most appropriate rate may be the cost of capital.

discounted cash flow: a method of project evaluation, based on discounting future cash flows at a specific interest rate in order to arrive at their present value as at the calculation date.

discovery well: the first oil or gas well drilled in a new field; the well that reveals the presence of a petroleum-bearing reservoir. Subsequent wells are development wells.

discretionary trust: a trust under which the trustee is given power to make choices or is required to decide from time to time which beneficiaries are to receive income and/or capital distributions from the trust fund and also what amounts each beneficiary is to receive and the make-up of those amounts.

discriminatory language: words which stereotype people on the basis of their sex, age, religion, political beliefs, nationality, race, colour, ethnic background, marital status, physical or mental disability, lifestyle or the like.

displacement fluid: in oil-well cementing, the fluid, usually drilling mud or salt water, that is pumped into the well after the cement to force the cement out of the casing and into the annulus.

disseminated ore: ore carrying small particles of valuable minerals, spread more or less uniformly through the gangue matter, as distinct from massive ore, where the valuable minerals occur in almost solid form with very little waste material included.

distillate: the product of the condensation of vaporised fractions of oil.

distress sale value: see fire sale value.

distribution: money or its equivalent paid by a trustee to a beneficiary of a trust (including a deceased estate).

distribution reinvestment plan: a scheme similar to a dividend reinvestment plan (qv), offered by a unit trust to its unit holders.

diversifiable risk: see non-systemic risk.

diversification: the spreading of the assets of a portfolio among a number of alternative investments in order to reduce risk - see spread. See also naive diversification, effective diversification.

divestment: the selling off of an investment.

dividend: the amount paid out of profits to shareholders.

dividend and interest reinvestment plan (DIRP): a dividend reinvestment plan.

dividend bonus plan (DBP): a dividend election plan.

dividend cover: the number of times that the profit after tax covers the dividend amount.

dividend election plan (DEP): a scheme similar in concept to a dividend reinvestment plan but one involving the company issuing bonus shares out of a capital source in lieu of declaring the normal dividends.

dividend investment plan (DIP): a dividend reinvestment plan.

dividend option plan (DOP): a dividend election plan.

dividend payable date: see ex dividend.

dividend payout ratio: the percentage of earnings distributed as dividends.

dividend per share (dps): the annual dividend expressed in cents per share.

dividend per share (dps): the annual dividend expressed in cents per share.

dividend ranking: the entitlement of newly issued shares to dividends - for example, from a particular date.

dividend reinvestment plan (DRP): a scheme offered by many companies to their shareholders as an alternative to their receiving dividends in cash, allowing them at their option to take up newly created shares (usually) instead (or to take a mixture of cash and shares). Such shares are generally offered at a discount of 1 to 5 per cent of the market price at the time, although some issues are made at no discount. No brokerage is incurred. Such issues can be attractive to both parties. Dividend reinvestment plans also flourish in some other countries.

dividend stripping: a form of tax avoidance whereby an investment is taken up in a company which has substantial accumulated profits from which non-taxable or rebatable dividends are about to be paid. The investment is subsequently sold after it goes ex dividend, probably for less than its cost, leaving the purchaser with a capital loss on the sale of the investment, which is tax deductible, and a non-taxable or rebatable dividend.

dividend withholding tax: a flat rate of tax deducted at source from dividends paid to non-residents of the country concerned.

dividend yield: the dividend return from an investment in shares. It is calculated by dividing a company's dividends per share by the current market price of the share and multiplying by 100. It should, however, be noted that dividing a historical dividend figure by a current market price can be misleading. The apparent annual return from ordinary shares as measured by the dividend yield is not at all comparable with the return from fixed interest investments, as the true return from shares includes a capital growth element.

division: the voting on a question before the chair in a way which allows the names of those voting "aye" or "no" to be separately recorded.

DIY superannuation fund: see "do it yourself".

DJIA: abbreviation for Dow Jones Industrial Average.

DKK: symbol for the Danish krone.

dl: abbreviation for deferred delivery.

DLC: abbreviation for dual listed company.

"do it yourself" (DIY) superannuation fund: an investment portfolio to provide retirement benefits for an investor which is set up under a superannuation trust deed but which is managed by the investor rather than by an outside organisation. This may or may not produce cost savings, but it gives greater investment freedom - for example, such a superannuation fund can include amongst its assets properties chosen by the investor.

However, this does not overcome the prohibition on borrowing which is imposed on superannuation funds, so that gearing of the type common for non-superannuation property investments is not practicable.

The setting up of DIY superannuation funds is often encouraged by lawyers and accountants - professionals who, while they may be giving bona fide taxation advice, also have a vested interest in generating fee income from their clients.

dollarisation: the adoption by one country of another country's currency as its official legal tender currency (especially but not exclusively the adoption of the United States dollar in this way).

domain: on the Internet, a set of related network addresses. For example, a computer with an address of "http://www.xyz. com."

has a unique "host name", namely "xyz", and a "domain name", namely "xyz.com.".

dome: a symmetrical upfold with the beds dipping in all directions.

don't sell advice: a public announcement by directors not to sell shares in a company pending a subsequent announcement. It usually indicates that takeover discussions are being held which may lead to a bid for the shares at a higher price than the prevailing market levels.

donee: see power of attorney and proxy.

donor: see power of attorney and proxy.

DOP: abbreviation for dividend option plan.

double entry bookkeeping: the system of accounting most commonly used where each transaction has a debit and a credit component of equal size.

double taxation: any taxation of the same transaction more than once.

double taxation agreement: an arrangement between a national Government and any other government to ensure that dividends and other income payments flowing across borders are not taxed at the full rate in both countries.

doubtful debts: debts the collection of which is uncertain. Bad debts actually written off are a tax deduction.

Dow company: a company which is one of the 30 United States companies included in the Dow Jones Industrial Average.

Dow Jones Industrial Average (DJIA): an index which is often used as a proxy for the United States equity market. The Dow covers only 30 stocks, most but not all of which are listed on the New York Stock Exchange. Its construction (based as it is on an unweighted average of the individual share prices rather than the market capitalisations of the companies concerned) leaves a lot to be desired.

Dow Theory: a concept which is recognised as one of the major theories of charting. It states that price movements comprise primary, secondary and minor trends.

down-tick: see tick.

down time: that period during which machinery and plant are not working because of repairs, strikes, etc.

downside risk: the perceived likelihood that the price of a stock will fall. The term limited downside risk indicates the belief that the perceived loss will be minimal. See also upside potential.

dps: abbreviation for dividend per share.

dragline: an earth lifting machine used in open pit mining. It works by dragging a bucket through overburden or blasted ore and relocating the material. A dragline is capable of moving up to 7000 tonnes per hour.

drawdown: the use of a credit facility.

dredge: a vehicle for raising silt, loose sand, etc., generally in water in a scoop or by suction. Used to mine such minerals as alluvial gold, tin, diamonds, manganese and mineral sands.

drift: a drive following the course of a reef or vein. In coal, it is an incline from the surface to a coal seam.

drifting: stock market activity where share prices move very little and involve light turnover.

drill stem test: a test used to study the productive capacity of a well at an early stage in its development.

drilling mud: a mineral suspension, usually of bentonite and barite, which is pumped down through the drill pipe to seal off porous zones and counterbalance the pressure of oil or gas.

drilling rig: see rig.

drive: a horizontal passage underground. A drive usually follows the vein or ore structure, as distinguished from a crosscut, which intersects it.

DRP: abbreviation for dividend reinvestment plan (or distribution reinvestment lan, in the case of unit trusts or stapled securities).

DRS: abbreviation for Direct Registration System (used by some United States companies for scripless trading).

dry: a supporter of free trade and an opponent of government interference in the economy; an economic rationalist. Opposite of a wet.

dry gas: gas which contains no commercial amounts of liquid hydrocarbons.

dry hole: a well which fails to produce commercial quantities of oil or gas.

DSS: abbreviation for Department of Social Security.

DT: abbreviation for discretionary trust.

DTP: abbreviation for derivatives trading platform.

dual listed company (**DLC**): one of a pair of related companies incorporated in two different countries but effectively administered as though they were a single company. Several local companies of this type exists: Rio Tinto was the first; Brambles and BHP Billiton are other examples. To illustrate: Shares in Rio Tinto Limited, an Australian company, are linked to shares in Rio Tinto plc, a United Kingdom company. Legally these two corporations are separate, but effectively they are treated as a single entity by virtue of carefully devised reciprocal arrangements and complementary constitutions. On a "per share" basis the shares in both companies rank equally, except that dividends are paid in the local currency and with the benefit of local franking rules. Well-known overseas examples include Unilever and Shell, both operating in both the United Kingdom and the Netherlands.

due diligence: an exercise to determine the attractiveness of a proposed investment and an assessment of the risks involved. It also involves verifying the data on which the investor intends to rely and ensuring that there are no hidden liabilities or the like.

dump: tailings or stockpiled ore which is left on the surface.

duplicate title: see certificate of title.

DVA: abbreviation for Department of Veterans Affairs.

DVP: abbreviation for delivery versus payment.

dyke: an essentially vertical, tabular body of igneous rock that cuts across the structure of adjacent rocks. Formed by an intrusion.

e-mail (electronic mail): the exchange of computer-stored messages over the Internet. These are automatically and inexpensively passed from one computer user to another, through computer networks, telephone lines and modems.

EAN: abbreviation for European Article Number.

earned for ordinary profit: consolidated net operating profit after deducting the profit attributable to minority shareholders and preference shareholders. Includes abnormal items but excludes extraordinary items.

earned premium: the part of a general insurance policy premium which relates to the portion of the policy period which has already expired.

earnings: consolidated net operating profit. Often used interchangeably with earned for ordinary profit.

earnings per ordinary share (eps): the portion of earnings attributable to each ordinary share, a figure obtained by dividing a company's net profit (notionally adjusted where contributing shares exist) less the preference dividends (if any) by the total number of ordinary shares on issue. Such a figure is best expressed in cents per share. (An earnings rate expressed as a percentage of nominal capital is meaningless.) Suitable adjustments are also required if the company has made any issues or repaid any capital during the year, and also if convertible securities or options exist - see diluted earnings per share. For a correct and meaningful series of historical results all prior year data should similarly be adjusted.

earnings yield: what the return from an investment in ordinary shares would be if all earnings (net of preference dividends) were paid out as ordinary dividends, a figure obtained by dividing a company's earnings per share (in cents per share) by the current market price of the share (also expressed in cents) and multiplying by 100. It should, however, be noted that dividing a historical earnings figure by a current market price can be misleading. The earnings yield is a measure of the performance of the company to an investor and can be compared with interest rate levels generally. It is a much more useful yardstick than the dividend yield, which - because it is a function of the payout ratio - ignores the fact that ordinary shareholders benefit from a company's earnings irrespective of whether these are actually distributed or not. Yields are normally expressed as percentages (thus eps 10.8 and market price 150 give an earnings yield of 7.2 per cent). The earnings yield per cent multiplied by the price earnings ratio always equals 100.

easement: a limited right to use a portion of land in a particular way which is available to a person who is not its owner and which is indicated on the title documents. Easements often relate to water or sewerage pipes, electric cables or the like. See also right of way.

EBIT: abbreviation for earnings before interest and tax.

EBITA: abbreviation for earnings before interest, tax and amortisation.

EBITDA: abbreviation for earnings before interest, tax, depreciation and amortisation.

EBT: abbreviation for earnings before tax.

EBTDA: abbreviation for earnings before tax, depreciation and amortisation.

EC: abbreviation for European Community.

ECAS: abbreviation for electronic company announcement system.

ECB: abbreviation for European Central Bank.

econometrics: the empirical study of economics.

economic entity: a group of companies consisting of a holding companies and all its subsidiaries.

economics: the science that studies the distribution of resources to satisfy wants.

economies of scale: those economies or savings that may be made through large scale operations, a frequent reason for horizontal integration.

EDP: abbreviation for electronic data processing.

EEC: abbreviation for European Economic Community.

effective diversification: a portfolio management technique which minimises non-systemic or diversifiable risk.

effective marginal tax rate: the amount of income tax payable by individuals under the sliding scale in use, plus the amount of social security benefits foregone under the income test, in respect of each *additional* income.

effective tax rate: the proportion of a company's taxation expense that is attributable to profit, after allowing for permanent and timing differences. It is often different from the prima facie tax rate. It is calculated by dividing taxation expense by group pre-tax profit.

efficiency frontier: the points or range of combinations of investments which maximise return from any given value of risk.

efficient capital market theory: a theory that argues that all available information is incorporated in the share price and as a result the share price prevailing represents the true value of that share. It concludes that in the long term abnormal profits cannot be gained from the stock market and that the best result that can be expected is the market return adjusted for risk. Because trading involves outlays for brokerage and stamp duty and the incurring of capital gains tax it follows that a buy and hold strategy produces the best return.

EFT: abbreviation for electronic funds transfer.

EFTPOS: abbreviation for electronic funds transfer at point of sale.

EGM: abbreviation for extraordinary general meeting.

EIA: abbreviation for Ethical Investment Association.

eiusdem generis: of the same kind.

EL: abbreviation for exploration licence.

elastic supply and demand: the supply of and demand for goods and services which increase or decrease markedly with changes to the price.

electric logging: the process of obtaining a geological profile of an area by lowering electrodes into a hole and measuring the responses.

electrolytic refining: the process of refining metals by conducting an electric current through a solution with the metal being deposited on the cathode.

electromagnetic survey: a surveying method based on the detection of electromagnetic radiation. The survey utilises varying degrees of conductivity between metals, basalt, etc. EM equipment introduces electrical currents from above ground into the earth, and this electrical activity is measured during and after the currents have passed through rocks or mineral deposits.

electrostatic separation: a method of concentrating ore using the conductivity properties of the ore to separate it from the gangue.

element: a substance which cannot be decomposed into other substances.

elephant in the room: an obvious but embarrassing development which everyone pretends to ignore.

eligible termination payment (ETP): a lump sum payment made in consequence of the termination of employment. Such a payment does not incur lump sum taxation if suitably rolled over.

eluvial: materials that are carried to lower depths.

embargo: a restriction on information until the company lodges the news with the Stock Exchange. This applies to price-sensitive information such as half yearly statements, preliminary final statements, mineral deposits found, etc.

EMI: abbreviation for equity market instrument.

emolument: fee.

EMTR: abbreviation for effective marginal tax rate.

EMVONA: abbreviation for excess of market value over net assets.

encumbrance: a charge or liability on a property - for example, a mortgage.

endorse: to confirm. With bills of exchange it means to sign the face as evidence of the assumption of liability.

endorsement: the recording, on a policy document or on an annexure to it, of any alteration to the terms or conditions of a policy.

endowment insurance: a policy under which the sum insured, plus any bonuses, is payable when the life insured reaches a specified age (or date), on death if it occurs beforehand, or on total and permanent disability (if applicable).

endowment warrant: a form of derivative, a warrant without a specific exercise price or expiry date. The word "endowment" in this context has no legal significance, but was coined by certain promoters for marketing reasons and to distinguish the product from more conventional warrants. An endowment warrant resembles other warrants in that it is issued by a third party (an entrepreneur referred to as the *issuer*) and not by the company which issued the underlying shares to which the endowment warrant relates; it involves a standardised contract; it is therefore readily tradeable; and it involves the right but not the obligation for its holder to acquire the underlying shares.

enduring power of attorney: an instrument which, unlike an ordinary power of attorney, remains operative regardless of the severity of any disability affecting the donor and which continues in force even after the appointment of a trustee over the donor's affairs if the donor becomes incompetent.

enrichment: the process of increasing the metallic content of an ore.

Enronitis: the impact of the world's biggest ever bankruptcy, that of the United States energy giant, Enron, on 2 December 2001. In just 15 years, Enron had grown from nowhere to be America's seventh largest company, employing 21,000 staff in more than 40 countries. But the group's apparent success turned out to have resulted from an elaborate scam. Enron had lied about its profits and its balance sheet items. It now stands accused of a range of shady dealings. Yet the company's auditors, Andersen, had given the company a clean bill of health, a factor which subsequently led to that firm's own demise. Following on shortly after the terrorism attacks of 11 September 2001 the Enron collapse was a significant further blow to investor confidence. See also Sarbanes-Oxley.

enterprise value (EV): a measure of a company's value. It is calculated as the company's market capitalisation for its ordinary shares, plus its debt, minority interests and preferred shares, minus its total cash and cash equivalents.

enterprises (GST): businesses, trades and professions, property investments, real estate leases, bodies corporate under strata title subdivisions and the like, but not hobbies and private recreational pursuits.

entities (GST): individuals, companies, partnerships, trusts, superannuation funds, incorporated organisations and unincorporated organisations.

entitlement issue: any pro-rata issue of shares to existing shareholders. See share issue.

entry fee: a fee charged to an investor in a managed fund at the time of purchase, possibly on a sliding scale based on the size of the investment being made.

EP: abbreviation for exploration permit.

eps: abbreviation for earnings per (ordinary) share.

eps growth: earnings per share growth measured fiscal year on fiscal year, and expressed in percentage terms.

equitable mortgage: an unregistered transfer of an interest in land as a security for the repayment of a loan, as when a certificate of title is merely deposited with the lender.

equity (companies): that part of the assets of a company owned by its ordinary shareholders (in other words, the ordinary shareholders' funds).

equity (in a property): the beneficial interest in a property, as distinct from the legal ownership; or the stake in an asset available to its owner after allowing for all liabilities relating to that asset.

equity (investments): an investment involving a variable and performance based return, such as an ordinary share or property, as distinct from a fixed interest security.

equity-linked policy: contract with benefits expressed in units, each representing a share in an investment portfolio. The unit price fluctuates with market values and allows for investment income.

erosion: the weathering and wearing away of a geological structure.

escalation clause: a clause in a selling contract which provides for the seller to be offered a higher price should the buyer or another party make a higher bid in the market within a certain period.

escrow: a legal term of general application. It refers to a writing sealed and delivered to a person who is not a party to it, to be held by that person until certain conditions are fulfilled, at which time it takes effect as a deed. However, in stock exchange parlance the term usually refers to vendor securities which are held *in escrow* - for a period of either 12 or 24 months after a new listing - by a bank or other recognised trustee.

ESP: symbol for the Spanish peseta.

estate: the net assets left behind by a person at the time of death (in the case of a deceased estate) or the net assets belonging to a trust (in the case of a trust estate).

estate duty: a tax levied on the net assets of a deceased estate.

estoppel: the principle that a person's previous words or actions later on preclude that person from acting inconsistently.

et sequentes (abbreviated *et seq* or *seqq*): and those that follow.

ETF: abbreviation for exchange traded fund.

ethane: gaseous hydrocarbon of the paraffin series.

ethical investments (property): investments favoured by certain property investors on moral grounds. Typically, such investors seek not to acquire properties being used as hotels, betting shops or brothels. Similarly, such investors do not lease their premises to tenants proposing to engage in such activities.

ethical investments (stock exchange): investments favoured by certain persons on the basis of moral principles rather than purely on profit motive considerations - for example, shares in companies using wind farms for power generation or companies that manufacture environmentally friendly products. Such investors try not to put money into the shares of companies involved in alcohol, tobacco, gambling, pornography, wood chips, animal testing, uranium, the manufacture of arms or the like, or into the shares of companies operating in certain countries which practise racial discrimination, which abuse human rights or which exploit cheap child labour.

ETO: abbreviation for exchange traded option.

ETP: abbreviation for eligible termination payment.

EU: abbreviation for enforceable undertaking.

EU: abbreviation for European Union.

EUR: symbol for the euro (qv).

euro: see Euroland.

eurobond: a long term loan denominated in a European currency other than that of the country or market in which it was issued.

Euroland: the 11 EU countries using the euro, the "single" European currency which came in on 1 January 1999, namely, Austria, Belgium, Finland, France, Germany, the Republic of Ireland, Italy, Luxembourg, the Netherlands, Portugal and Spain, together with Greece, which joined the others on 1 January 2002 and Slovenia, which joined the others on 1 January 2007.The three other European Union members - Denmark, Sweden and the United Kingdom - continue to use their national currencies. The term is an unofficial one.

European Article Number (EAN): a 13-digit universal barcode for retail products, originally intoduced in Europe. From 1 January 2007 each EAN used for a book is also its ISBN.

European Community (EC): now the European Union.

European Economic Community (EEC): now the European Union.

European style: options or warrants which are exercisable only *on* their expiry date; contrast *American style.*

European Union (EU): Commencing on 1 May 2004, 27 countries, namely, Austria, Belgium, Bulgaria, Cyprus, the Czech Republic, Denmark, Estonia, Finland, France, Germany, Greece, Hungary, the Republic of Ireland, Italy, Latvia, Lithuania, Luxembourg, Malta, the Netherlands, Poland, Portugal, Romania, Slovakia, Slovenia, Spain, Sweden and the United Kingdom. The members of the EU have agreements to facilitate trade between themselves, making it difficult for others to penetrate their markets. Formerly known as the European Economic Community or the European Community. See also Maastricht Treaty, convergence (political).

EV: abbreviation for enterprise value.

EVA: abbreviation for economic value added (that is, profit less cost of capital).

evergreening: in relation to pharmaceutical products, the lodging of bogus patent applications by drug companies, in order to delay the introduction of cheap generic drugs manufactured by competitors. The device can be used repeatedly.

EVM: abbreviation for enterprise value multiple.

ex: without something - for example, shares bought ex rights or ex dividend do not entitle a purchaser of shares to those benefits, which remain with the seller. Contrast cum. (Latin for "without".)

ex curia: out of court.

ex dividend (xd): dividend announcements involve two dates - the "books closing date" or "record date" (which determines who is entitled to the payment, namely, holders on the company's register at that time) and a "dividend payable date" some weeks later, when the actual cheques are posted or electronic credits are put through. For securities listed on the stock exchange a third date is also used. Five working days before and including the books closing date the stocks go "ex dividend" (xd), meaning that the sellers of shares rather than the buyers become entitled to the payment. Before that the stock is traded on a "cum dividend" (cd) basis, meaning the reverse. However, the market price for the shares ex dividend will usually be lower (other things being equal) than the previous cum dividend price in order to reflect the change of status. It should be noted that books close at the close of business on the named date, while in contrast shares trade ex dividend as from the start of trading on the specified ex dividend date. Thus, in the absence of public holidays, the ex dividend date precedes the books closing date by six calendar days where a weekend intervenes and by four calendar days where it does not.

ex gratia: purely as a favour.

ex officio: by virtue of his office.

ex parte: by only one party to a dispute in the absence of the other.

ex post facto: retrospectively.

excess (general insurance): the amount of loss that is to be borne by the insured when claiming under a policy.

exchange rate: the price of one currency in terms of another.

exchange traded fund (ETF): a listed unit trust which is usually designed to replicate a particular stock exchange index. However, they have been available for some years in Europe and the United States, where they are quite popular, partly because they can be bought on margin and sold short. Such trusts are open-ended at the wholesale level.

exchange traded options (ETOs): They are *synthetic* instruments (*derivatives*) created by the interaction of third parties - writers (sellers) and takers (buyers) - without reference to the company which issued the underlying share (the shares to which the option relates). Such options have standardised expiration dates and standardised exercise prices. Transactions are processed through a clearing house. Investors can trade out of their positions before the expiration date. See also call option and put option.

excise: a tax levied internally upon some phase of the production process.

executive director: a director who is also employed full-time by the company.

executor: a person charged with winding up a deceased estate in accordance with a valid will.

executrix: (feminine of "executor".)

exempt: see input taxed (GST).

exercise notice: a notice issued by the Options Clearing House obligating a client to deliver the securities covered by the option against payment of the exercise price.

exercise of option: the payment of a predetermined amount (the exercise price) to take up shares covered by the option in accordance with its terms.

exercise price: the price at which an underlying security may be purchased or sold on the exercise of an option or warrant.

exhaustion: the completion of the mining of a deposit.

exit fee: a fee charged to an investor in a managed fund on withdrawal, possibly on a sliding scale based on the time that the investment was held.

expense ratio (general insurance): expenses (including commission but excluding costs relating to claims) as a proportion of earned premiums.

expiration date: the last day, or maturity date, on which an option may be exercised.

exploitation well: a well drilled to permit more effective extraction of oil from a reservoir. It is sometimes called a development well.

exploration licence: the exclusive right to explore over an area.

exploration permit: the exclusive right to explore over an area.

exploration well: a wildcat well.

extended deeming: a social security concept. In order to counter a perceived abuse of the system a concept known as "extended deeming" or these days just "deeming" now applies in the case of certain assets called "financial investments". For these the actual investment return is disregarded for the purpose of the income test and a notional or *deemed* rate of return applied to the current value of the asset is used instead.

extraordinary general meeting: a non-regular meeting of shareholders to consider special resolutions.

extraordinary items: items of revenue or expenses which arise outside the normal course of business, non-recurring items. They are disclosed separately in the profit and loss account and are excluded from the operating profit. Contrast abnormal items.

F&L: abbreviation for food and liquor.

face: as applied to a drive, cross-cut or stope, it is the end in which work is progressing.

face value: see par value.

factoring: the sale or acquisition of debtors' balances at a discount.

family company: a company, often formed with a purely nominal amount of capital, all or most of which is held by members of a family.

family income benefit: an additional life insurance benefit providing income for dependants if the life insured dies within a specified period.

family trust: a trust, set up by a deed of settlement for the benefit of beneficiaries all or most of whom are members of the one family.

FAQ: a list of frequently asked questions and their answers. Such lists are a popular feature of the Internet.

farm-in: the entry of a new partner or partners into an existing prospect. This arrangement usually results in the farminee either bearing a greater than proportionate share of costs or agreeing to repay a portion of the costs incurred prior to its joining the venture.

farm-out: this is a farm-in from the point of view of the original title holder.

FAS: abbreviation for free alongside ship.

FAST: abbreviation for Flexible Accelerated Security Transfer.

fault: a break in the subsurface strata. Often strata on one side of the fault line have been displaced (upward, downward, or laterally) relative to their original positions. It can cause a trap.

FBT: abbreviation for fringe benefits tax.

FCDRS: abbreviation for Financial Co-operative Dispute Resolution Scheme.

FDI: abbreviation for foreign depository interest.

FDI: abbreviation for foreign direct investment.

feasibility study: an examination of the facts relating to the mining of a deposit to see whether the project is economically viable.

Fed, the: slang for the United States Federal Reserve System.

Federal Open Market Committee (FOMC): the committee of the Federal Reserve System, the United States central bank, which from time to time, by action in the market place, initiates changes in the federal funds rate in that country.

fee simple: land held in fee simple is freehold land, with its proprietor having virtually absolute ownership (subject to the payment of various annual rates and taxes), although the possibility of compulsory acquisition by a government or by a government agency always exists.

feeder: a mechanical device, usually a conveyor, which transports ore to a machine, usually a crusher or concentrator.

feedstock: the raw materials for primary processing.

fees: see management fees.

ferro alloy: a metal that is mixed with iron to give properties of hardness, strength, resistance to corrosion, etc.

ferrous: containing iron.

fertility rate: the number of live births per 1000 women aged 15 to 44 years in a given year.

Fibonacci series: an infinite sequence of numbers in which each number after the first two is the sum of the preceding two numbers (1, 1, 2, 3, 5, 8, 13, 21, 34, 55, 89 ... This series has many fascinating properties and is related to various other mathematical concepts, including the golden section, sin 18 degrees, the logarithmic spiral, the regular pentagon, Pascal's triangle and Penrose tiling. However, there is no reason to think, as some investors do, that the Fibonacci numbers can be used to make accurate forecasts of the stockmarket.

FICS: abbreviation for Financial Industry Complaints Service Limited.

FID: abbreviation for financial institutions duty.

fidelity fund: a fund formerly maintained by the stock exchange to protect the interests of investors from the collapse of a stockbroker. Now replaced by the National Guarantee Fund. There is also a separate fidelity fund for futures trading.

fiduciary: a trustee or other person who holds a position of trust with respect to a beneficiary and who must therefore act in good faith solely in that beneficiary's best interests.

fiduciary duty: the legal duty of a fiduciary to act in the best interests of the beneficiary.

field: an area of interest. This could refer to a specific area such as an individual oil field or a general area such as a gold field.

FIFO: first in, first out. An accounting method for valuing inventories. Basically it works by treating the first item of stock purchased as the first item of stock sold. The valuation of stock affects the determination of profit. Contrast LIFO.

filibuster: a series of speeches designed to fill in time so that a particular motion cannot be put to a vote.

filtration: a process of separating solids from liquids.

FIM: symbol for the Finnish markka.

final dividend: that dividend paid after the conclusion of the financial year when the profit for the year is known.

final salary plan: a superannuation plan in which the member's retirement benefits are related to a combination of the salary at or near retirement (or over some other period) and the years of service or membership. Contributions at a level sufficient to purchase these benefits need to be paid. Contrast accumulation plan.

finance: funds raised to fund a project. Can be debt or equity finance.

finance company: a non-bank financial institution which raises money through debentures or unsecured notes (often on prospectus) and which lends money for a variety of purposes.

financial debt: interest bearing borrowings.

financial engineering: creating new financial products, possibly by combining or modifying existing products. This is usually done to satisfy a real or perceived investment need or for the better management of risk.

financial intermediary: an institution operating in the financial and capital markets.

financial investments: see deeming.

financial products: securities, derivatives, general insurance, life insurance, superannuation, deposit accounts and means of payment facilities. Typically such products are sold through financial intermediaries including securities advisers and dealers, insurance agents and brokers, and futures brokers.

financial supplies (GST): certain items set out in the GST legislation, such as money, stock exchange type securities, life insurance and health insurance, but not general insurance.

Financial Times Index: an index covering the prices of 30 representative industrial companies listed in London. abbreviation to FT 30. There is also an FT 100, similarly based on 100 companies.

financial year: a 12-month period for financial reporting and tax purposes. For most taxpayers, it is the period running from 1 April to the following 31 March, both days inclusive. Income tax is levied separately in respect of the transactions occurring during each financial year. Some company and other taxpayers work on a "substituted year"; in some cases this is done in order to conform with the reporting practices of an overseas parent, in others because of seasonal factors affecting a particular industry. Appropriate returns have to be filed with the

Department Income Tax, normally by 30 June each year for individuals.

fines: a well crushed ore, as distinct from lump ore.

FIRB: abbreviation for Foreign Investment Review Board.

fire refining: metal is liquefied in a reverberatory furnace and the impurities are oxidised and slagged off.

fire sale value: a method of valuation of assets at their readily realisable value. Usually far less than their book or market value.

firm: see partnership.

first mortgage: a charge on land by way of a mortgage which ranks ahead of other mortgages.

FIS: abbreviation for Financial Information Service (part of Centrelink).

fiscal policy: economic policy, the prime tool of which is the budget, as distinct from monetary policy.

fiscal year: the financial year.

fishing: the attempted recovery of implements lost in a well, causing drilling to be impeded.

fissure: an extensive fracture or crack in the rock.

FITB: abbreviation for future income tax benefit.

fittings: items which can be removed from a property without causing damage either to it or to them, as distinct from fixtures.

fixed assets: assets that can be used repeatedly in the production process. Except for land they are usually depreciated over their useful life. Examples of fixed assets are: land, buildings, plant, equipment, vehicles and leasehold improvements. See also assets.

fixed charge: a charge over specific assets.

fixed costs: costs which do not vary with the level of output.

fixed deposit: a deposit with a bank or similar organisation for a fixed period at a fixed interest rate.

fixed exchange rates: exchange rates fixed by government edict and kept constant for considerable periods of time, as distinct from those arrived at by the interaction of buyers and sellers, users and speculators. Periodical devaluations or revaluations occur.

fixed interest security: an investment involving a defined and guaranteed periodical return, as distinct from an investment known as an equity which involves a variable and performance based return. Examples include bonds, debentures, notes, deposits, mortgages and most preference shares. Issuers can include governments at all levels as well as companies. While the return to an investor who holds the security throughout its life is known at the start (apart from the possibility of default) investors buying or selling on the market may experience a different rate of return.

fixed rate loan: a loan with the interest rate set at the outset of the transaction and then kept constant for the entire duration of the loan regardless of subsequent market changes.

fixed trust (non-discretionary trust): a trust under which the deed spells out the specific beneficiaries and their precise entitlements.

fixed trust (non-flexible trust): a unit trust investing in a share portfolio involving a certain number of specified listed companies in fixed proportions.

fixtures: items which cannot be removed from a property without causing damage either to it or to them, as distinct from fittings.

FJD: symbol for the Fijian dollar.

flag: a charting formation which appears as a small, compact parallelogram of price fluctuations, which slopes back moderately against the prevailing trend.

flaring: burning of dry gas produced at the wellhead for which there is no immediate market or use.

flat yield: a crude measure of the return from a fixed interest investment. It is calculated by dividing the nominal interest per annum by the market price. The redemption yield gives a much more useful indication of the worth of a fixed interest security.

flexible trust: a unit trust investing in a portfolio of assets chosen with regard to their merit and varied from time to time.

float (banking): the money within the banking system representing cheques or overseas drafts still in the process of being cleared.

float (stock exchange): an initial public offering and capital raising; the offer of shares to investors who apply for them under a prospectus, with a view to the issuing company becoming listed on the stock exchange shortly after the new shares have been allotted to the successful applicants.

floaters: loose fragments of ore, rock and reef in the soil.

floating charge: a charge over assets at large; the creditor is able to choose which asset or assets to make a claim over if a default situation arises. See also charge.

floating exchange rates: exchange rates arrived at from minute to minute by market forces, as distinct from exchange rates fixed by government edict.

floating rate loan: a loan with the interest rate made subject to periodical changes (up or down) in line with market changes or according to some formula.

floor price: the lowest price possible because no seller will accept less.

floor, to have the: to have the right to address a meeting.

flotation (mining): a method of mineral separation where certain particles in a solution attach themselves to bubbles and float to the surface while other particles sink. Through flotation the valuable minerals are separated from the valueless ore.

flow: the movement of oil and gas from a reservoir to the well head.

flux: a chemical or mineral used in smelting to assist fusion.

fluxing ore: an ore which does contain valuable metals or minerals but which is smelted because it contains minerals required in the reduction of richer ores.

flying by the seat of one's pants: an action based on emotion and intuition rather than reasoned judgement.

FMRA: abbreviation for further market-related advice.

fob: abbreviation for free on board. Opposite of cif.

fold: a bend in strata structure.

footwall: the mass of rock beneath a fault plane, vein, lode or bed of ore.

force majeure: circumstances beyond the control of a party to a contract which prevent the completion of the contract - for example: acts of God, fire, flood, earthquakes, war, terrorism, sabotage, strikes, riots and insurrection.

foreshadowing: the notice given during the course of a debate of a further motion or amendment dealing with the same subject matter and which it is proposed will be moved at the earliest opportunity after the motion or amendment before the chair has been disposed of.

forex: foreign exchange.

forfeited shares: shares in a no liability company which the previous owner has forfeited by failing to pay a call.

formation: a bed or deposit composed throughout of substantially the same kinds of rock. Each different formation is given a name, frequently as a result of study of the formation outcrop at the surface and sometimes based on fossils found in the formation.

formation fracturing: a method of stimulating oil and gas production by increasing the permeability of the producing formation. Under extremely high hydraulic pressure, a fluid (such as water, oil, alcohol, dilute hydrochloric acid, liquefied petroleum gas, or foam) is pumped downward through tubing or drill pipe and forced into the perforations in the casing. The fluid enters the formation and parts or fractures it. Sand grains, aluminium pellets, glass beads or similar materials are carried in suspension by the fluid into the fractures. These are called propping agents or proppants. When the pressure is released at the surface, the fracturing fluid returns to the well, and the fractures partially close on the proppants, leaving channels for oil to flow through them to the well. This process is often called a frac job.

forward contract: a bilateral contract between a specific producer and a specific consumer for the delivery of some defined commodity at a defined price at some defined future date, thus facilitating forward planning and reducing uncertainty for both parties. Contrast futures contract.

forward exchange contract: an agreement to exchange at a specified date the currencies of two countries at a predetermined rate.

fossil fuel: coal and petroleum.

fossiliferous: containing organic remains.

founder shares: shares issued by a company as consideration for the acquisition of property from associated parties, usually at the time of a float. There are restrictions on trading such securities immediately after a public issue. Also called vendor shares.

fractal: an irregular geometric pattern that appears similar at all scales of magnification. The term was coined in 1975 by Benoit B Mandelbrot, the discoverer of the Mandelbrot set, from the Latin *fractus*, meaning "broken".

fracture: breaks in rocks and strata due to folding or faulting.

franchise: an independent business established or operated under an authorisation to sell or distribute a company's goods or services and to use its brand name and systems in a particular locality in return for a franchise fee or royalty.

franchisee: the proprietor of a business granted a franchise by a company (the franchisor).

franchisor: a company granting a franchise to the proprietor of a business (the franchisee).

franked dividends: dividends with attaching franking credits under the dividend imputation system.

franking credit: an amount associated with a dividend and representing income tax paid by a company; this is treated as assessable income to the individual shareholders concerned, but it can also be claimed as a tax rebate or tax refund by Australian resident individual shareholders receiving that dividend.

franking ratio: the franked dividend as a proportion of the total dividend payout, expressed as a percentage. For fully franked dividends the franking ratio is 100 per cent.

franking rebate: see franking credit.

franking tax offset: see franking credit.

FRC: abbreviation for Financial Reporting Council.

free float: the portion of a company's capital which is in the hands of pure portfolio investors - individuals or institutions that have large holdings of shares in many different companies - as distinct from the portion of the capital which is held by certain other groups with a different perspective. The latter holdings can include vendor shares held in escrow (qv) for a period after the float of a company; shares held by a business associate, such as those owned by an overseas parent or by a customer or supplier or joint venturer; cross-holdings held by a pair of friendly companies that are not professional investors (possibly by way of takeover defence); and those shares in partly privatised companies that are still in government hands.

free-carried: a joint venture interest where one or more parties are not required to make financial contributions till a specified stage of development or expenditure has been reached.

freehold: land owned outright, as distinct from leasehold. See also fee simple and leasehold.

FRF: symbol for the French franc.

friable: easily crumbled.

Friedman: Milton Friedman, the leading proponent of the monetarist school of economic thought. Monetarists stress the significance of monetary policy in controlling the economy.

friendly societies: mutual organisations, formed under special State legislation on the basis of group interests, and offering assorted benefits - for example, hospital cover, savings and investments, death benefits, retirement villages, trustee services.

friendly society bonds: friendly society policies, usually subject to single premiums and usually without death benefits, which are backed by professionally managed fixed interest and/or equity portfolios. They can be either capital guaranteed or investment-linked and either superannuation or non-superannuation. They do not involve cash distributions, but pass on the investment returns either through bonuses added to the nominal sum insured or, in the case of unit-linked contracts, through a rising unit value. In some ways they resemble unit trusts, but income tax is paid by the friendly society and not the investor. Withdrawals within the first ten years also attract tax in the policyholder's hands in respect of the net gain, but this is subject to a special rebate.

friendly takeover bid: one supported and agreed to by the board of the target company.

FRN: abbreviation for floating rate note.

front-end fees: fees charged at entry when acquiring a managed investment, usually as a percentage of the assets being acquired.

front-end loader: an earth moving machine, similar to a tractor with a loading bucket on the front.

frozen: applicable to bank accounts and assets which cannot be used pending legal examination or action.

FSA: abbreviation for Financial Services Authority (a regulator in the United Kingdom).

FSAC: abbreviation for Financial Sector Advisory Council.

FSG: abbreviation for Financial Services Guide.

FSR: abbreviation for floor space ratio (plot ratio, building area as proportion of land area).

FTA: abbreviation for Free Trade Agreement between two countries or among a group of countries.

Fuller's earth: a fine earth, resembling clay.

fully paid: refers to shares on which there is no uncalled liability.

FUM: abbreviation for funds under management.

functus officio: having discharged his duty and thus ceased to have any authority over a matter.

fund of funds: a managed fund investing in other managed funds, rather than directly in shares or property. While such an approach provides diversification and possible access to wholesale funds not otherwise open to individual investors it also results in two lots of charges rather than one.

fundamental analysis: the determination of the intrinsic value of a share by reference to fundamentals such as expected future profits, dividends, cash flow, assets, growth, etc. A principal tool of this analysis is ratio analysis, that is, the study of past financial performance. Contrast charting.

fundamentalist: a proponent of fundamental analysis. See also technical analysis and efficient market theory.

funds statement: a statement which details where a company's cash has been derived and what it has been used for in a period.

fungible: of such a nature that one unit can be replaced by another - for example, all shares in a particular company are interchangeable. In contrast, each plot of land is unique. Money is fungible.

future tax benefit: the estimated amount of future savings in income tax likely to arise from the recoupment of tax losses or the reversal of timing differences. See also tax effect accounting.

futures contract: a contract tradeable on a futures exchange. It produces a similar economic effect to a forward contract but does so indirectly. The use of standardised terms in futures contracts facilitates the matching of demand from buyers and supply from sellers, without the two parties even knowing each other. While such contracts can be used speculatively, in conjunction with cash sales they are frequently used for hedging and to iron out fluctuations in price. A futures exchange, in addition to facilitating the trade in contracts involving real commodities as mentioned below, also enables dealings in certain artificial "commodities" - for example, financial instruments or stock exchange indices where physical delivery would not be practicable and where appropriate cash settlements therefore have to be used instead. Buyers and sellers on a *physical* market normally exchange commodities for cash, with an immediate transfer of ownership taking place. By way of contrast, trading on a *futures* market involves, not physical commodities, but rather *standardised contracts* for the delivery of a given quantity of a commodity (of a defined quality) at some specified future date, at a price agreed on at the time of the deal. This price can be either higher or lower than the *spot price* (the price for immediate delivery). The buyers usually contract to take delivery and to make payment at the settlement date and the sellers contract to effect delivery at that time. Originally futures contracts related to rural products, such as wool, live cattle, boneless beef, and so on, or to minerals, especially gold. Producers and consumers of such commodities often desire to guarantee for themselves a price negotiated long before the intended date of delivery, frequently before the commodity even comes into existence.

futures exchange: see futures market.

futures fund: a unit trust which is dedicated to trading in futures contracts and options.

futures market: an auction market in which participants buy and sell commodity/future contracts for delivery on a specified future date. Volume in the futures market usually increases when the stock market outlook is uncertain.

G7: the Group of Seven, the seven largest industrialised countries: United States, Japan, United Kingdom, France, Germany, Italy and Canada. It is a forum for the discussion of economic policy issues.

G8: the Group of Eight, the eight largest industrialised countries: United States, Japan, United Kingdom, France, Germany, Italy, Canada and Russia. It is a forum for the discussion of economic policy issues.

GAAP: abbreviation for generally accepted accounting principles.

gabbro: a plutonic rock consisting of calcic plagioclase and clinopyroxene.

gag: the procedural motion, more properly known as the closure: "That the question be now put."

galena: lead sulphide, the principal ore of lead.

galvanometer: an instrument for measuring or detecting a small electric current.

gamma: measure of magnetic intensity.

gamma-ray well logging: an alternative method of logging when electric logging cannot be used because the holes are cased.

gangue: the noneconomic minerals contained in the ore being mined.

gas: a fluid of low density and high compressibility having neither independent shape nor volume.

gas field: a tract or district yielding natural gas.

gas sand: a stratum of sand or porous sandstone from which natural gas is obtained.

gas show: the gas that appears in drilling fluid returns, indicating the presence of a gas zone.

GATT: abbreviation for the General Agreement on Tariffs and Trade (now the World Trade Organization (WTO)).

gavel: the hammer traditionally used by the chairman of a meeting as a symbol of authority, ceremoniously banged by the chairman in order to indicate the start and finish of the meeting or to call a disorderly meeting to order.

GAW: abbreviation for general advice warning.

gazumping: the immoral practice under which the vendor of a property repudiates an oral agreement to sell it to a prospective purchaser, usually because he has received a better offer from another party.

GBP: symbol for the British pound.

GDP: abbreviation for Gross Domestic Product.

gearing: leverage; the use of borrowed funds in order to supplement an investor's own money when acquiring an asset or the proportion of funding obtained by debt. The higher the gearing, the higher the use of debt. It is measured by a number of ratios such as debt to equity and shareholders' interest. In the stock market gearing often refers to the purchase of options or contributing shares in a stock rather than its fully-paid shares. Thus an investor can buy a larger volume of securities than the fully-paid shares for the same capital outlay. In a market swing the options and contributing shares, because of their financial convertibility into fully paids, will tend to be more volatile.

gearing ratio (companies): a company's total outside liabilities divided by its shareholders' funds.

gearing ratio: the borrowed funds divided by the investor's own stake (equity) in a project.

geiger counter: an instrument used in the search for radioactive minerals.

general bequest: a bequest which is a gift of money or which involves a category of goods, as distinct from a particular item.

general interest charge (GIC): the interest penalty imposed on taxpayers to compensate the government for the interest lost by receiving tax monies late. The GIC is tax deductible.

general meeting: see annual general meeting and extraordinary general meeting.

general reserve: see reserve.

generation X: the generation of persons born in Western countries during the period from the early 1960s to the late 1970s - persons widely regarded as being disillusioned, cynical and apathetic. See also baby boomers.

generation Y: the generation of persons following generation X, usually taken as persons born in Western countries during the period from the late 1970s to the turn of the century.

geochemical exploration: prospecting methods depending on the chemical analysis of rocks, soil or of plants.

geologist: a scientist who procures and interprets data pertaining to the strata of the earth's crust.

geology: the science that relates to the study of the structure, origin, history, and development of the earth and its inhabitants as revealed in rocks, formations, and fossils.

geometric mean return: a statistical method used to calculate the compound rate of growth of funds invested. It is also called the average compound rate of return or the time-weighted return. It is the best measure of a portfolio's performance.

geophysical survey: the use of one or more geophysical techniques to determine subsurface conditions by analysis of such properties as specific gravity, electrical conductivity, and magnetic susceptibility; the results may be displayed in map-form and are interpreted in geological terms.

Gesellschaft mit beschrnkter Haftung (GmbH): a limited company in Germany.

GIC: abbreviation for general interest charge.

gift: a transfer of property from one person to another with the giver receiving nothing in return.

GIGO: abbreviation for garbage in, garbage out.

gilt-edged securities: government securities and blue chip stock where it is felt there is little likelihood of the security issuer facing financial difficulties. Gilt-edged securities are nearly but not completely risk free.

GLA: abbreviation for gross leasable area.

GLC: abbreviation for a government-linked company (Singapore).

glory hole: a large open pit from which the ore is or has been extracted.

GmbH: abbreviation for Gesellschaft mit beschrnkter Haftung.

GNP: abbreviation for Gross National Product.

goaf: that part of a coalmine from which coal has been mined and the space more or less filled.

going concern value: a method of valuing the assets of a business on the assumption that the operations will continue for the foreseeable future. Has a higher value than "fire sale" or "distress sale" value.

going public: the listing of a private company on the stock exchange through a prospectus.

gold: a precious metal, usually found in a natural state. Principal uses include bullion or coinage, as a store of wealth, and for jewellery. Chemical symbol: Au.

golden parachute: a provision in a key executive's employment contract specifying that the executive will receive certain significant benefits if that executive's employment is terminated, especially if control of the company changes.

good delivery: the settlement of a purchase of securities to which a valid title is held by the vendor.

good till cancelled: an instruction to a stockbroker which is operative till cancelled.

goods and services tax (GST): a tax based upon the value added to products and services. This tax in other countries is usually called a value added tax (VAT).

goodwill: the difference between the tangible value of assets and the price buyers are prepared to pay for them. It may reflect anticipated future earnings, the reputation of a brand name, or time and place utility. Goodwill is an intangible asset.

goodwill on consolidation: in group accounts, the shortfall in the value of the subsidiary companies' net assets over their cost to the parent. The opposite of premium on consolidation.

googol: 10 to the power of 100.

googolplex: 10 to the power of one googol.

gossan: a hydrated oxide of iron that forms a superficial cover on masses of pyrite. Also known as iron hat. Many metallic ores contain a proportion of iron sulphides and while other minerals may be leached the iron oxides remain.

GP: abbreviation for gross profit.

gr: abbreviation for growth units.

grab sample: a sample of rock taken more or less indiscriminately at any place.

grade: measure of inclination. Also an expression of relative quality.

grammar slack: the tolerance exhibited by most Internet users for small spelling and grammatical errors.

grandfathering: a concession under which an activity which was being carried out by some persons before the commencement of a new law can continue to be carried out by those persons in the same way as before rather than becoming subject to the new rules which apply to persons commencing similar activities after the commencement of the new law. An example is the exemption from the capital gains tax net of assets acquired before the commencement of that tax.

granite: a light coloured, coarse grained igneous rock composed essentially of quartz and feldspar.

grant of probate: an official certificate authorising the executor of an estate to administer a valid will.

grant of representation: a grant of probate or letters of administration.

grantor: the person who legally creates a trust by executing (signing) the trust deed and by feeding in the initial assets of the trust fund (often only a nominal amount of cash sufficient to satisfy a legal fiction).

gravimeter survey: a survey by an instrument that measures gravitational attraction on the principle that different rocks have different specific gravities and thereby affect the gravitational pull of the earth. Formations with different specific gravities can thus be determined and plotted on a geophysical chart.

gravity concentration: a form of concentrating ore by agitating, resulting in the separation of the ore from the gangue due to different specific gravities.

GRD: symbol for the Greek drachma.

green chip stock: a stock with a small market capitalisation, say in the bottom decile.

green paper: a consultation document, especially a parliamentary paper setting out proposals on which the government wishes to obtain public views and opinion. Contrast white paper.

green shoe option: an overallotment and market stabilisation provision in an underwriting agreement when a company floats. It allows the underwriter to place up to 10 or 15 per cent more shares than the nominal issue size if the demand from investors is unexpectedly heavy. The underwriter then covers this short position within 30 days - either by purchases on the market (if the after-float market price is less than the issue price), thus also supporting the market price, or by exercising a call option in the underwriting agreement requiring the company to supply shares to the underwriter at or under the issue price (in the reverse situation). The name of this legal method of manipulating share prices comes from the Green Shoe Company of the United States (which made real shoes), the company which first granted such an option to an underwriter.

Gresham's law: the principle that bad money drives out good - for example, if counterfeit and genuine coins are in circulation simultaneously people will tend to pass the former and hoard (or melt down) the latter, thus driving them out of circulation.

grid: survey lines to determine the location or co-ordinates of drill holes, samples, geophysical surveys, etc.

Gross Domestic Product (GDP): the value at current prices of the total annual output of final goods and services produced in a country.

Gross National Product (GNP): in relation to India, the Gross Domestic Product plus the income earned by India residents from their overseas investments less the income earned by non-residents from India investments.

gross profit: the margin between the selling price and the cost of goods sold. Selling, administrative and finance expenses and certain other charges are deducted from the gross profit in order to arrive at the net profit before tax.

gross value: dollar value of metal in situ.

ground rent: the rent at which vacant land is leased to a tenant for a long term or in perpetuity, for the right to occupy it and to improve it by erecting a building.

group accounts: the consolidated financial accounts of a group of companies reflecting the interests attributable to shareholders in the parent company and the minority shareholders.

group insurance: individual life policies, the premiums for which are paid in instalments by deductions from an employee's salary or wages and remitted by the employer to the life insurer in bulk.

growth investor: an investor who typically seeks to acquire assets with the potential for capital growth, even if the immediate yield from income alone is low. Contrast value investor.

growth stocks: stocks with prospects for good growth in earnings per share and in the share price.

growth units: units in a split unit trust which are entitled to all or most of the capital appreciation. Contrast income units.

GST: abbreviation for goods and services tax.

GST-free: goods and services which are completely exempt from the goods and services tax because that tax is not payable by consumers and the suppliers of those goods and services are able to claim back the tax paid on their inputs. Examples include health, education, religious services and exports. Other countries use the term "zero rated" to describe this type of activity. Contrast input taxed.

GTC: abbreviation for good till cancelled (orders on the stock exchange).

guardian (generally): a person appointed by a will or court order to care and manage the affairs and person of a child during its minority or of an adult with a disability who is not capable of making personal decisions.

guardian (trusts): in the case of some trusts, a person given a power of veto over certain types of transaction, a power to remove or appoint trustees, a right to be consulted in relation to certain investments, a power to act as an arbitrator in the event of certain disputes and/or a power to nominate a successor as guardian.

gut feeling: an emotional reaction, with or without reason.

GVSR: abbreviation for general value shifting regime (income tax).

GVSR: abbreviation for general value shifting regime.

HACC: abbreviation for Home and Community Care.

half on half: a company's results for one half-year compared with the results for the same period of the previous year.

half-year: the first or second six months of a company's financial year. All listed companies have to submit a half yearly statement (with information on the revenue, profit before tax, tax, interest, depreciation, extraordinary items, any minority interests and numbers of shares issued) for the current year and the previous corresponding period. Dividends for the first half year are called interim dividends.

hammer: to declare a member of a stock exchange a defaulter. Used mainly in relation to the London stock exchange, from the practice of making three taps of a hammer on the rostrum.

handling fee: the fee charged by a stockbroker to a company for handling its issue.

hanging wall: the wall on the upper side of a vein or deposit.

hard rock: rock which requires drilling or blasting for its economic removal.

head and shoulders: a charting formation representing three rallies, the second of which is the largest, with prices after the first two rallies returning to a base level, known as a neckline. After the third rally prices are expected to fall. A head and shoulders formation can also form in reverse with the second decline being the lowest, etc.

head grade: the metal value in ore on reaching the surface.

head lease: the original lease granted by a freeholder to a lessee (the "head lessee"), as distinct from a separate lease (the "sublease") granted in turn by the head lessee to a sublessee. The sublease may cover a smaller area and/or involve a shorter duration than the head lease.

headframe: the structure above the mine shaft.

headline inflation: inflation as measured by the Consumer Price Index, without adjustment for irregular influences - contrast

heavy sands: see mineral sands.

heavyweight stock: shares in large companies.

hedge fund: a managed fund designed to take speculative positions in currencies, etc., especially on a large enough scale to force exchange rates in a desired direction. Because leverage is involved there is the scope to make substantial profits or substantial losses in relation to the equity held. There are also hedge funds operating in stock exchange securities, characterised by the fact that they take short positions as well as long positions; the theory is that by holding short positions they, unlike conventional managed funds, will make profits in a falling market.

hedging: in relation to futures, taking an opposite position in the futures market to the one held in the physical market, so that any loss in the physical market will be offset by a corresponding profit in the futures market, thus providing a form of price insurance. However, while the hedger has the advantage of being able to budget in the knowledge that a specific price has been locked in regardless of any future fluctuations, it follows that any profit in the physical market - which would otherwise have been a windfall gain - will then be offset by a corresponding loss in the futures market. Through hedging producers can be assured of future sales while manufacturers can be guaranteed supplies at a future point in time at a fixed price. This risk minimisation strategy can also be used in options trading or in relation to foreign currencies. Contrast speculating.

heir (deceased estates): a person who is entitled by right of blood to receive property from an ancestor's deceased estate, in accordance with the laws relating to intestacy; (loosely) any person who is, or who expects to be, entitled to receive property as legal successor to its former owner on that person's death.

hematite: iron oxide, the principal ore of iron.

heptane: a liquid hydrocarbon of the paraffin series.

hexane: a liquid hydrocarbon of the paraffin series.

Hg: chemical symbol for mercury.

hidden reserves: accumulated wealth that is not readily disclosed as such in the balance sheet. It may take the form of undervalued assets, various expense provisions that are unlikely to be needed or overestimated depreciation.

high: the highest price paid for a stock during a period.

high flyer: a speculative stock the price of which has risen substantially.

hire purchase: a means of acquiring assets on terms. The user does not acquire ownership until the final payment. See also leasing.

historical cost accounting: an accounting method based upon the original costs of assets and which does not take into account their current replacement cost or their current market value. It tends to understate the value of assets and to overstate the profits in real terms.

hive-off: see spin-off.

HKD: symbol for the Hong Kong dollar.

HMO: abbreviation for health maintenance organisation (a prepaid health insurance plan).

HoH: abbreviation for half on half.

hoist: an arrangement of pulleys and wire rope or chain used for lifting heavy objects.

hold: advice to maintain holdings in a stock and to neither buy nor sell.

holding company: a company which owns shares in other companies - known as "subsidiary companies" - which actually run the business (the "operating companies"). The holding company may or may not also run part of the business. The holding company is the "parent company" of the group and the other companies are either wholly-owned subsidiaries (where 100 per cent of the shares is held, and the companies are virtually divisions of the parent) or partly-owned subsidiaries (where more than 50 per cent but less than 100 per cent of the shares is held and/or where the board of directors is controlled). Other companies in which significant shareholdings are held (other than as a pure investment) and over which some influence is exerted are called "associated companies". A holding company and its subsidiaries are all said to be "related" to each other.

holding costs: outgoings relating to a property, such as rates, land tax, insurance premiums and body corporate charges, together with maintenance costs and interest, which are incurred by a developer or other owner of property pending the receipt of income from a tenant or the sale to another party.

holdrs: trust-issued receipts that represent an investor's beneficial ownership of a specified group of listed stocks, typically those in a particular industry, sector or group in the United States. These receipts can be traded on the stock exchange in the same way as shares. The acronym stands for HOLding company Depositary ReceiptS.

hollow log: the hiding place of a corporate asset - for example, an off-balance sheet vehicle.

hollow swap: a practice such as company A selling something to company B and vice versa, without any cash changing hands but with both companies immediately claiming sales figures and profits. These profits will then inevitably be cancelled out by losses in future years.

home equity conversion loan: a first mortgage loan secured on a residential property typically owned and occupied by an elderly person or couple, on the basis that all interest and charges are accumulated against the property, with the loan being discharged only after the death of the owner (or of the survivor of two joint owners), or when the property is vacated and sold for other reasons, such as permanent entry into a nursing home.

home equity conversion loan: a loan secured by a mortgage of the borrower's home under an arrangement which does not require periodical payments of either interest or capital, the intention being that the total debt will be repaid on the death of the home owner (or on the death of the survivor of a married couple).

home page: an organisation's main page on a World Wide Web site.

honeymoon rate: a concessional rate of interest charged for a relatively short initial period (typically 6 to 12 months) to persons borrowing for purposes such as housing, in order to induce them to take out a long term loan with a particular bank or other lending institution. Much higher rates then apply during the remainder of the term of the loan, a factor which can trap unwary borrowers.

horizons: the various layers that comprise a soil. Also the different levels in a mine.

horizontal integration: the absorption by a company of its competitors in order to get a better market penetration and thus a bigger market share, enabling economies of scale, lower unit costs and greater profits. Depending on the elasticity of demand, there may also be scope for price increases.

horizontal monopoly: that trading situation where one stage of supply in the production process is owned by only the one organisation which thus has a monopoly power over a market.

horoscope, corporate: a horoscope prepared for a company as though it were a human being who was born on the day that the company was incorporated. There is no reason to believe that any such astrological document has any value whatsoever in forecasting performance on the stock exchange. Using a computer to prepare such a horoscope is a great perversion of a marvellous scientific device.

horse: a large block of unmineralised rock included in a vein.

horst: a block of strata bounded by two or more faults and thrust upward.

host rock: the rock containing an ore deposit.

hostile takeover bid: one opposed by the board of the target company.

hot money: extremely short term funds, especially wholesale amounts owned by organisations operating internationally, that are deposited where the interest rate and exchange rate outlook are considered the best at any one time and which are uplifted as soon as the scenario changes.

hot-desking: the practice in offices of workers using whatever desk an employer has available rather than an assigned desk for each employee. Workers are allocated work space according to their needs. They keeping their personal belongings in lockers or filing cabinets when they are not in the office. Computers are often used to re-route telephone calls, to allocate resources and to maintain individual working files.

house stocks: companies for which a broker acts as underwriter.

householding: the practice of mailing a single copy of a listed company's annual report to only one of a group of shareholders living at the same address, where the remaining shareholders have requested or authorised this cost-saving measure.

HSEC: abbreviation for Health, Safety, Environment and Community.

hurdle: a yardstick in an employment contract for executives - for example, one which entitles them to exercise options on favourable terms. Hurdles can have regard to increases in items such as total profit; or earnings per share; or market value per share (possibly adjusted for dividends); or return on equity. The yardstick can be absolute or relative to some share index or accumulation index or the performance of other companies in the same industry.

hurdle rate: that rate of return on an investment that is considered to be the minimum acceptable return.

hybrid securities: securities such as convertible notes, which exhibit some of the characteristics of two distinct asset classes (in this case, of fixed interest securities and of the underlying ordinary shares).

hybrid trust: a trust which is non-discretionary for some or all capital and/or for some or all income and which is discretionary for the balance.

hydrocarbon: a compound composed of only carbon and hydrogen (for example, any member of the paraffin series, hexane, octane, butane, etc.). These compounds may be gases, liquids or solids at normal temperatures.

hydrocarbon shows: the hydrocarbon that appears in drilling fluid returns, indicating the presence of a gas or oil zone.

HYFGR: abbreviation for high yield for good reason.

hypothecated taxes: taxes earmarked for a particular purpose, usually in a vain attempt to make them more acceptable to the voters. They are generally regarded by economists as being regressive (qv) and far less efficient than ordinary taxes. One example is the Medicare levy, which actually gives the public a totally misleading impression of the actual cost of providing health services and which probably encourages overutilisation ("as we have paid for this we might as well use it").

IAS: abbreviation for instalment activity statement.

IASC: abbreviation for International Accounting Standards Committee.

IBA: abbreviation for Indian Banks' Association.

IBNR claims (general insurance): claims incurred but not reported.

IC: abbreviation for Industry Commission.

ICAI: abbreviation for Institute of Chartered Accountants of India.

IDR: symbol for the Indonesian rupiah.

IEE: abbreviation for interposed entity election.

IEP: symbol for the Irish punt.

IFRS: abbreviation for International Financial Reporting Standards.

IFSA: abbreviation for Investment and Financial Services Association Limited.

igneous intrusion: an injection of molten rocks into solid rocks forming sills, dykes, and larger bodies of irregular shape.

igneous rocks: rocks formed by solidification from a molten state.

IISL: abbreviation for India Index Services & Products Ltd.

illiquid: in a poor position with regard to cash, near cash or the ability to obtain cash to meet current needs.

ilmenite: iron titanium oxide, the principal ore of titanium.

ILR: abbreviation for indicator lending rate.

IMF: abbreviation for International Monetary Fund.

immediate annuity: an annuity under which the periodical payments are already payable. Payments at regular intervals continue until the death of the annuitant (or the death of the survivor of joint annuitants) or for some other specified period.

import quota: the right to import a fixed amount of a specified good.

imprest account: an account used for advances of petty cash up to an agreed amount to a person, on the basis that appropriate vouchers will be submitted as the money is expended, at which stage further cash will normally be advanced sufficient to restore the original balance.

improved value: the value of land, allowing for the value of the buildings erected on it (cf. "site value").

improvements: the buildings erected on land, as distinct from the land itself.

imputation credit: an amount associated with a dividend and representing income tax paid by a company; this is treated as assessable income to the individual shareholders concerned.

imputation rebate: see imputation credit.

imputation trust: a unit trust invested mainly in shares paying franked dividends.

imputed rent: the market rent that an owner-occupier would pay as the tenant of an equivalent house owned by an arm's length landlord and would receive as the landlord of an equivalent house occupied by an arm's length tenant.

in: abbreviation for income units.

in camera: in private session.

in curia: in court.

in extenso: at full length.

in situ: in its original situation; in the ground.

in specie (1): in its own form and not in an equivalent.

in specie (2): in coins and not in paper money.

in the black: in a profitable trading condition.

in the money: in relation to options, the situation where the holder of an option can get an immediate benefit by exercising it. Thus a call option is *in the money* if the market price of the underlying share exceeds the exercise price of the option; a put option is *in the money* if the market price of the underlying share is less than the exercise price of the option.

in the red: in an unprofitable trading condition.

in toto: entirely.

income: (1) profit or (2) sales (according to context).

income account: see profit and loss account.

income securities: see perpetual floating rate notes.

income splitting: the allocation of a sum of assessable income to a number of different taxpayers in order to attract a lower marginal rate of tax on that income.

income tax: a government charge on earnings.

Income Tax Department: functioning under the union ministry of finance, the department is responsible for collecting income tax and various other taxes from individuals and businesses.

income test: a criterion, the level of income each week, which is applied in order to determine eligibility for social security pensions and benefits.

income units: units in a split unit trust which are entitled to all or most of the periodical income, as distinct from the capital appreciation. Contrast growth units.

incompetent rock: weak rock which would collapse if unsupported.

incorporate (of an organisation): to acquire status as a legal person either by registering as a company or in some similar way.

incubator: a company or facility designed to encourage and support entrepreneurship and to help startup companies, especially fledgling high technology enterprises, to grow through the use of shared resources, management expertise and intellectual capital.

independent director (listed companies): a non-executive director elected by shareholders to a company's board of directors who is not affiliated with the company directly or indirectly.

This includes affiliation as an employee or personal services contractor or auditor or adviser or consultant (or as an employee or partner of such entities), or by virtue of any family relationship, or otherwise.

It covers affiliation with the company or its related parties or their executive officers, or their major customers or suppliers or charitable beneficiaries, in any other capacities than as director and shareholder.

A past affiliation should be regarded as relevant for a further period of, say, three to five years after it ceases.

An independent director should be a person who makes judgements on the merits of a case, in good faith, in the best interests of the company, and not as the result of any outside influence. There should be no known relationships or circumstances which could affect, or might appear to affect, that director's judgement.

An independent director should not rely solely on the company's management to provide information to enable the monitoring and evaluation of that management.

An independent director's remuneration from the company (apart from dividends) should not constitute a significant portion of that person's annual income. See also share qualification.

Preferably such an independent director should not also be an employee of another company where any of the company's executives serve on that company's board of directors.

index: in stock market usage, a measure of share prices: The index number represents the market capitalisation of all the shares concerned, expressed as a number relative to the base number mentioned above. Thus if an index is 1500.0 on a particular day and the shares concerned in total go up 1 per cent in value (after adjustment for any capital raised or repaid) then the index will be up 15 points at 1515.0. Indices thus give a quick picture of the weighted average price movements in the market as a whole. The *percentage movement* up or down - rather than the precise number of points - gives the message. While such indices have some conceptual limitations they can be used as yardsticks by which the performance of a particular portfolio can be measured objectively. Movements in indices can also be used to make comparisons between any country and international markets. In compiling these indices brokerage is ignored. No adjustments are made for either the sudden price drops as particular shares go ex dividend or the gradual build up of prices between successive dividend distributions.

index fund: a managed fund which is invested in a basket of shares which closely replicates the composition of some specified stock exchange index. Various local and overseas indices can be used for this purpose, according to taste. Institutional portfolios administered by full-time professional fund managers who devote all their energies to the task - and who have access to all published information and to security analysis - should in theory produce investment returns which are well above the average of those obtained by all investors or those obtainable by picking stocks at random.

In practice this has often not happened, hence the moves to make greater use of index funds. The managers of such funds use computers to build up a portfolio. The intention is to avoid conscious decision making and its associated expenses on research and to replace these by a computer-based automatic stock selection process. The proponents of this theory claim that it is far better in this way to avoid mistakes by *ensuring* an average performance, rather than to have the possibility of producing a below average performance.

However, such a theory would work only if the fund concerned and/or its investors incurred no administration expenses, no brokerage or GST when buying or selling and no income tax on realised capital gains. In the real world an index fund is inevitably going to underperform the index to which it relates. Nor is it clear why investors would want to pay for the privilege of specifically *aiming* at achieving only an ordinary performance.

Index Funds

- Principal Index Fund, an index fund scheme on S&P CNX Nifty launched by Principal PNB AMC Pvt. Ltd in July 1999.
- UTI Nifty Index Fund launched by UTI AMC Pvt. Ltd in March 2000.
- Franklin India Index Fund launched by Franklin Templeton AMC (India) Pvt.Ltd. in June 2000.
- Franklin India Tax Fund launched by Franklin Templeton AMC (India) Pvt.Ltd. in February 2001.
- SBI Magnum Index Fund launched by SBI Funds Management Ltd in December 2001.
- ICICI Prudential Index Fund launched ICICI Prudential AMC Ltd in February 2002.
- HDFC Index Fund - Nifty Plan launched by HDFC AMC Ltd. in July 2002.
- Birla Index Fund launched by Birla Sun Life AMC Ltd in September 2002.
- LICMF Index Fund - Nifty Plan launched by LIC Mutual Fund AMC Ltd in November 2002.
- Tata Index Fund-Nifty Plan launched by Tata AMC Pvt. Ltd in February 2003.
- ING Vysya Nifty Plus Fund launched by ING Investment Management (I) Ltd in January 2004.

- Canara Robeco Nifty Index Fund launched by Canara Robeco AMC Ltd. in September 2004.
- Principal Junior Cap fund launched by Principal PNB AMC Pvt. Ltd in May 2005.
- Reliance Equity Advantage Index Fund launched by Reliance Capital AMC Ltd. in June 2007.
- Religare Banking Fund launched by Religare AMC Pvt. Ltd. in May 2008.
- Reliance Quant Plus Fund launched by Reliance Capital AMC Ltd in June 2008.
- Taurus Ethical Fund launched by Taurus AMC Ltd in February 2009.
- Edelweiss Nifty Enhancer Fund launched by Edelweiss AMC Ltd in May 2009.
- JM Nifty Plus Fund launched by JM Financial AMC Pvt. Ltd. in June 2009.

index options: index option gives a person the right but not the obligation to buy or sell something. An option is a contract between two parties wherein the buyer receives a privilege for which he pays a fee (premium) and the seller accepts an obligation for which he receives a fee. The premium is the price negotiated and set when the option is bought or sold. A person who buys an option is said to be long in the option. A person who sells an option is said to be short in the option.

India Index Services & Products Ltd. (IISL): is a joint venture between the National Stock Exchange of India Ltd. (NSE) and CRISIL. IISL has been formed with the objective of providing a variety of indices and index-related services and products for the capital markets. IISL has a licensing and marketing agreement with Standard and Poor's (S&P), the world's leading provider of equity indices, for co-branding IISL's equity indices.

indicator lending rate (ILR): the base lending rate set by a bank from which interest rates on its variable interest loans are derived.

indicator mineral: a mineral which is not sought itself, but if followed may lead to a deposit of the sought mineral.

indirect taxation: broadly speaking, taxes levied on money spent - the sale, purchase, production or use of goods or services - for example, sales tax, customs duties, excise duties and the goods and services tax. The impact of such taxes is usually passed on to the end consumer. Contrast direct taxation.

induced polarisation: a method of geophysical prospecting.

industrial minerals: non-metallic minerals used in industry.

industrial property: warehouses and factories.

industrial stocks: stocks other than mining and oil.

inelastic supply and demand: the supply of and demand for goods or services which do not increase or decrease markedly with changes to price.

infant mortality rate: the number of deaths to infants under one year of age per 1000 live births in a given year.

inflation: the state of affairs when the value of money falls and the prices of goods and services increase, other things being equal.

infrastructure: the non-mining utilities required to bring a project into production - for example, roads, a township, water supply, electricity, etc.

initial potential: the rate at which a well produces during first production tests.

initial public offering (IPO): a float; the raising of capital through an offer of shares to investors who apply for them under a prospectus, with a view to the issuing company becoming listed on the stock exchange shortly after the new shares have been allotted to the successful applicants.

input tax credits (GST): the goods and services tax paid on their inputs by suppliers of goods and services which those suppliers are able to claim back. Such claims can be made in respect of both taxable and GST-free items. However, input tax credits are not allowed for the GST paid by businesses on inputs used in activities that are input taxed. Nor are input tax credits allowed for GST paid on goods and services for the personal use of proprietors.

input taxed (GST): goods and services which are only partly exempt from the goods and services tax because, while that tax is not payable directly by consumers, the suppliers of those goods and services are not able to claim back the tax paid on their inputs and thus have to reflect that in their price structure. Examples include financial services and residential rents. Other countries use the term "exempt" to describe this type of activity. Contrast GST-free.

inquorate: not constituting a quorum (an inquorate conference is one lacking a quorum).

INR: symbol for the Indian rupee.

inscribed stock: see Commonwealth bonds.

inside information: information, ultimately from company sources, which is not publicly available.

insider trading: buying or selling shares on the basis of inside information. This is illegal.

insolvency: the inability to meet debts as they fall due.

instalment: a part of the issue price of a security. Companies sometimes make share or debenture issues which are payable by a series of two or more instalments rather than requiring the total application money to be paid by the applications closing date.

instalment receipt: an instrument traded on the stock exchange and resembling a contributing share. Typically, it arises when existing fully-paid shares in a company are offered to the public under a prospectus with the vendor agreeing to accept payment for them in stages.

instalment warrant: a form of derivative, designed to resemble a contributing share.

institutional adviser: an adviser in a stockbroker's office who specialises in dealing with institutional clients.

institutional investors: organisations with vast sums of money to be invested on behalf of clients. Largely made up of superannuation funds, unit trusts, investment companies and life insurance companies.

instrument: a legal document in writing. In a financial context it refers to a debt which may or may not be negotiable.

insurance bonds: life insurance company or friendly society policies, usually subject to single premiums and usually without death benefits, which are backed by professionally managed fixed interest and/or equity portfolios. They can be either capital guaranteed or investment-linked and either superannuation or non-superannuation. They do not involve cash distributions, but pass on the investment returns either through bonuses added to the nominal sum insured or, in the case of unit-linked contracts, through a rising unit value. In some ways they resemble unit trusts, but income tax is paid by the institution and not the investor. Withdrawals within the first ten years also attract tax in the policyholder's hands in respect of the net gain, but this is subject to a special rebate.

intangible assets: a class of assets which is generally a right rather than a physical object. Examples of intangibles include: goodwill, patent rights, copyrights, trademarks, trade names, licences, newspaper mastheads, concessions, preliminary and share issue expenses. It is common for these assets to be written off over time. See also assets.

intellectual property (IP): intangible assets derived from original thought and protected by law - ideas, discoveries and inventions. The protection comes about from laws covering patents, copyright (literature, music, art, software and so on) and trademarks.

inter alia: among other things.

inter se: among themselves.

inter vivos: during a person's lifetime.

inter vivos trust: a trust set up by a living person, as distinct from a trust set up by will.

inter-company market: the short term borrowing and lending of surplus cash at interest between major companies.

interest (financial transactions): the periodical payment by a borrower to a lender for the use of money. See also compound interest, simple interest, yield (investments generally).

interest (legal transactions): a right, claim or share in property.

interest cover: the number of times that earnings before interest and tax (EBIT) cover interest. It is one measure of the security of those payments. The interest cover ratio is calculated by dividing EBIT for the year by the annual interest payments.

interest indexed bonds: Commonwealth treasury bonds involving quarterly interest payments under which the investors get a low coupon, but with the amount of interest paid each three months representing the sum of the quarterly coupon and the consumer price index (CPI) movement for that quarter. The capital at maturity remains unaltered at its original face value.

interest rate: the percentage of par value paid out per annum as interest. Sometimes called the coupon rate. It is distinct from yield.

interest rate swap: an exchange where one party is obliged to pay a fixed interest rate to the other party in return for a floating interest rate. A net interest payment flows one way or the other in each interest period, depending on the relative levels of the two rates.

interest withholding tax: a flat rate of tax deducted at source from interest paid to non-residents of the country concerned.

interim: relating to the first six months of a financial year, as in interim profit report and interim dividend announcement.

internal rate of return (IRR): the interest rate which equates the present value of the amounts invested in a project with the present value of the expected future cash flows. It is a measure of the return from an investment.

International Financial Reporting Standards (IFRS): a set of accounting standards which aim at international harmonisation. They are "principles-based" standards, in that they establish broad rules rather than dictating specific treatments.

International Monetary Fund (IMF): an international organisation which draws on a pool of funds contributed by its member countries in order to assist developing countries having balance of payments problems.

International Standard Book Number (ISBN): a unique 10-digit code for the identification of printed books and pamphlets and various other material (but not serial publications - see next item). ISBNs are scheduled to consist of 13 digits as from 1 January 2007.

International Standard Serial Number (ISSN): a unique 8-digit code for the identification of serial publications, including periodical newsletters produced by organisations.

Internet: a co-operative public network of shared information stored on computers.

Internet service provider (ISP): an organisation controlling appropriate computers, modems and other equipment which for a fee provides access to the Internet to its subscribers.

intersection: the length of mineralisation encountered in a drill hole.

intestacy: the state of dying without leaving a valid will.

intra vires: within the power.

intrinsic value (options): the market price of the underlying share less the exercise price of the option, but not less than zero. See also time value.

intrinsic value (shares): a fundamentalist's valuation of a share. See fundamental analysis.

intrusion: see igneous intrusion.

inventory: stocks of finished goods, work in progress and raw materials. For tax purposes trading stock can be valued, at the option of the taxpayer, at cost or at market selling value or at its replacement price.

inverse yield curve: see yield curve.

investment: an act of immediate sacrifice in the expectation of future reward; the exchange of money for some income earning and/or appreciating asset in order to gain a future return. An investment entails risk. A wide range of assets from coins and art to property and shares can be purchased as investments. See also assets.

investment account policy: a contract under which premiums, less the cost of life cover and expenses, are paid into an individual investment account to which interest, net of tax, is credited.

investment adviser: a person or company licensed as such.

investment bonds: see insurance bonds.

investment company: a specially formed company acting in a similar fashion to a unit trust, involving money subscribed by members of the general public. Investment companies are usually listed on the stock exchange. They are like all other listed companies except that their assets, instead of being plant, stock, land, debtors, etc., consist primarily of ordinary shares in non-investment companies listed on the stock exchange. Investment companies thus resemble closed end (listed) unit trusts in terms of activity, but not in legal form or taxation status. They are often aimed at smaller investors and provide spread (qv) and management know-how.

investment grade: fixed interest securities regarded as unlikely to default. Contrast junk bonds.

investment spread: see spread.

investment-linked policy: a contract with benefits expressed in units, each representing a share in an investment portfolio. The unit price fluctuates with market values and allows for investment income.

investments (balance sheets): shares and debentures in listed and unlisted companies; loans to associates and affiliates and government securities which have been purchased with the intent of holding for a long period and not for immediate or near term resale. Short term investments are classified as current assets.

Insurance Regulatory and Development Authority: set up by an act of Parliament, this statutory body regulates, promotes and ensures orderly growth of the insurance industry and to protect the interests of the policyholders in India.

investor: one who invests.

invisibles: invisible imports and exports - for example: interest, dividends, royalties, insurance, banking services, tourism, transport costs, foreign aid, etc. These are intangible items involving payments corresponding to those for visible imports and exports.

ion exchange: a method for recovering metals in solution.

IP: abbreviation for intellectual property.

IPO: abbreviation for initial public offering (a float).

IQD: symbol for the Iraqi dinar.

IRDA: abbreviation for Insurance Regulatory and Development Authority.

iron: a primary metal produced mainly from iron oxide. Usually processed into pig iron, steel and specialised steels in combination with other metals such as cobalt, manganese and tungsten. Chemical symbol: Fe.

IRR: abbreviation for internal rate of return.

IRR: symbol for the Iranian rial.

IRS: abbreviation for interest rate securities.

IRS: abbreviation for Indian Revenue Service.

ISBN: abbreviation for International Standard Book Number.

ISK: symbol for the Icelandic krona.

ISO: abbreviation for International Organization for Standardisation.

isopach map: a contoured map showing variations in thickness of a geological feature.

ISP: abbreviation for Internet service provider.

ISSN: abbreviation for International Standard Serial Number.

issue: lineal descendants - children, grandchildren, and so on.

issue: see share issue.

ITA: abbreviation for International Tin Agreement.

ITC: abbreviation for input tax credit.

ITC: abbreviation for International Tin Council.

ITEC: abbreviation for income tax exempt charity.

ITF: abbreviation for in trust for.

ITL: symbol for the Italian lira.

ITO: abbreviation for International Trade Organisation.

jaw-boning: words by a central bank to condition expectations.

jig: a device for concentrating minerals using water action.

jobber: a UK share wholesaler who deals as principal only with stockbrokers. This role does not exist in the Australian sharemarket. Jobbers deal with brokers as principals. Jobbers do not charge brokerage, but instead make profits and cover costs by always trading at two different prices simultaneously - a lower one, at which they are willing to buy, and a higher one, at which they are willing to sell. The margin or difference between the two prices came to be known as the "jobber's turn". The jobber is never told whether the broker wishes to buy or sell.

joint (law): involving two or more persons in conjunction, as distinct from several.

joint (mining): a small scale fracture along which there has been no movement.

joint holding: a shareholding registered in the name of more than one person.

joint stock company: a company the capital of which is divided into numerous transferable shares. All listed companies are in this category, but mutual life offices are not.

joint tenancy: the ownership of land by two or more persons collectively in such a way that on the death of one the ownership passes to that person's survivor or survivors, as distinct from a tenancy-in-common. A joint tenant is one of the co-owners and is not a "tenant" in the sense of "lessee".

joint tenant: (see joint tenancy); not a "tenant" in the sense of "lessee".

joint venture: an arrangement for two or more parties to explore or develop a prospect.

joule: a unit of energy.

journal: day book. An accounting book of original entry.

JPY: symbol for the Japanese yen.

junk bonds: corporate fixed interest securities characterised by high apparent interest rates and a greater than average risk of default (very often involving poor interest cover and low asset backing). Contrast investment grade.

Jurassic Period: the middle one of the three periods comprising the Mesozoic era. In time, 140 to 195 million years ago.

kaolin: a group of clay minerals.

kerogen: the solid, bituminous mineraloid substance in oil shales which yields oil when the shales undergo destructive distillation.

kerogen shale: see oil shale.

Keynesian economics: the advocacy of monetary and fiscal programs by governments in order to increase employment and spending and to stimulate business activity. This economic theory was originally put forward by John Maynard Keynes in his book *The General Theory of Employment, Interest and Money* (1936). Keynes was of the view that high employment and controlled inflation could best be achieved by the authorities varying interest rates, tax rates and public expenditures rather than relying on market forces.

kick back: commission earned by a third party for facilitating a deal. Often used for that part of the commission earned by an intermediary which is passed back to the client.

killing: an exceptionally good speculative profit on the market.

kimberlite: a variety of mica, usually in the form of dykes, sills and pipes.

kimberlite pipe: a volcanic vent, çircular in shape with a diameter up to several kilometres, the host body for diamonds.

knockout event: the fall in a company's share price to below a defined "knockout price", leading to adverse consequences for the company - for example, an increase in the interest rate payable on certain of its existing loans.

KRW: symbol for the Korean won.

KWD: symbol for the Kuwaiti dinar.

Laffer curve: a curve named after the American economist Arthur Laffer, plotting the revenue collected by a government on the horizontal axis against the income tax rate on the vertical axis. The optimum collection of tax in any country does not occur at very high rates of tax.

A tax rate of zero would clearly produce no revenue. However, a tax rate of 100 cents in the dollar would also produce no revenue - because no sane person would find it worth while to earn any income under such a regime. The maximum amount of revenue is thus gathered at some intermediate point - although nobody knows precisely what that particular point might be.

laissez-faire: a policy of non-interference by the government in the economy.

land: a solid part of the earth's surface. Technically, the word encompasses also the buildings erected on the soil.

land tax: a tax on property imposed by a State Government and based on the total site values of all properties owned by one person in the State concerned.

Landsat: an unmanned satellite which was launched into a near polar orbit and designed to provide multispectral imagery of the earth's surface on a repetitive basis. The Landsat imagery has the traditional advantages of distant remote sensing in that large areas are visible within a single frame. This facilitates examination of the geological fabric of continents and discovery of major lineaments. The use of imagery complements the traditional sources of data.

lapsed policy: a policy terminated because of the non-payment of premiums before the policy has acquired a cash or other non-forfeiture value.

large cap: a term used by the investment community to refer to companies with a minimum issue size of Rs.10 crore. Large cap is an abbreviation of the term "large market capitalization".

last: the last sale price paid for a stock at the conclusion of a period. It is common to adjust the last price for a subsequent higher bid or lower sell offers in order to provide a more meaningful closing price.

lateritic deposit: deposits formed by the leaching away of soluble minerals leaving behind in the laterite a valuable ore such as nickel or bauxite.

laundering of money: the chanelling of money obtained either fraudulently or from illegal activities such as drug dealing, or alternatively from legitimate activities but not declared for income tax purposes, through a stockbroker, solicitor, casino or other respectable organisation in order to disguise its true source and to enable its use without arousing suspicion.

law of large numbers: in statistics, the principle that the probability of an event occurring, as derived from a sample, is likely to be a good approximation for the true probability only if the number of items in the sample is sufficiently large.

lazy balance sheet: the state of affairs when a company has assets which are not producing a proper rate of return. In such a case the company should sell the assets and either reinvest the proceeds or pass the cash on to its shareholders by way of capital return or through a buyback (qv).

lazy money: money kept in low interest or zero interest bank accounts on a permanent or semi-permanent basis, through either investor inertia or investor ignorance.

LBO: abbreviation for leveraged buyout.

LCI: abbreviation for labour cost index.

leaching: the removal of minerals from ore by their dissolution in water and subsequent percolation. May be a natural process on in situ deposits or a chemical process used in milling.

lead: a primary metal whose principal characteristics are its density and resistance to corrosion. Used mainly in batteries and as an additive to petrol. Chemical symbol: Pb.

lead-time: the length of time between making a decision to undertake a project and the actual commencement of production or mining.

lease (mining): a legal document granting the holder or holders certain exploration and development rights. Also refers to the area subject to the lease.

lease (real estate): a contract under which one party (the lessor) allows another party (the lessee) to use a property for a defined period subject to the payment of rent and the observance of other conditions; or the document evidencing such a contract.

leaseback: the sale of a property subject to a lease from the purchaser to the vendor.

leasehold: land held for a limited period under a lease, at the expiry of which the land reverts to its owner, the freeholder.

leasehold improvements: improvements made to leasehold property.

leasing (businesses): a form of finance under which the supplier of funds (the lessor) buys an asset required and chosen by a business (the lessee) and makes it available to the business for an agreed period at an agreed rental. The lessor retains ownership of the asset.

least squares regression: a statistical method of calculating a trend line from a set of scores by fitting a line which best represents the observations. The line, which may be straight or curvilinear, is calculated by minimising the sum of the squares of the difference between the actual and the predicted values.

ledger: an accounting record summarising and classifying transactions.

legacy: property left to a person by another person's will.

legacy currencies: the currencies that were used by the European countries that adopted the euro before that unit took over - for example, the French franc, the German mark and the Italian lira.

legal deposit: the statutory requirement for all publishers in many countries to deposit free of charge on its issue one copy of each of their publications with the appropriate designated Library and also with the National Library of the country. These provisions apply to both commercial and non-commercial publishing activities. Applicable in UK, Canada, Australia, New Zealand, etc.

legal ownership: the nominal or registered interest in a property, as distinct from the beneficial or equitable ownership

lender of last resort (LLR): an institution, usually a country's central bank, that offers loans to banks or other eligible institutions that are experiencing financial difficulty or are considered highly risky or near collapse. The lender of last resort functions both to protect individuals who have deposited funds, and to prevent panic withdrawing from banks who have temporary limited liquidity.

lens: a body of ore that is thick in the middle and tapers toward the ends.

LEPO: abbreviation for low exercise price option.

lessee: the tenant or occupier under a lease.

lessor: the landlord or owner under a lease.

letter of awareness: see letter of comfort.

letter of comfort: a non-binding statement expressing support for one company by another. Used to support borrowing applications.

letter stock: a distinct series of ordinary shares which participates in the profits of only a defined division of a company rather than in those of the entire enterprise.

letters of administration: authority granted by a court to a person to wind up the estate of a deceased person who did not leave a valid will

letters of administration with the will annexed: authority granted by a court to a person to wind up the estate of a deceased person who left a valid will but who appointed as executor a person who is unable or unwilling to act as such

leucoxene: a mineral formed from weathered ilmenite.

levels: openings at each of the different horizons in a mine.

leverage: gearing; the use of borrowed funds in order to supplement an investor's own money when acquiring an asset or the proportion of funding obtained by debt. The higher the leverage, the higher the use of debt. It is measured by a number of ratios such as debt to equity and shareholders' interest. In the stock market leverage often refers to the purchase of options or contributing shares in a stock rather than its fully-paid shares. Thus an investor can buy a larger volume of securities than the fully-paid shares for the same capital outlay. In a market swing the options and contributing shares, because of their financial convertibility into fully paids, will tend to be more volatile.

leveraged buyout (LBO): a takeover bid made not by an outsider but rather by a syndicate involving the management team of the company concerned. Typically it involves the use of large amounts of borrowed funds, to be charged on the assets of the enterprise itself, possibly supplemented by equity funds from an organisation specialising in packaging such deals. However, a panel of owners running their own business has a strong motivation to make the venture succeed. In the case of professional managers who were previously repressed by an incompetent board of directors the chance to be free to make commercial decisions can also be a factor lifting profitability significantly.

leveraged lease: a form of tax-efficient funding where most of the funds for a project are in effect borrowed by the lessor. Leveraged leases tend to be used for large projects and are generally for longer periods than ordinary leases.

LGS ratio: the ratio of liquid and government securities that trading banks used to maintain in respect of their deposits. Liquid and government securities comprise cash, treasury bills, government securities and deposits with the Reserve Bank of India.

liabilities: obligations to another party. Shareholders' funds are not a liability of a company. Liabilities can be divided into a number of different categories based upon their maturity. These classifications are:

- *current liabilities* (shown in the balance sheet; due within one year)
- *deferred liabilities* (shown in the balance sheet; due after one year)
- *contingent liabilities* (shown by way of notes to the accounts).

Liabilities include provisions (qv) but not reserves.

LIC: abbreviation for listed investment company.

lien: the right to hold property belonging to another person as security for the payment of some debt or the performance of some obligation - for example, the right of a broker over shares until a buying client has paid for them.

life expectancy: the average number of additional years a person would live if current mortality trends were to continue. The life expectancy at birth is frequently quoted as an indicator of mortality trends.

life insurance bonds: life insurance company policies, usually subject to single premiums and usually without death benefits, which are backed by professionally managed fixed interest and/or equity portfolios. They can be either capital guaranteed or investment-linked and either superannuation or non-superannuation. They do not involve cash distributions, but pass on the investment returns either through bonuses added to the nominal sum insured or, in the case of unit-linked contracts, through a rising unit value. In some ways they resemble unit trusts, but income tax is paid by the life office and not the investor.

life interest: an entitlement to the income of some fund for a period ending on the death of some person (the *life tenant*).

life tenant: the holder of a life interest (qv).

LIFFE: abbreviation for London International Financial Futures and Options Exchange.

LIFO: last in, first out. An accounting method for valuing inventories. Basically it works by treating the last item of stock purchased as the first item of stock sold. The valuation of stock affects the determination of profit. Contrast FIFO.

limestone: a sedimentary deposit consisting largely of calcium carbonate. Used in the manufacture of lime for cement.

limit: see at limit.

limitation of action: the principle that there should be a period defined by legislation within which a legal action to enforce a right must be taken. After this period any such action is regarded as statute barred. For example, in the case of simple contracts (those not under seal) the period ends six years after the cause of action arose.

limited downside risk: see downside risk.

limited liability: see company.

limited partnership: a special type of partnership available and requiring to be registered as such. A limited partnership consists of one or more general partners with unlimited liability and one or more limited partners. These latter have liability for the debts and obligations of the partnership only in proportion to the amounts they invest, as long as they do not participate actively in the management of the business. Only the general partners have the power to bind the limited partnership.

limited recourse financing: the financing of a project by an institution on the basis of the project rather than the participants in the project.

limonite: iron oxide, an ore of iron.

liquefied natural gas (LNG): gas which has been compressed, and thereby liquefied, for easy transportation.

liquefied petroleum gas (LPG): petroleum gas which has been compressed for transportation.

liquid asset: cash and any asset which is readily convertible to cash.

liquid assets ratio: a measure of liquidity. Basically, it compares the sum of a company's cash and debtors and those securities which are readily convertible into cash with its current liabilities. This ratio differs from the working capital ratio in that it disregards stock (inventories). If the ratio is too high, then this indicates idle funds which could be better employed; if it is too low, then this gives a warning sign as to a potentially dangerous situation. Two alternative approaches are in use:

- ratio = (CA-S)/CL
- ratio = (CA-S)/(CL-OD)

where

CA = current assets
CL = current liabilities
S = stock
OD = bank overdraft

Also known as the acid test, the liquid ratio, the quick test, the quick ratio, the quick assets ratio.

liquid ratio: see liquid assets ratio.

liquidation: the winding up of a company by a liquidator - the conversion of its assets into cash and the payment of that cash to creditors and, if there is any surplus after that, to shareholders. Most liquidations are compulsory and relate to insolvent situations. However, a liquidation can also be voluntary and merely represent a reorganisation of a group structure. Defunct companies with no assets or liabilities can be struck off without being formally liquidated.

liquidity (companies): the closeness of an asset to cash. The term also refers to the ability of a company to meet its liabilities. Liquidity is often measured in terms of the current ratio, the liquid ratio, the interest cover and the cash flow ratio.

liquidity (stock exchange): the ease with which a share can be traded on the market.

liquidity preference: a desire to remain in a state of liquidity.

listed company: a company at least one of the securities of which is listed on the stock exchange.

listed investment company (LIC): a specially formed company acting in a similar fashion to a unit trust, involving money subscribed by members of the general public. Investment companies are usually listed on the stock exchange. They are like all other listed companies except that their assets, instead of being plant, stock, land, debtors, etc., consist primarily of ordinary shares in non-investment companies listed on the stock exchange. Investment companies thus resemble closed end (listed) unit trusts in terms of activity, but not in legal form or taxation status. They are often aimed at smaller investors and provide spread (qv) and management know-how.

listed property trust: a unit trust with the bulk of its assets invested in property and which is listed on the stock exchange.

listed securities: securities which can be traded on the stock exchange. A company may have all, or part, of its securities listed.

listing requirements: a set of rules and regulations that need to be fulfilled in order to gain and maintain the listing of securities on the stock exchange.

lithology: the physical and mineralogical characteristics of a rock.

living trust: a trust set up by a living person, as distinct from a trust set up by will

living will: an enduring power of attorney (medical treatment), an instrument which allows a donor to appoint an agent who can make decisions about medical treatment on the donor's behalf when the donor has become incapable of making such decisions personally.

LKR: symbol for the Sri Lankan rupee.

LLR: abbreviation for lender of last resort.

LMI: abbreviation for listed managed investment.

LNG: abbreviation for liquefied natural gas.

loading: an addition to a normal premium charge because of extra risk involved through occupation or health, etc.

loan to asset ratio: the borrowed funds divided by the total assets (the sum of the investor's own stake in a project and the borrowed funds).

loan to equity ratio: the borrowed funds divided by the investor's own stake in a project.

LOC: abbreviation for letter of credit.

locked in: a situation that arises after a raid or takeover, where non-accepting minority shareholders may have difficulty in selling their holdings. Also used in the context of shareholders who are reluctant to sell because of the incidence of capital gains tax on realised profits.

locus standi: the right to be heard in court.

lode: generally tabular mineral deposit, usually relatively narrow and occurring between well defined walls.

London Metal Exchange: the major world market place for free traded metals.

long position (futures market): a contract promising to take. Because futures trading is a zero sum game, for every contract to buy (a long position) there must be a corresponding contract to sell (a short position).

long position (share market): the status when shares are owned. Contrast *short position*.

long term: in accounting, involving a period of more than twelve months; in regard to investments, probably involving a horizon of at least three to five years.

long term assets: assets which in the ordinary course of business would not be consumed or turned into cash within 12 months. See also assets.

long term liabilities: liabilities which in the ordinary course of business would not be consumed or turned into cash within 12 months. Examples include provision for deferred tax, other non-current provisions, long term financial debt. See also liabilities.

long ton: see tonne.

longwall mining: a system of working a seam of coal in which slices of coal are cut from a long ore face.

loss: a deficit on trading; the failure of revenue to cover costs. See also profit.

loss ratio (general insurance): incurred claims as a proportion of earned premiums.

low: the lowest price paid for a stock during a period.

low doc loan: a low document loan under which the lender determines the borrower's eligibility for finance by relying mainly on statements by the borrower to the effect that the borrower can meet the periodical repayments, rather than by sighting a proof of income such as a tax assessment or pay-slips.

A higher interest rate than for conventional loans is usually charged to compensate for the additional risk involved and mortgage insurance (qv) will usually also be required.

low exercise price option (LEPO): a European style option over underlying securities with an exercise price of no greater than 10 cents which is traded on the stock exchange.

LPG: abbreviation for liquefied petroleum gas.

LPT: abbreviation for listed property trust.

LSE: abbreviation for London Stock Exchange.

Ltd.: abbreviation for limited. See company.

lump ore: a physical state of ore - often the case immediately after mining or some crushing, as distinct from fines.

LVR: abbreviation for loan-to-valuation ratio.

M&A: abbreviation for mergers and acquisitions.

M1; M2; M3: see money supply.

Maastricht Treaty: the Treaty of 7 February 1992, setting up the European Union (qv). The parties resolved to achieve the strengthening and the convergence of their economies and to establish an economic and monetary union including, in accordance with the provisions of the Treaty, a single and stable currency, later named the euro (qv). See also convergence (political).

magma: molten material that cooled and formed into rock.

magnetic anomaly: see anomaly.

magnetic separation: a form of concentrating ore using the magnetic qualities of ore to separate it from the gangue.

magnetite: iron oxide which is magnetic.

magnetometer: a device for measuring the different magnetic properties of an area.

MAI: abbreviation for Multilateral Agreement on Investments.

majority: the greater part of; that is, more than half.

make good: on vacating premises to return them to their state at the commencement of a tenancy.

managed funds: funds marketed to the public, promising to provide spread and expertise. Those currently available include:

- listed unit trusts (including property trusts)
- unlisted unit trusts
- listed investment companies
- investment bonds issued by life insurance companies
- investment bonds issued by friendly societies
- exchange traded funds
- pooled development funds (PDFs)
- infrastructure funds
- public superannuation funds
- property syndicates
- hedge funds.

Most managed funds are invested in a wide range of assets so as to minimise the risk for investors.

management and investment company (MIC): an intermediary which under former legislation was licensed by the government to raise funds from the public in order to take shares in or lend to high-tech industries. This entailed relatively high risks for the investors who in return derived a tax benefit.

management buyout (MBO): a takeover bid made not by an outsider but rather by a syndicate involving the management team of the company concerned. Typically it involves the use of large amounts of borrowed funds, to be charged on the assets of the enterprise itself, possibly supplemented by equity funds from an organisation specialising in packaging such deals. However, a panel of owners running their own business has a strong motivation to make the venture succeed. In the case of professional managers who were previously repressed by an incompetent board of directors the chance to be free to make commercial decisions can also be a factor lifting profitability significantly.

management expense ratio (MER): the total fees per annum charged to investors in a managed fund, expressed as a percentage of the assets.

management fees: money paid out by investors to somebody else for doing something in connection with an investment and which are thereby permanently lost to those investors. Furthermore, such money is no longer part of a portfolio capable of generating future income and growth. For example explicit fees to a financial planner or implicit fees through a commission structure; fees in connection with a master fund (qv) or a wrap account (qv); the usual retail or wholesale fees for using managed funds; and brokerage indirectly when the chosen fund managers trade on the stock exchange. Investors may also encounter exit fees and switching fees. It needs to be remembered that notwithstanding all this outlay half of all managed funds perform below the average.

mandamus: a writ issued by a court requiring a person (for example, the chairman of a meeting) to carry out that person's duties in accordance with the law.

manganese: a primary metal whose principal uses are in dry batteries and as a ferro alloy in steel manufacture. Chemical symbol: Mn.

manipulation: actions which create a false or misleading market; actions designed to artificially raise or lower the market price of listed securities, futures contracts, etc., and/or to give a false or misleading appearance of active trading, in order to make an unfair profit. See also cornering, green shoe, pool, wash sales.

Mareva injunction: an injunction preventing a person from dissipating property or moving property or assets out of the relevant jurisdiction.

margin call: a formal demand for some remedial action issued by a lender to a borrower under a margin lending arrangement when the market value of the total portfolio which has been pledged drops so that the amount of cover for the loan falls below a defined ratio; or a similar request for more funds to cover adverse price movements in the futures market.

margin lending: see Chapter 5.

marginal cost: the extra cost incurred in producing an extra unit of output.

marginal costing: see direct costing.

marginal profit: the difference between marginal cost and marginal revenue.

marginal rate of abatement: the amount of income tax payable by individuals under the sliding scale in use, plus the amount of social security benefits foregone under the income test, in respect of each *additional* dollar of income.

marginal revenue: the extra revenue made from selling one extra unit of output.

marginal tax rate: the amount of income tax which is payable by a person in respect of income earned in a financial year; this rate - rather than a person's average rate of tax - is relevant when making investment decisions.

mark to market: the requirement to show assets in a company balance sheet at their true market value on the balance date, rather than at their historical cost or at a previous book value. This means putting corresponding items into the company's profit and loss account. Critics of this system claim that this distorts profit figures year by year, especially in the case of listed shares, the value of which can fluctuate widely over the course of an accounting period. The approach can indeed do that, but it is far more important that shareholders and creditors should not be misled as to the true worth of an enterprise. Some boards of directors also rather naively like to pretend that no capital loss arises until an asset that has gone down in value is actually sold. Individuals tend to be more realistic - for example, they often base their own spending patterns on how rich they feel having regard to the current market value of their house rather than its original purchase price.

market: a place where buyers and sellers meet to trade, especially subject to recognised rules. With the growth in technology, some markets need not have a physical marketplace, trading taking place, for example, on the telephone or through the Internet. The term is also used as a synonym for the stock exchange.

market bid: the price differential per share allowed in stock exchange transactions.

market capitalisation: the worth of a listed company as set by the stock market. It is calculated at any given point of time by multiplying the number of ordinary shares on issue by the market price per share, possibly with adjustments for securities other than fully paid ordinary shares. Eligibility for inclusion in various stock exchange indices can depend on a company's market capitalisation.

market depth: the outstanding buying and selling orders recorded at any particular time for the shares of one class in a company at each of various price limits.

market failure: the situation where market forces do not lead to an efficient allocation of resources.

market maker: a stockbroker or institution willing to buy and sell a specified security as principal even in the absence of client orders.

market manipulation: actions which create a false or misleading market; actions designed to artificially raise or lower the market price of listed securities, futures contracts, etc., and/or to give a false or misleading appearance of active trading, in order to make an unfair profit.

market overt: an unregulated market for goods or services, with free competition between buyers and sellers matching supply and demand.

market participant: a stockbroking organisation.

market portfolio: a theoretical portfolio of all stocks in the market. By definition the size of each holding is in proportion to each company's capitalisation.

market price (listed securities): the last sale price of a security on the stock exchange or the buyer price, if higher, or the seller price, if lower.

market raid: see raid.

market rigging: see market manipulation.

market risk: that element of risk which cannot be removed by diversification and which arises from political events and other forces which affect the whole market rather than a particular stock. It is also known as non-diversifiable risk, systemic risk and systematic risk. Beta is a measure of the market risk.

market value: the price at a given point of time which a willing but not anxious buyer is prepared to pay, and which a willing but not anxious seller is prepared to accept, in an open market transaction, with both parties being prudent and properly informed in regard to the matter, and at arm's length to each other, with neither party being under any abnormal pressure to buy or to sell.

marketability: the ease with which a purchase or a sale can be made in a particular security. It is affected by costs of the trade, the ease of physical transfer, research costs, the number of securities in circulation and the willingness of existing shareholders to sell at that price.

marketable parcel (loosely): a parcel of shares in a company worth at least $500. The number of holders of such parcels has to be shown in annual reports.

marketable parcel (technically): the smallest parcel of shares in a company normally tradeable on the stock exchange, currently a single share. In former times it was often 100 shares, but a sliding scale was involved. Sometimes the term is still used colloquially to reflect that concept. In the pre-computer age smaller parcels of shares were called odd lots and incurred an additional fee when bought or sold.

marriage (stock exchange): see crossing.

massive: without definite crystalline structure, as distinct from porphyry. Also describes an ore body which is big in all directions.

master fund (also called master trust): an "umbrella" service, a special type of managed fund that for a fee enables investors to direct money into one or more conventional wholesale or retail managed funds (and in some cases also listed shares). Some master funds are discretionary funds, with the investor (if desired, with the help of a financial planner) choosing the specific investment products from a list drawn up by the master fund manager and with the investor also having the right to switch these from time to time. Others master funds are "funds of funds", with the investor specifying his tolerance to risk and his preferences in regard to growth and income and with the master fund manager then selecting the specific investment products. Investing through a master fund can give access to a range of wholesale investment funds which would otherwise not be available to individual investors and which generally involve lower charges. A further attraction is the availability of a single comprehensive and consolidated report. See also wrap accounts.

MAT: abbreviation for moving annual turnover.

maternal mortality rate: the number of deaths to women due to pregnancy and childbirth complications per 100,000 live births in a given year.

matte: smelter output, being metal still containing some impurities requiring refining to obtain pure metal.

maturity date: the redemption date; the date on which a fixed interest security is due to be repaid by its issuer.

MBO: abbreviation for management buyout.

McLibel Trial: an infamous British court case involving libel. McDonald's Corporation (a company listed on the New York Stock Exchange) and McDonald's Restaurants Limited (one of its subsidiaries) sued Helen Marie Steel and David Morris. The case ran for some two-and-a-half years and became the longest ever English trial. The judge, Mr Justice Roger Bell, delivered his verdict on 19 June 1997. It was a public relations disaster for McDonald's. The judge ruled that they had exploited children with their advertising, had produced misleading advertising, were culpably responsible for cruelty to animals, were antipathetic to unionisation and paid their workers low wages. But Steel and Morris had failed to prove all their points and so the court ruled that they had indeed libelled McDonald's. He awarded damages of 60,000 pounds. They refused to pay and McDonald's knew better than to pursue the matter. In March 1999 the Court of Appeal made further rulings against McDonald's in relation to heart disease and employment.

MCR: abbreviation for minimum capital requirement (insurance).

mean: the mathematical average of a set of scores. It is calculated by adding the value of the scores and dividing the total by the number of scores. Sometimes the scores are multiplied by a second variable to reflect the frequency of occurrence and the mean of the sum of those values is then known as a weighted average.

mean age: the mathematical average age of all the members of a population.

means test (social security): an assets test and/or an income test.

media release: a written communication setting out a statement which is intended for publication as a news story in newspapers and/or on radio and television.

median: the middle value in a set of ranked data.

median age: the age that divides a population ranked by age into two numerically equal groups.

mediation: the process under which a neutral third person attempts to bring two disputing parties to a situation where they can reach their own agreement.

meeting: a gathering of persons, especially one called to discuss matters of common interest and to make formal decisions.

member: a shareholder.

memorandum of association: a document drawn up on creation of a company, setting out its initial objectives, capital, name and address. See also articles of association.

MER: abbreviation for management expense ratio.

merchant bank: a financial institution specialising in advising and arranging finance for companies.

merger: a union agreed to by two or more companies to join all or part of their operations.

merger of equals (MOE): a euphemism for a takeover offer not involving a premium. Typically such transactions:

- are largely or entirely scrip based, with the share exchange ratios reflecting recent share trading levels
- result in each set of shareholders owning approximately 50 per cent of the combined company
- enable the financial benefits of the transaction to be shared equally among all shareholders of the two companies
- draw on the best skills available from each management team
- combine both boards of directors into one unified board.

MESI: abbreviation for monthly economic and social indicators.

Mesozoic Era: an era 70 to 230 million years ago. Includes the Cretaceous, Jurassic and Triassic Periods.

metallurgy: the science of treating and deriving metal.

metamorphic: rock which has changed its structure and properties through the effects of heat and pressure over time.

methane: a gaseous hydrocarbon of the paraffin series.

mezzanine finance: loan finance that is halfway between equity and secured debt.

MIC: abbreviation for management and investment company.

mid cap: is an abbreviation for the term "middle capitalization". As the name implies, a mid cap company is in the middle of the pack between large cap and small cap companies.

mid price: the price half-way between the buying and selling quotes.

migration: the process by which hydrocarbons are moved under pressure through permeable rocks until trapped.

mill: a plant in which ore is ground and treated for the recovery of the valuable metals. Originally called a battery.

millionaire factory: (a disparaging term for) Macquarie Bank Limited. The bank is well known for the extremely large remuneration packages that it pays to its key executives.

mine: generally any excavation for minerals. May be open-cut or underground.

mine face: that surface which is available to be worked.

mineral: a naturally occurring homogeneous substance having definite physical properties and chemical composition.

mineral claim: the exclusive right of exploration for minerals.

mineralisation: the process of conversion into a mineral. Also refers to the presence of a mineralised zone.

minimum bid: see market bid.

minimum subscription: the minimum level (in the aggregate) and the minimum parcel size (for individual applications) that will be accepted for new share issues and fixed interest offerings.

mining lease: the right to mine an area.

mining licence: the right to mine an area.

minor trend: see trend.

minority interest: that portion of a company or its net assets or profits as is attributable to minority shareholders.

minority shareholders: parties that hold shares in a company in which some other party holds a controlling interest.

minutes: the formal brief summary of proceedings at meetings and especially of the decisions made.

mission statement: a concise summary describing the general aims, core values and overall operating plan of a company or organisation, especially for the inspiration of employees and the information of customers, investors and other stakeholders.

ML: abbreviation for mining lease.

MMBOE: abbreviation for million barrels of oil equivalent.

MMP: abbreviation for mixed member proportional representation.

mode: in statistics, the most frequently occurring value in a set of scores.

modus operandi: the way in which an operation is carried out.

MOE: abbreviation for a merger of equals.

molybdenum: a primary metal the principal quality of which is its high melting point. Used primarily as a ferro alloy. Chemical symbol: Mo.

monazite: a mineral, the principal ore of thorium. Found in mineral sands.

monetarist: an economist who believes that changes in a country's money supply are the most important determinants of economic activity and economic cycles and by implication that governments should manipulate the money supply. Even if this theory were true - which is disputed - controlling the money supply when there are as many forms of credit as there are today is virtually impossible in a democracy.

monetary policy: the financial policy of managing a nation's or a region's money supply by a central bank in order to achieve specific goals - such as reducing inflation or achieving full employment. These days the primary tool of monetary policy usually involves open market operations to set the short term interest rate - see cash rate - although in some overseas countries exchange rate manipulation and controls over the money supply are also used.

money: bank notes or coins of convenient form stamped by a public authority and issued as a medium of exchange and a measure of value. The term can also include deposits, etc., convertible into money.

money accumulation plan: a superannuation plan involving defined contributions which are invested and accumulated at interest in order to produce a retirement benefit. Contrast defined benefit plan.

money illusion: the subconscious view held by many unsophisticated consumers and investors that value of money always remains same and that inflation can be ignored. Thus a pensioner getting 4 per cent on his money might think that he is doing all right by keeping his capital intact. However, if the cost of living is rising by 5 per cent then he is really going backwards, even on a pre-tax basis.

money laundering: the chanelling of money obtained either fraudulently or from illegal activities such as drug dealing, or alternatively from legitimate activities but not declared for income tax purposes, through a stockbroker, solicitor, casino or other respectable organisation in order to disguise its true source and to enable its use without arousing suspicion.

money market: that market which deals in the wholesale borrowing and lending of money. There are several markets within the money market - for example, the official short term money market, the inter-company market, the bill market.

money supply: the amount of money in the economy. It has three main levels of measurement which are in order of increasing breadth: M1 (all currency and current deposits with trading banks); M2 (all currency and total deposits with all trading banks); M3 (M2 plus deposits with all savings banks).

monopoly: a situation in which a single organisation has control over the supply of a product or service.

Moody's Investor Services: a corporate credit rating agency. See also rating agencies.

Moore's Law: the fact that the cost of technology declines by about 50 per cent every 18 to 24 months. (The Intel co-founder, Gordon Moore, had in 1965 observed that the number of transistors per square inch on integrated circuits had doubled every year since the integrated circuit was invented; in subsequent years the pace slowed somewhat.)

mortality table: a statistical table used by life insurance companies to estimate the chance of a life insured living to or dying at a given age.

mortgage: the formally registered transfer of an interest in land for the purpose of securing the repayment of a loan or other debt; or (loosely) the loan secured in this way itself. If the mortgagor (the borrower) defaults then the mortgagee (the lender) has certain rights, including the right to sell up the property in order to clear the debt. (Any balance, after deducting all costs, is paid to the borrower, the former owner of the land concerned.) A "first mortgage" creates a charge which ranks ahead of other charges known as second, third, etc., mortgages; unless qualified, the word "mortgage" by itself implies a first mortgage.

mortgage insurance: a special form of insurance which protects a lender on the security of property against any loss of capital or interest arising from defaults by a borrower, either absolutely or above a certain limit. The single premium is usually paid by the borrower; however, the policy is purely for the benefit of the lender, not the borrower.

mortgagee: the lender under a mortgage (contrast mortgagor).

mortgagor: the borrower under a mortgage (contrast mortgagee).

most favoured nation status: a status awarded by one nation to another in international trade. It means that a receiving nation is granted all trade advantages, such as low tariffs, that any third nation also receives.

motion: a proposed resolution before it has been adopted (that is, passed or carried) by a meeting.

mover: the person who proposes a motion to a meeting.

moving annual turnover: sales for a 12-month period calculated on a monthly rolling basis.

moving average: an average of scores involving a fixed time interval which moves with the passage of time.

MTAWE: abbreviation for male total average weekly earnings.

MTL: symbol for the Maltese lira.

MTN: abbreviation for medium term note.

mud: see drilling mud.

mullock: debris or waste rock taken out of a mine.

Multilateral Agreement on Investments (MAI): a proposed international treaty, later abandoned, designed to prevent member countries discriminating against foreign investors.

multiplier theory: an economic theory which explains the relationship between expenditure and the creation of income. It recognises that expenditure by one party is income for its recipients, leading to a further round of expenditure, and so on.

mum and dad investors: small individual investors, especially those relatively unsophisticated.

mutatis mutandis: the necessary changes being made.

mutual fund: an unlimited company performing a role similar to that performed by an unlisted unit trust, but without the use of a trustee.

MXN: symbol for the Mexican peso.

MYEFO: abbreviation for mid-year economic and fiscal outlook.

MYR: symbol for the Malaysian ringgit.

Naamloze Vennootschap (NV): a limited liability company (Dutch).

NAB: abbreviation for net asset backing.

naive diversification: diversification achieved by increasing the number of investments without regard to their relationship.

naming: the declaration by the chairman made when a member has disobeyed an order by the chairman, usually leading to that member's suspension in the absence of an apology.

naptha: a distillation product between petrol and refined oil.

NASD: abbreviation for National Association of Securities Dealers.

NASDAQ: abbreviation for National Association of Securities Dealers Automated Quotation system.

National Association of Securities Dealers: an organisation for United States brokers and dealers in the over the counter market.

national currency units: the domestic currency units of the European countries which were replaced by the euro.

national debt: the total debt of a country.

National Guarantee Fund (NGF): a fund maintained by the Australian Securities Exchange to compensate clients of brokers in respect of money or securities lost through broker fraud or insolvency.

National Stock Exchange (NSE): is the largest stock exchange in India and the third largest in the world in terms of volume of transactions. It operates in debt market, capital market and in derivatives. NSE, created at the behest of Government of India, is owned by a set of leading financial institutions, banks, insurance companies and other financial intermediaries in India. It is located in Mumbai.

native metal: a metal which occurs naturally in a pure state - for example, gold or silver.

natural gas: a highly compressible, highly expansible mixture of hydrocarbons having a low specific gravity and occurring naturally in a gaseous form.

natural gas liquids: those liquid hydrocarbons which are gaseous in the reservoir but are recoverable by condensation or absorption. Natural gasoline, condensate and liquefied petroleum gases fall in this category.

natural hedge: a hedge which is available to a business without its having to use an artificial hedging vehicle such as a futures contract - for example, by borrowing in the same currency as that to be generated by its future sales (so that any losses on one of these two transactions are matched by gains on the other, when measured in the local currency).

natural increase: the surplus of births over deaths in a population in a given period.

natural justice: the common law rules and procedures to be followed in order to ensure that decisions affecting others are made fairly.

NAV: abbreviation for net asset value.

NBFI: abbreviation for non-bank financial institution.

NCD: abbreviation for non-callable deposit.

NCSC: abbreviation for National Companies and Securities Commission.

NCU: abbreviation for national currency units.

NDA: abbreviation for non-disclosure agreement.

"near cash": assets which are readily convertible into cash (usually without loss), such as bank accounts, interest-bearing deposits at call, marketable government securities and short term bank bills.

"near money": assets which are readily convertible into cash (usually without loss), such as bank accounts, interest-bearing deposits at call, marketable government securities and short term bank bills.

neckline: see head and shoulders.

NED: abbreviation for non-executive director.

negative gearing: the situation when an investment such as property or shares is purchased with the assistance of borrowed funds and where the rental or dividend income (after the deduction of expenses) is less than the interest commitment in the course of a financial year; for tax purposes this negative net income can then be offset against any positive income from other sources.

negative pledge: an undertaking given by a borrower to a lender that the borrower will not undertake further loans without the lender's approval or in excess of a defined ratio and that the future borrowings will not rank ahead of existing loans.

negotiability: the ability to transfer ownership, usually in reference to debt instruments.

negotiable certificate of deposit: a negotiable receipt issued by a bank in exchange for the deposit of funds. The issuing bank agrees to pay the amount deposited plus interest to the bearer of the certificate on the date specified on the certificate.

negotiable instrument: a bearer bond, bill of exchange, promissory note, certificate of deposit or similar instrument which is transferable by delivery.

nemine contradicente: unanimously.

nemine dissentiente: unanimously.

net annual value (NAV): the notional rent of a property, covering both the land and the buildings erected on it.

net asset value (NAV): the total assets of a company, including intangibles, less the total liabilities.

net capital ratio (banking): see minimum capital standards.

net change: the closing price of a share on a day less its closing price on the preceding day, adjusted for any difference in the dividend entitlement, etc.

net present value (NPV): the sum of the projected cash flows from an investment, with each item discounted from the relevant date to the date of calculation. For example, the present value of Rs. 121 due in two years' time at 10 per cent per annum is Rs. 100. Theoretically, if the net present value is positive then the investment should be undertaken, and if it is negative then it should not be undertaken. Results can vary significantly with the discount rate used.

net profit: the difference between revenue and the costs of earning that revenue. In many contexts "net" means net of taxation.

net realisable value: a method of valuing inventory, taking into account its market price less the costs of sale.

net tangible asset backing (NTA): the net worth of a share, the theoretical value of the net assets attributable to each ordinary share on issue. It is calculated by dividing the company's total shareholders' funds, net of any minority interests, preference share capital and intangible assets, by the number of ordinary shares on issue. Adjustments need to be made to allow for contributing shares and for the dilutive effect of any company options and convertible securities. The exercise of such options and the conversion of the convertible securities should always be assumed where this produces a lower NTA figure per share.

net worth (companies): see net tangible asset backing; see also balance sheet.

net worth (individuals): the value of a person's assets, at current market value, less the value of that person's liabilities (including housing loans, credit card and store debts, personal loans, outstanding tax obligations and so on).

net worth tax: a tax levied on a taxpayer's assets less liabilities, usually above a threshold.

netizen: a person who uses the Internet frequently.

neutral gearing: the situation when an investment such as property or shares is purchased with the assistance of borrowed funds and where the rental or dividend income (after the deduction of expenses) is exactly equal to the interest commitment in the course of a financial year.

new: abbreviation for new shares.

new shares: shares arising out of a recent issue or placement which have a different dividend entitlement than the corresponding "old" shares.

NGF: abbreviation for National Guarantee Fund.

niccolite: nickel arsenide, an ore of nickel.

nickel: a primary metal whose principal qualities are its hardness, strength and resistance to corrosion. Used primarily for stainless steel and electroplating. Chemical symbol: Ni.

Nifty: it is an indicator of 50 top and most traded stocks on National Stock Exchange.

Nigerian scam: a much publicised fraud emanating from Nigeria and elsewhere. This scheme has been around on paper for years, but it is now being propagated to potential investors by e-mail on a large scale. While there are numerous variations to the theme the message often purports to come from a group of top officials of some government agency in Nigeria. They claim to have defrauded their own government of $US31 million or somesuch. They are seeking the use of the investor's bank account in Australia in order to launder the money. In return they offer a 20 per cent share of this large amount. Those who show interest are then asked to provide various sums in advance, to cover some necessary expenses, taxes and bribes. This happens more than once. Correspondents who by their own admission go in for defrauding their own government seem to lack proper business credentials. It is not clear why any investor who deals with such criminals would expect to be treated honourably by them.

Nikkei Index: Indicator of Japanese Stock Exchange.

NL: abbreviation for no liability.

NLA: abbreviation for net leasable area.

NLG: symbol for the Dutch guilder.

no confidence motion: a very serious motion which if carried proclaims that the persons to whom it refers are not fit to hold their positions.

no liability: see company.

no par value (NPV): shares without a nominal or face value.

"no shop" agreement: a contract under which the directors of a target company in a takeover agree not to solicit rival bids.

"no talk" agreement: a contract under which the directors of a target company in a takeover agree not to talk to or negotiate with potential or actual rival bidders.

nodules: the form in which ocean floor deposits of metals are found.

noes: those voting against a particular motion.

NOHC: abbreviation for non-operating holding company.

noise: random fluctuations in statistics.

NOK: symbol for the Norwegian krone.

nominal: see real.

nominal value: see par value.

nominee: a party who represents another. For example, shares may be registered in the name of a nominee company, either to disguise the identity of the beneficial owner or for ease of management.

non-active assets: for CGT purposes, passive investments, as distinct from assets that are used in the course of carrying on a business.

non-bank financial institutions (NBFIs): organisations such as merchant banks, finance companies, building societies, credit unions and life offices - and any other institutions involved in finance which do not hold banking licences.

non-conforming usage: the use of land in a manner not normally allowed by current regulations, but permitted by way of special concession in the case of persons in occupation before the rules were changed.

non-cumulative: see cumulative.

non-current assets: assets which in the ordinary course of business would not be consumed or turned into cash within 12 months. See also assets.

non-current liabilities: liabilities which in the ordinary course of business would not be consumed or turned into cash within 12 months. Examples include provision for deferred tax, other non-current provisions, long term financial debt. See also liabilities.

non-discretionary trust: a trust under which the deed spells out the specific beneficiaries and their precise entitlements.

non-diversifiable risk: see systemic risk.

non-forfeiture: the system under which unpaid premiums are automatically advanced on the security of the surrender value of a life policy in order to keep it in force.

non-recourse loan: a loan charged against a specific asset as the sole security for that loan, with no right for the lender in the event of a default to benefit from any other assets owned by the borrower.

non-renounceable rights issue: a new issue of shares, made pro rata to existing shareholders, the entitlements to which cannot be traded.

non-systemic risk: that risk which arises from the unique characteristics of a specific investment. This risk can be reduced by effective diversification. It is sometimes called diversifiable risk.

normal distribution (statistics): a distribution of scores around an expected value where variations are caused by random factors. Plotted, the scores form a symmetrical bell-shaped curve.

normal yield curve: see yield curve.

notes to the accounts: a series of notes that explain in detail parts of the balance sheet and profit and loss account.

NPAT: abbreviation for net profit after tax.

NPR: symbol for the Nepali rupee.

NPV: abbreviation for net present value.

NPV: abbreviation for no par value.

National Securities Clearance Corporation Ltd. (NSCCL): wholly owned subsidiary of NSE, it is responsible for carrying out clearing, settlement and transfer of funds and securities on the settlement date.

NSCCL: abbreviation for National Securities Clearance Corporation Ltd.

NSE: abbreviation for National Stock Exchange.

NTA: abbreviation for net tangible assets or net tangible asset backing per share.

nts: abbreviation for convertible notes.

nugget: a naturally occurring water-worn piece of precious metal.

NV: abbreviation for Naamloze Vennootschap.

nx: abbreviation for new, ex interest.

nx: stock exchange quotation symbol for new ex interest.

NYSE: abbreviation for the New York Stock Exchange.

NZD: symbol for the New Zealand dollar.

o: abbreviation for options. Figures after the letter indicate the calendar year of expiry.

obiter dictum: a saying by the way.

occupational superannuation plan: a superannuation plan covering employees in a particular occupation or the employees of a particular business or group.

occupier: a person in possession of land. The word usually refers to a tenant, but in some contexts can also mean an owner.

OCR: abbreviation for official cash rate.

octane: a liquid hydrocarbon of the paraffin series.

odd lot: see marketable parcel.

OECD: abbreviation for Organisation for Economic Co-operation and Development.

off the plan: see buying off the plan.

off the record: remarks made to a reporter for background information only and not attributable.

offer (stock exchange): a selling quote; an offer to sell.

offer documents: see takeover.

offeree: the subject of a takeover offer, the target company or one of its shareholders.

offeror: the company making a takeover bid, the bidder.

official interest rate: see cash rate.

official list: the list of securities that are traded on the stock exchange.

official short term money market: see short term money market.

offshore drilling: drilling for oil in the ocean.

oil field: the surface area overlying an oil reservoir or reservoirs. Commonly, the term includes not only the surface area but also the wells and production equipment.

oil permit: the right to explore for oil in an area.

oil sand: a sandstone that yields oil.

oil shale: shale containing kerogen, a solid, bituminous substance which yields oil when the shales undergo destructive distillation.

oil zone: a formation or horizon of a well from which oil may be produced. The oil zone is usually immediately under the gas zone and on top of the water zone if all three fluids are present and segregated.

old shares: see new shares.

oligopoly: the trading condition where there are only a small number of sellers of a particular commodity in a market.

OMR: symbol for the Omani rial.

on demand: see at sight.

on the record: remarks made to a reporter which can be quoted freely.

one name paper: certificates of deposit or promissory notes issued by companies to raise funds and not endorsed by anyone else. This paper is tradeable in the money market.

onerous lease: a lease which imposes more disadvantages than advantages on the lessor.

ONO: abbreviation for or nearest offer.

onshore exploration: exploration activity taking place on land.

OP: abbreviation for oil permit.

OPEC: abbreviation for Organisation of Petroleum Exporting Countries.

open cut mine: a mine worked at the earth's surface. Distinct from an underground mine.

open end unit trust: a unit trust under which the manager creates new units as and when investors apply for them and under which the manager redeems or repurchases units for investors wanting to quit their holdings for cash.

open hole: any wellbore in which casing has not been set.

open interest: the number of outstanding contracts in a particular class or series existing in the options market.

open market: an unregulated market for goods or services, with free competition between buyers and sellers matching supply and demand.

open market operations: the buying and selling of government securities by the Reserve Bank of India and other central banks around the world, in order to affect the money supply and thus the level of interest rates.

open order: an order for an unlimited number of shares which is good till cancelled.

opening purchase: a transaction in which an investor becomes the taker of an option.

opening sale: a transaction in which an investor becomes the writer of an option.

operating company: see holding company.

operating profit/loss: the after tax profit/loss made from normal trading activities.

operating revenue: the total amount receivable by a company in the ordinary course of its business for goods and services supplied by it during a financial year, excluding any inter-group transactions. Deducting all expenses including the net increase in the provisions from this figure gives the profit.

operator (industry): the person or company, either proprietor or lessee, actually managing a project.

operator (stock exchange): under the former trading floor system, the person on the trading floor who actually effected the buying and selling orders.

oppressive conduct: action by a board of directors to harm one group of shareholders (usually a minority) in order to benefit another (usually a majority). The courts can interfere in such situations.

opt: abbreviation for options.

option (property): the right but not the obligation to purchase land at a defined price by a specified date.

option (stock exchange): a security which gives its holder the right but not the obligation to acquire a share in a company at a specified price (called the *exercise price*) on a stipulated date (called the *exercise date*) or, sometimes, at any time up to a maximum date; an option which is not exercised by the latest possible exercise date lapses and becomes worthless. Options are usually transferable and can be themselves traded rather than used as a means to obtain the underlying security. See also call option, put option and exchange traded option.

order fee: a fixed charge on every order executed by some stockbrokers.

ordinary insurance: all classes of life insurance other than superannuation.

ordinary shares: see shares.

ore: a mixture of minerals, host rock and waste material the mining of which is expected to earn a profit.

ore blocking: the process of collecting and assaying samples on a sufficiently closely spaced grid to allow the reliable estimation of the ore grades and tonnage.

ore body: a fairly continuous mass of ore which may include low grade and waste as well as pay ore but is separate in form and character from the country rock.

organic growth: the increase in assets and profit from the existing activities of a business, as distinct from those obtainable through the raising of additional capital and acquiring further assets or engaging in takeovers or mergers.

Organisation for Economic Co-operation and Development (OECD): an international body consisting of the developed nations and having policies to encourage economic growth, high employment and financial stability among its members. The ultimate aim is to contribute to the development of non-members and members who are less advanced. The 30 OECD countries are: Australia, Austria, Belgium, Canada, Czech Republic, Denmark, Finland, France, Germany, Greece, Hungary, Iceland, the Republic of Ireland, Italy, Japan, Korea, Luxembourg, Mexico, the Netherlands, New Zealand,

Norway, Poland, Portugal, Slovak Republic, Spain, Sweden, Switzerland, Turkey, United Kingdom and United States.

Organisation of Petroleum Exporting Countries (OPEC): a cartel of members who attempt to control the price of oil through maintaining oil production at pre-set quota levels.

OSDP: abbreviation for overseas shareholders dividend plan.

OTC: abbreviation for over-the-counter.

other method: the way used for calculating capital gains tax when assets which have been held for less than 12 months are disposed of. In the absence of offsetting capital losses investors pay tax on the full nominal gain.

out of the money: in relation to options, the situation where the holder of an option is unable to can get an immediate benefit by exercising it. Thus a call option is *out of the money* if the market price of the underlying share is less than the exercise price of the option; a put option is *out of the money* if the market price of the underlying share exceeds the exercise price of the option.

outcrop: an exposure of rock or a mineral deposit that can be seen on surface.

outgoings: expenditure relating to a property, such as rates, land tax, insurance premiums, body corporate charges, repairs and the like, which may or may not be passed on to a lessee.

outperform: said of a share that increases in market value more than the market as a whole or that decreases in market value less than the market as a whole. Opposite of underperform.

outstanding shares: stocks currently held by investors, including restricted shares owned by the company's employees, as well as those held by the public.

over-the-counter market (OTC): a decentralised market in the United States for securities not listed on a stock exchange, using geographically dispersed dealers who are linked together by telephones and computer screens.

over-the-counter securities (OTC): derivatives which are individually tailored to the specific requirements of investors. While unlisted they can usually be sold back to the issuer.

overbought: a commodity for which the price has been pushed up to unrealistically high levels.

overburden: the waste overlying a mineral deposit.

overburden to ore ratio: the proportion of overburden that has to be removed, prior to mining, relative to the amount of mineable ore.

overdraft: the facility to borrow funds from a bank through writing cheques on a cheque account for more than has been deposited into it.

overhead: a fixed indirect cost that cannot be attributed to any particular profit centre.

overholding: the state of affairs when a lessee remains in occupation of a property after the formal expiry date of a lease without executing a new lease.

overriding royalty: see royalty.

oversold: opposite of overbought.

oversubscribed: the situation where applications for a new issue exceed the amount available. In fixed interest issues it is common for a specific level of oversubscriptions to be accepted. In equity issues oversubscriptions are not usually accepted and allotments are made at the discretion of the company.

owners corporation (in relation to strata title complexes): a special sort of company, a non-profit organisation, jointly owned and controlled by and run for the benefit of the property owners concerned. However, it is not subject to the normal companies legislation. It also owns the common property shown on a plan of subdivision. The owners have a number of votes each, as set out in the plan of subdivision. Also known as body corporate.

oxidation: a chemical reaction between any substance and oxygen. Most refining and smelting activities are directed at reversing this process to yield the pure metal.

oxide: the compound that arises from the oxidation (adding of oxygen) of an element, usually a metal.

pa: stock exchange quotation symbol for protection available.

paddock: ore stacked on the surface, which is said to be "in the paddock" or "at grass".

paid-up policy: a life policy on which no further premiums are payable.

Palaeozoic Era: an era 230 to 570 million years ago that incorporates the Permian, Carboniferous, Devonian, Silurian, Ordovician and Cambrian Periods.

panning: the washing of gravel or soil to separate valuable metals from the waste.

paper: securities - for example, government paper, commercial paper.

paper profit: a surplus or gain over the purchase price that has not yet been realised.

par value: the nominal or face value that applies to fixed interest securities. Prices in excess of a par value are said to be at a premium; prices below a par value are said to be at a discount.

paraffin: a saturated hydrocarbon.

parent company: a company that has subsidiaries. In accounting for its operations it will present both a consolidated (group) situation and that of the parent company, excluding the results of subsidiaries, apart from dividends actually received. The consolidated accounts are more significant and exclude inter-company transactions.

parent entity: a holding company.

Pareto principle: the "80-20 rule", which states that for many phenomena 80 per cent of the consequences stem from 20 per cent of the causes - for example, that 80 per cent of wealth is owned by 20 per cent of the population, or that 80 per cent of turnover comes from 20 per cent of customers.

pari passu: equally.

part: abbreviation for participating.

participating policy: a policy with the right to share in a life insurance company's surplus.

participating preference shares: see shares.

partly-paid share: a contributing share, a share on which only part of the capital (and/or, formerly, the share premium) has been paid.

partnership: the relationship between two or more persons carrying on business in common with a view to profit (other than as shareholders in a company). Every partner shares in the risks and rewards of the enterprise. Each is personally liable (jointly with the other partners) for the entire debts of the partnership. A partnership (also known as a "firm") is not an incorporated body and is not a legal entity. However, it is an entity for GST purposes.

pass (mining): see chute.

pass a dividend: to decide not to declare a dividend at the usual time.

passed (of motions): adopted by a meeting following the receipt of the required majority of the votes.

passed in: relating to property offered for sale at an auction but not sold because the highest bid did not reach the reserve price set by the vendor.

passing rent: the actual current rental income of a property, as distinct from the income which would be achieved if the property were fully let at current market rents.

passing rent: the current actual rent of a property under a lease, as distinct from the current market rent.

passing yield (property): the return from an investment in property. The passing yield is obtained by dividing the passing rent per annum by the price and multiplying by 100, without any adjustment for future growth.

PAT: abbreviation for profit after tax.

patent: the grant of exclusive rights to a product which has been invented.

pay as you earn (PAYE): the system used up to 30 June 2000, also known as "group tax", under which tax was paid by salary and wage earners and annuitants in the form of compulsory deductions from the periodical sums due to them by employers and certain other payers during the course of a financial year, these being then applied towards their ultimate income tax liability for that year.

pay as you go instalment (PAYG): the system under which tax is paid by individuals on business and professional incomes and on investment income such as interest, dividends and rent (net of expenses). The tax is collected by way of instalments during the course of a financial year and is applied towards the taxpayer's ultimate income tax liability for that year.

pay limit: a grade of ore below which mining is uneconomic.

pay sand: the producing formation, often one that is not even sandstone. Also called pay zone and producing zone.

payback period: the length of time required for an investment to recover the initial cash outlay.

payday lending: small unsecured personal loans that low income consumers use to finance emergency needs. Such loans involve high interest rates and charges. Typically, the borrower is required to write out a post-dated cheque in favour of the payday lender covering the capital and interest, on the basis that the cheque will not be cashed until the consumer's next payday.

payday loans: small loans made quickly and with little paperwork but at relatively high interest rates, to low income borrowers in order to tide them over till their next payday.

PAYE: see pay as you earn.

PAYG: see pay as you go.

payments, allowing for compound interest.

payout ratio: the percentage of earnings distributed as dividends.

payroll tax: a tax levied on employers, based on their outlays for salaries and wages and certain other employment costs.

pcp: abbreviationfor previous comparable period.

PDF: abbreviation for pooled development fund.

PDS: abbreviation for product disclosure statement.

PE: abbreviation for price earnings ratio.

pecuniary interest: an interest that someone has in a matter by virtue of a reasonable likelihood or expectation of an appreciable financial gain or financial loss. See also conflict of interest.

pecuniary legacy: money left to a person by another person's will.

pedente lite: pending the suit.

peg: to mark out a claim or lease.

PEG ratio: the price earnings ratio divided by the company's growth rate.

pegmatite: igneous rock of very coarse grain containing feldspar and quartz with usually some mica and often some rare minerals.

PEL: abbreviation for petroleum exploration licence.

pellet: a marble-sized ball of iron ore bonded by clay material and fused for hardness.

penalty: a charge added to the cost of toll smelting for impurities in the ore.

pennant: in charting, a formation. The difference between a flag and a pennant is that a pennant is bound by converging boundary lines rather than by parallel lines.

penny dreadful: a low priced speculative share, usually in a company engaged in mining or oil exploration.

pentlandite: nickel iron sulphide, an ore of nickel.

PER: abbreviation for price earnings ratio.

per capita: individually; in equal shares per person.

per diem: per day.

per stirpes: by stock - a method of dividing the assets of an estate such that, if a member of the group among whom the assets are being divided happens to be dead at the time of that division, the children of that deceased member of the group collectively will receive the share which their parent would have received had that parent remained alive.

percentage point: the unit expressing the difference between two percentages - for example, if the rate of inflation falls from 5 per cent to 4 per cent, then the reduction is one percentage point (and not 1 per cent). It actually represents a 20 per cent reduction, but this fact is probably not very helpful.

percentile rank: a level, in a ranked series of scores, where each level represents a one-hundredth part of the observations.

percussion drilling: a drilling process which involves hammering the drill bit down the hole, while the cuttings are forced upwards to the surface.

perforate: to pierce the casing wall and cement of an oil/gas well to provide holes through which formation fluids may enter, or to provide holes in the casing so that materials may be introduced into the annulus between the casing and the wall of the borehole. Perforating is accomplished by lowering into the well a perforating gun, or perforator, that fires electrically detonated bullets or shaped charges from the surface.

performance hurdle: a yardstick in an employment contract for executives - for example, one which entitles them to exercise options on favourable terms. Hurdles can have regard to increases in items such as total profit; or earnings per share; or market value per share (possibly adjusted for dividends); or return on equity. The yardstick can be absolute or relative to some share index or accumulation index or the performance of other companies in the same industry.

permanent difference: a difference between the pre-tax profit and the taxable income caused by an item which is treated differently in a company's accounts from the way in which it is treated under the taxation legislation and which will never enter the tax calculation - for example, the amortisation of goodwill. Permanent differences, as opposed to timing differences, are not reversible.

permeability: a measure of the ease with which fluids can flow through a porous rock.

Permian Period: a period 230 to 280 million years ago.

perpetual floating rate notes: income securities offering a variable interest rate, usually defined as the 90 day bank bill rate each quarter plus a specified margin, and often with a guaranteed minimum rate for a specified initial period - for example, one year. These notes have no fixed maturity date but the issuing company usually reserves the right to redeem them at par plus accrued interest at a time of its choosing as from some specified date - for example, after five years from the date of issue. Until redeemed they can be traded on the stock exchange. Their market value will fluctuate. The quarterly interest amounts are usually non-cumulative. The notes are unsecured, but they rank ahead of the company's ordinary and preference shares.

Perseroan Terbuka (PT): a limited liability company (Indonesian).

persona non grata: a non-acceptable person.

personal accident and sickness: an insurance contract which provides a benefit in the event of death, total or permanent disability or loss of eye(s) or limb(s) caused by accident, or an income benefit if the life insured is temporarily disabled by sickness or accident.

personal property: goods and chattels; movable property as distinct from land (but leasehold interests in land are also regarded as personal property).

personal representative: an executor or administrator of a deceased estate

personal services income (PSI): the income of a contractor that is mainly a reward for the contractor's personal effort or skill. Such income is taxed in the hands of the contractor even if it is nominally earnt through a company, through a trust or through a partnership. The intention of the relevant legislation is to tax contractors on a similar basis to employees doing comparable work.

personal statement: a form issued by life insurance companies in which the life to be insured gives medical history details. With the proposal, this statement is the basis of the contract.

petroleum: oil or gas obtained from the rocks of the earth.

petroleum exploration licence: the right to explore for petroleum over an area.

petrophysics: a branch of geophysics that deals with the nature and quantification of the physical characteristics of rocks.

pf: abbreviation for preference shares.

PGK: symbol for the Papua New Guinea kina.

phosphate rock: a sedimentary rock containing calcium phosphate. Primarily used as a fertiliser.

PHP: symbol for the Philippines peso.

physical market: a market on which real securities or commodities are traded, as distinct from a market in futures contracts.

pig iron: crude cast iron from a blast furnace.

pillar: a column of rock remaining after removal of the surrounding rock.

pinch: the narrowing of a vein or a deposit.

pipe: cylindrical rock body, usually vertical.

pit: the excavation in open cut mining.

pitch: see dip.

pitchblende: uranium oxide, an ore of uranium.

PJC: abbreviation for Parliamentary Joint Committee.

PJCCFS: abbreviation for Parliamentary Joint Committee on Corporations and Financial Services.

PJSCCS: abbreviation for Parliamentary Joint Statutory Committee on Corporations and Securities (now Parliamentary Joint Committee on Corporations and Financial Services).

PKR: symbol for the Pakistani rupee.

placement: the allotment of shares for cash to outsiders, as distinct from through a pro rata rights issue to existing shareholders.

plat: the floor of a level near its intersection with a shaft.

platinum: a precious metal. Chemical symbol: Pt.

play: the testing of a hunch or concept of geological structure.

plc: abbreviation for public limited company, the United Kingdom equivalent of Ltd.

plot ratio: the total floor areas of a building divided by the area of the land. The plot ratio will normally exceed 1 for a multi-storey building.

plough-back: the balance in the profit and loss account, profits which have not been distributed to shareholders but which are being retained for use in the operations of a business. Also known as accumulated profits, undistributed profits, retained earnings or unappropriated profits. They form part of the shareholders' funds.

plugged: the practice of cementing in holes that are left when a petroleum exploration hole is abandoned, required by law.

plugged and abandoned: in relation to a petroleum exploration hole that has been abandoned.

plunger: a speculator; one who takes a plunge.

plunging anticline: an anticline which has the long axis inclined.

pocket: a small body of ore or an enlargement of a lode or vein, or an irregular cavity containing ore.

point: the unit of measurement in a stock exchange index.

point of order: the official bringing to the attention of the chairman of a meeting of some alleged irregularity in the proceedings.

points: a means of expressing interest rates. A point equals 0.01 per cent per annum. Thus a move from 13.29 per cent to 13.41 per cent can be described as a 12-point increase.

poison pill: a restrictive clause inserted into a company's constitution or alternatively some corporate move primarily made in an endeavour to deter unwanted takeover bids. Such provisions usually help to keep the market price of the company's shares down, by reducing buying pressure both from potential bidders and from investors acquiring shares in the expectation of some bid. Devices include large scale expansion moves and the issue to existing shareholders, ahead of an actual bid, of securities with special privileges which come into play when a hostile bid is made - all of which are actions designed to make the total cost of acquisition higher.

policy: the legal document issued by the insurer to the policyholder which outlines the conditions of the insurance contract.

policyholder: the person who owns an insurance policy, the insured. In life insurance, the policyholder is often the same person as the life insured, but not necessarily so.

poll: the voting on a question before the chair in writing, in a way which allows accurate figures to be ascertained, but without the names of those voting "aye" or "no" becoming available.

Ponzi scheme: a fraudulent investment scheme that promises unrealistically high returns. It involves the early entrants into the scheme being indeed paid the promised returns, but not from real profits. Instead the returns are paid out of the funds being subscribed by later entrants into the scheme. The early entrants, highly satisfied with their profits, enthusiastically recommend the scheme to other people, so that growth continues for some time. However, inevitably sooner or later the scheme runs out of new investors and at that stage the whole house of cards collapses. Greedy investors invariably overlook the maxim: "If it looks too good to be true then it probably is."

pool: an arrangement between parties who are normally competitors to fix the price of a commodity and/or to control its production and marketing.

pooled development fund (PDF): an investment company specialising in providing equity capital to small and medium enterprises and registered as a pooled development fund under the relevant legislation. This status confers certain income tax benefits and capital gains tax exemptions on both the company and its shareholders.

pooled investment vehicle: a managed investment - for example, a unit trust.

population growth rate: the increase in the population per 1000 population in a given year due to natural increase and net migration.

porosity: the amount of pore space in the sand or other reservoir rock which determines the amount of oil, gas or water the rock can hold.

porphyry deposit: a deposit in which the minerals occur in crystalline form or in veinlets throughout a great volume of rock, as distinct from massive.

portability: the facility for transferring superannuation entitlements on a change of job from the superannuation fund of the previous employer to the fund of the new employer, usually with a credit for past service. See also preservation.

portal: the entrance to an adit.

portfolio: a collection of investments owned by an investor.

portfolio theory: a theory for risk-averse investors acting rationally, enabling them to construct their portfolios to maximise their expected returns for a given level of market risk.

positive gearing: the situation when an investment such as property or shares is purchased with the assistance of borrowed funds and where the rental or dividend income (after the deduction of expenses) is more than the interest commitment in the course of a financial year.

possession: the actual holding or occupying of land.

post meeting report: a report issued all too rarely by listed companies. Ideally it covers much more than just the chairman's formal address, although that would be one item. Each question asked by any shareholder can be included, together with the answer given. Elaborations on these impromptu replies can also be put on the public record in this way.

poverty trap: the situation where the marginal rate of abatement (tax plus loss of social security benefits) exceeds 100 cents in the dollar, thus leaving a person actually worse off on a net basis when gross income rises.

power of attorney: a legal document which authorises one person (known as the "donee" of the power or as the "attorney" under it) to make decisions and to execute documents on behalf of another person, the "donor" of the power.

PPF: abbreviation for Public Provident Fund.

PPF: abbreviation for purchased payment facility (for example, stored value cards, travellers' cheques).

PPP: abbreviation for public private partnership.

preamble: words at the beginning of a motion or a contact or a trust deed which give some background to it or set it in context.

Precambrian Period: that period from 600 million years ago to the beginning of the earth.

precipitation: a process of separating minerals from a solution.

predatory lending: consumer loans granted to unsophisticated low income borrowers at outrageous interest rates and fees, especially loans by lenders in the non-conforming market, loans which ignore the statutory Uniform Consumer Credit Code and which are usually targeted at poor persons who cannot afford them. Some predatory loans are also made for housing purposes; these can involve punitive interest rates in the event of any default and pose the very real prospect that the house concerned will be sold from under the borrower.

predatory pricing: the use by a company of its market power to reduce prices for a time, selling below cost in a bid to drive out or damage a competitor, with a view to raising prices again later on when the competitor has disappeared.

pref: abbreviation for preference shares.

preference shares: shares, where a company has them, which provide a fixed rate of return and which have priority over the ordinary shares in regard to dividend payments and to the company's assets in the event of a winding up. They rank after all the company's liabilities. They can take various forms - for example, with or without cumulative dividend entitlements; with or without participating or partial participating rights. They can be redeemable or irredeemable; convertible or non-convertible; voting or non-voting.

preliminary expenses: expenses incurred in establishing a business.

preliminary report: a report to the stock exchange setting out a company's provisional estimate of the results for the previous financial year. It usually includes the announcement of the final dividend.

premium (insurance): the amount payable by the policyholder to an insurance company under an insurance policy as consideration for the benefits insured.

premium (options): the price of an options contract.

premium (securities): the excess of a price over the nominal or face or par value of a security. The opposite of discount.

premium on consolidation: in group accounts, the excess of the value of the subsidiary companies' net assets over their cost to the parent. The opposite of goodwill on consolidation.

prescribed private fund: a form of charitable trust enjoying tax deductibility for donations made to it. The enabling legislation provides businesses, families and individuals with great flexibility to start their own trust funds for philanthropic purposes.

present value: the discounted value of a series of future.

preservation: an arrangement for employees on changing jobs enabling them to keep intact until retirement the superannuation benefits relating to service with their former employer. Such arrangements can involve the superannuation funds of either the old or the new employer, or special funds established for this purpose by life offices or other third parties. See also portability.

previous question: the procedural motion: "That the question be not now put."

prf: abbreviation for preference shares.

price cash flow ratio: a figure obtained by dividing a company's cash flow for the last year (expressed in cents per ordinary share) into the current market price of its share (also expressed in cents). It is used by security analysts as it gives a picture complementing that given by the conventional price earnings ratio.

price earnings ratio: a figure obtained by dividing the earnings per share into the current market price of the share; 100 divided by the earnings yield. The PE ratio shows the number of times the market price covers earnings and is a valuable tool for comparing profit performance relative to price. It should, however, be noted that dividing a historical earnings figure into a current market price can be misleading. The PE ratio can be an indicator of the market's anticipation of future earnings and the quality of the company's management and performance. See also earnings yield.

price leadership: a market situation where one supplier alters a price and the remainder of the industry follows suit.

price sensitive information: information that may have an effect on a listed company's share price. The continuous disclosure rules require all such information to be disclosed to the stock exchange.

price/NTA: a ratio reflecting the market price of a share relative to its asset backing.

prima facie: on the face of it; on a first view.

primary: original, when applied to the deposition of ore minerals, that is, not enriched or altered by processes of weathering, etc.

primary industry: agricultural and pastoral activities. Technically the term also includes mining. Compare secondary, tertiary industries.

primary market: the market for new issues, as distinct from the stock exchange. The term applies particularly to bonds and treasury notes sold by the Central Bank of country.

primary trend: see trend.

prime cost: see depreciation.

principal trading: buying or selling by a stockbroker for the stockbroker's own account, as distinct from trading as an agent for clients.

prior period adjustment: an accounting adjustment made to the current accounts but relating to an earlier period.

priority: see ranking.

priority issue: see spin-off.

private company: a proprietary limited company; a non-public company. Such companies are not allowed to offer shares to the general public.

private equity: an investment of risk capital, usually by a large group and with the substantial use of borrowed funds, in assets in which the equity after acquisition is not tradeable on a stock exchange. The investors generally restructure the business thus acquired and after a few years receive their return through initial public offerings and/or trade sales and/or management buyouts of various parts of the business. On disposal the parts are often significantly more valuable than the previous whole. The profit realised rewards the investors for the risks undertaken, the lack of liquidity during the holding period, the management skills provided and the use of leverage.

private placement: a share issue made to selected investors in large parcels at negotiated prices. This is seen by some companies to be a more efficient way of raising funds rather than going to the public or to all shareholders, but it can unfairly water the equity of the existing ordinary shareholders.

private treaty sale: the sale of property by negotiation between the parties, as distinct from at auction.

privatisation: the sale of a government-owned enterprise to the private sector. The opposite of nationalisation. Contrast corporisation. The word is sometimes also used in a different sense, to cover the situation when the shares held by the public in a listed company are purchased by some person or group, effectively turning the enterprise into a private company.

pro forma: for the sake of form.

pro rata: in direct proportion.

probability: the chance of an event occurring.

probate: authority granted by a court to a person to wind up the estate of a deceased person who left a valid will.

probate duty: a tax levied on the net assets of a deceased estate.

procedural motion: a motion dealing with the conduct of the meeting itself (as distinct from a substantive motion).

producer's price: a price set by a producer. See also spot price.

product disclosure statement (PDS): a document similar in function to a prospectus for a new share issue but covering managed investments, superannuation and insurance products, derivatives, and so on. It sets out features of the product, fees including commission, risks, complaints mechanisms, cooling off period, and so on.

product ruling: a public ruling issued by the Income Tax Department in order to provide certainty to potential investors by confirming that the promised tax benefits of an investment product are really available. A product ruling deals only with the tax consequences of a particular product and does not act as an endorsement of its investment merits.

products, financial: securities, derivatives, general insurance, life insurance, superannuation, deposit accounts and means of payment facilities. Typically such products are sold through financial intermediaries including securities advisers and dealers, insurance agents and brokers, and futures brokers.

profit: revenue less costs. There are a number of different measures of profit. Trading, gross or operating profit is the difference between the selling price and the cost of goods sold. Selling and administrative expenses are deducted from trading profit to give EBIT (earnings before interest and tax). EBIT less interest gives the pre-tax profit, from which the taxation expense is deducted to give the net profit. The word "loss" is used for results which are negative.

profit and loss account: a table, also called a *statement of financial performance*, summarising the revenues, expenses, gains and losses of a company or other enterprise during a specific reporting period (usually the financial year) ending on the balance date. It also shows the net profit or earnings and the dividends declared (if any). The difference, which represents the *retained earnings* or *plough-back*, is a part of the total shareholders' funds. For listed companies profit and loss statements are usually published in the annual report about three months after the balance date. They complement the balance sheets.

profit margin: a company's earnings before interest and tax as a percentage of its turnover.

profit taking: the act of realising paper profits.

profitability: a measure of the relative return on an investment. There are a variety of ratios which attempt to measure profitability. The more common ones are:

- *EBIT/assets:* measures operational efficiency, before the effects of financing.
- *EBIT/sales:* measures profit per sales dollar before the effects of financing.
- *earnings on shareholders' funds:* measures profitability from the point of view of the shareholder. Calculates the return on the funds subscribed by shareholders together with the undistributed profits.
- *net profit/sales:* measures the net profit per sales dollar and includes the effects of interest and taxation.

programme trading: the placing of orders to buy or sell shares by computers using programmes which do not call for human intervention once installed. Orders are triggered automatically when specified stocks reach certain threshold prices, allowing large volumes of trading to take place at enormous speed. A by-product of this is that a severe market fall can occur very rapidly.

progressive tax: a tax levied at rates increasing with increases in the sum subject to the tax, as in the case of income tax. Contrast regressive tax.

project financing: see limited recourse financing.

promissory note: a written promise, legally enforceable, to pay on demand, or on a fixed date, a specified sum. It is a method of raising funds where no party incurs a contingent liability on the note.

propane: a gaseous hydrocarbon of the paraffin series.

property: either anything that is owned - see personal property, real property - or just real property (land and the buildings on it). See also intellectual property.

property deed: title to land recorded by an entry in a government register kept at the Land Registrar's Office and the issue of a certificate.

property tax: the tax levied by local corporations, municipal bodies on a property. This tax has to be paid by the legal owner of the property.

proposal: the formal offer to take out an insurance policy and the basis of the contract.

proposer: the person who proposes a motion to a meeting, the mover.

proprietary company: see company.

proprietary ratio: a company's shareholders' funds divided by its total assets, with the result usually expressed as a percentage. It is a measure of the how safe the company is - the greater the proportion of the total value of the company represented by the shareholders' equity the less the likelihood of creditors ever being able to institute receivership or liquidation proceedings.

proprietary trading: trading by a bank or other institution on its own behalf, as distinct from on behalf of its customers.

prospect: a mining property the value of which has not been proved by exploration.

prospectus: a legal document prepared by a company when raising money from the general public in connection with an issue of securities. The law requires that prospectuses must set out all information that investors and their professional advisers would reasonably require in order to make an informed assessment of the company's assets and liabilities, profits and losses and prospects. A modern prospectus must also set out in considerable detail the precise terms of the issue - its size, the issue price, the opening and closing dates, the asset backing, the proposed annual return to the investors, the dividend policy, the expected franking status of any dividends, the rights attaching to the securities being offered, the maturity dates (if applicable), and so on. The prospectus should also set out the existing capital structure and the background of the company and its directors, together with details of any proposed or existing dividend reinvestment, shareholder discount and employee share plans or the like.

protector: in the case of some trusts, a person given a power of veto over certain types of transaction, a power to remove or appoint trustees, a right to be consulted in relation to certain investments, a power to act as an arbitrator in the event of certain disputes and/or a power to nominate a successor as protector.

Proterozoic Period: the younger of the two geological periods in the Precambrian Era.

provision (accounting): an amount set aside in an organisation's accounts as a charge against profit in order to meet the estimated cost in present value terms of some future obligation - for example, a provision in respect of long service leave for employees. Unlike liabilities, such provisions do not refer to a debtor/creditor relationship; however, they are included on the liabilities side of a balance sheet. Provisions are also made to reflect an anticipated reduction in the value of some asset - for example, a provision for doubtful debts. Such provisions could be included as negative items on the assets side of a balance sheet. Provisions should be distinguished from *reserves,* which are part of the equity of an organisation.

provision (legal): a stipulation in an Act of parliament or regulation, or in a legal document such as a contract, a trust deed or a will.

provision for deferred tax: the estimated amount of future income tax likely to arise from the reversal of timing differences. See also tax effect accounting.

provisional tax: the system used for collecting tax on income. It is not an additional impost, but rather a *prepayment* of ordinary income tax.

provisions: amounts charged against profit and set aside in a company's books in anticipation of (or as an approximation for) expenses or liabilities - for example, in respect of obligations such as future taxation, depreciation, doubtful debts, long service and holiday leave, and so on. Contrast liabilities, reserves.

proxy: a person (the "donee") deputised to act for another (the "donor"), especially in regard to attending and voting at meetings; or the paper setting out such an appointment.

proxy statement: detailed information required to be sent to shareholders with the notice of an annual general meeting and a solicitation of proxies.

PSI: abbreviation for personal services income.

PSI: abbreviation for pounds per square inch.

PT: abbreviation for Perseroan Terbuka.

PTE: symbol for the Portuguese escudo.

Pty. Ltd.: abbreviation for proprietary limited company. See company.

pu: abbreviation for protection not available.

pu: stock exchange quotation symbol for protection unavailable.

public company: see company.

Public Limited Company (plc): a limited liability company (UK).

public private partnership (PPP): an arrangement under which an infrastructure project benefiting the community is funded and operated by a partnership involving a government and one or more private sector companies, often under a long term contract at the expiry of which the entire assets vest in the government free of debt. The theory is that a private sector organisation can manage such a project more efficiently than a government agency. Usually the intention is also for a smaller call on taxpayer funds and for the bulk of the business risks to be borne by private sector investors.

public relations: a communications process which strives to foster an audience's understanding about and acceptance of an organisation or an issue.

pullback: in charting, a return in price to the previous boundary line after a breakout.

pump and dump: a stock market scam, designed to catch greedy investors who are foolish enough to think that unsolicited e-mails from complete strangers in another country contain genuine stock tips. The idea is that the recipients will buy a stock based on messages which pump its virtues. The price will then surge, at which stage the promoters of the ruse dump their own holdings in the company concerned. After that the price collapses. The warning signs are clear enough - it should be obvious that if the originators of the e-mails concerned really had special insights then they would have been much better off exploiting these themselves in total secrecy rather than offering them free of charge to all and sundry.

punt: a gamble or speculation.

punter: a gambler or speculator.

pure endowment: a policy under which the sum insured, plus any bonuses, is payable only if the life insured lives for specified period. If not, some or all of the premiums are returned, generally with interest.

put option: a contract which entitles (but does not require) its holder to sell a fixed number of shares (usually 1000) in an underlying company at a stated price on or before a specified expiry date. See also option.

putting a question to a vote: the action of the chairman of a meeting when asking those eligible to vote on a particular motion to do so.

pyramiding: the practice of making further purchases of a stock in a rising market. It also refers to the practice of an entrepreneur with a limited but controlling stake in a company using the resources of that company to acquire a controlling stake in another company, and so on - with the result that the total assets ultimately controlled by the entrepreneur vastly exceed the original stake.

pyrite: iron sulphide. Sometimes called fool's gold.

qango: abbreviation for quasi-autonomous non-governmental organisation.

QAR: symbol for the Qatari riyal.

QoQ: abbreviation for quarter on quarter.

qua: in the capacity of.

quadruple witching day: the quarterly expiration of stock index futures, index options, options on individual stocks and single stock futures contracts, all on the same day in the United States. In practice many traders in derivatives close out their positions ahead of this day.

qualified accounts: financial statements that have been noted by the auditors to vary from normal accounting practice.

quarry: an opencut mine for extracting building materials.

quarter on quarter: a company's results for one quarter compared with the results for the same period of the previous year.

quarterly: a statement from companies setting out details of activities over the past three months.

quartile: every twenty-five per cent of a ranked series of scores.

quartz: silicon dioxide, a very common mineral.

quasi: as if.

Quaternary Period: a geological period dating from the present to about 1.8 million years ago.

query: a formal inquiry by the stock exchange of a listed company as to the reasons for an unusual movement in the price of a company's shares; this is done in order to maintain a fully informed market. Where the matter has significant consequences the company's shares may be suspended until a satisfactory reply is received.

query tag: a mark placed on the trading screen to indicate that the stock exchange is seeking further information from a company.

quick asset: cash and any asset which is readily convertible to cash.

quick assets ratio: a measure of liquidity. Basically, it compares the sum of a company's cash and debtors and those securities which are readily convertible into cash with its current liabilities. This ratio differs from the working capital ratio in that it disregards stock (inventories). If the ratio is too high, then this indicates idle funds which could be better employed; if it is too low, then this gives a warning sign as to a potentially dangerous situation. Two alternative approaches are in use:

- ratio = (CA-S)/CL
- ratio = (CA-S)/(CL-OD)

where

CA = current assets
CL = current liabilities
S = stock
OD = bank overdraft

Also known as the acid test, the liquid ratio, the liquid assets ratio, the quick test, the quick ratio.

quick ratio: see quick assets ratio.

quick test: see quick assets ratio.

quid pro quo: something for something.

quorate: constituting a quorum (a quorate meeting is one at which a quorum is present).

quorum: the minimum number of voting members required to be present at a meeting in order to constitute a valid meeting.

quote: the price which buyers or sellers have indicated as the price at which they are prepared to do business.

quote sheets: the daily official record of trading on the stock exchange.

quoted securities: shares, options, convertible notes, etc., of companies, which have been accepted for trading on the stock exchange. A company may have all, or part, of its securities listed.

radioactivity: the property of emitting alpha, beta and gamma rays.

raid: active share market purchases of one company's shares by another with the intention of seizing control. Also known as a market raid.

raider: a company that raids another company, usually with the intention of rationalising its business and/or stripping its assets.

raise: a vertical or inclined underground working that has been excavated from the bottom upward.

rally: strong price rises, generally across the board.

ramping the market: actions designed to artificially raise the market price of listed securities and to give the impression of voluminous trading, in order to make a quick profit.

random sample: a sample selected by chance.

random walk hypothesis: an hypothesis which describes share price movements as being independent of previous changes. Each movement is explained by new information as it comes to the market. It is a weak form of the efficient market theory.

range: the interval between the highest and the lowest observation in a set of scores.

ranking: the order and extent to which different classes of securities participate in an event. New shares may have an initial difference in dividend entitlement. This is known as dividend ranking. The word is also used to describe priority in the event of liquidation, for example, first ranking debentures rank before second ranking debentures, i.e., they are entitled to repayment of capital before another class of liability.

rare earths: oxides of a series of rare metals.

ratchet clause: a clause in a lease which provides for a periodical adjustment to the rent but with a proviso that the rent in any period will never be less than the rent in the preceding period.

rates: taxes on property imposed at a local government level by municipal councils and water and sewerage authorities (under various names); some rates are imposed on the site value of each property and others on the improved value or the net annual value.

ratings agencies: bodies such as Moody's Investors Service and Standard & Poor's which provide independent assessments of the credit worthiness of governments, companies, debenture issues, managed funds and so on. Ratings take into account aspects such as the size of the assets in relation to the size of the liabilities, cash flow projections, the cover for interest payments, the quality of the assets, the width of the investment powers, expansion plans and so on. The top rating is AAA.

ratio analysis: the analysis of financial statements as a means of determining the intrinsic value of a company. The analysis usually involves the comparison of liquidity, gearing and profitability ratios over time and between companies. It is a basic tool of fundamental analysts.

rationalisation: the business process of reorganising a company or industry in order to make it more efficient.

RBI: abbreviation for Reserve Bank of India.

RE: abbreviation for responsible entity.

re: stock exchange quotation symbol for reconstructed.

real: with an adjustment to take out the effect of inflation, in contrast to "nominal" - for example, the real rate of interest in a transaction is the nominal rate of interest net of an allowance for inflation; similarly for other concepts, such as the real growth rate, the real rate of return, real incomes, and so on.

real estate: property, including land, houses and commercial buildings.

real property: land and buildings, as distinct from movable items.

realisable: the amount of cash that can be obtained by liquidating an asset.

rear-end fees: fees charged at exit when disposing of a managed investment, usually as a percentage of the assets being disposed of.

reasonable benefit limit (RBL): a figure representing the maximum superannuation benefit allowable before a penal rate of taxation applies.

rebate: an amount which is subtracted from the income tax which would otherwise be payable by a taxpayer; however, except in the case of franking rebates, rebates cannot lead to a negative amount of tax and unused rebates cannot be carried forward. The official term for this currently is tax offset.

receivables: trade debtors, other debtors and money similarly owed to a company.

receiver: a person appointed to collect all incoming funds.

receiver and manager: a receiver who has also been appointed to manage the business affairs of a company.

recession: an economic condition in which the production of goods and services is slowing, unemployment is rising and interest rates are falling, perhaps preceding a depression unless the economy is stimulated. Some economists define a recession as two consecutive quarters of negative growth.

recipient created tax invoice (GST): a tax invoice issued by the person making a payment.

recommittal: any procedure designed to allow further debate on a motion so that an informed decision can be made as to whether or not it should be allowed to stand either in its original form or with some amendment.

reconnaissance: a preliminary examination survey of the ground.

reconstruction: a change to the existing capital structure of a company - for example, a share split or consolidation. The term is also used to describe a change in ownership or corporate direction.

record date: the date as at which the share register is closed for determining entitlements to a dividend, a vote, a share issue or some other reconstruction. The "ex dividend", etc., date is usually five working days prior to the books closing date. Shares purchased after that time do not participate in the dividend or issue.

recovery: the proportion of metal that is obtained from treating ore compared with the amount of contained metal, usually expressed as a percentage.

rectangle: a charting formation where the price moves between two parallel horizontal boundaries.

red: abbreviation for redeemable.

red: see in the red.

redeem: to repay principal.

redeemable preference shares: see shares.

redemption date: the maturity date; the date on which a fixed interest security is due to be repaid by its issuer.

redemption yield: the actual return obtainable from a redeemable fixed interest investment allowing for both the remaining interest payments and the difference between the purchase price (which may or may not be at par) and the redemption or maturity value. It is the internal rate of return on the cash flow from the investment. In contrast, the flat yield - in other words, the coupon divided by the market price - does not give a useful indication of the worth of a fixed interest security.

rediscount: the further discounting of commercial paper which has previously been discounted and which has reached its maturity date.

reduction of capital: a capital reconstruction which formerly required court approval that involved reducing the par value and/or the number of issued shares. It was made either to write off lost capital or as a means of paying some excess capital to the shareholders.

reef: similar to a lode.

reference motion: a procedural motion to send a matter to a committee with appropriate instructions.

refinancing: the extension or replacement of existing loans by loans on different terms.

refractory ore: ore that resists normal chemical processing and must be roasted to effect recovery of valuable minerals.

register: see share register. Companies also maintain a register of directors, managers and secretaries.

registered office: the legal residence of a company.

registrar: the organisation that maintains a company's share register.

regression analysis: see least squares regression.

regressive tax: a tax levied at a flat rate, irrespective of the means of the taxpayer, as in the case of the goods and services tax. Contrast progressive tax.

regulated entity: a bank or other authorised deposit-taking institution, a life or general insurance company, a superannuation fund or a non-operating holding company (NOHC) for any of these which is regulated by a country's Regulation Authority in order to minimise losses to depositors, policyholders and members of superannuation funds.

REIA: abbreviation for Real Estate Institute of Australia.

REIT: abbreviation for real estate investment trust.

related company: see holding company.

relative strength: a charting technique where an industry share price index or the price history of a stock is compared with the movements in a larger sector. One is divided by the other and the result is expressed as an index.

relinquishment: the abandoning of all or part of a prospect. May be voluntary or compulsory under the terms of the lease.

remainder interest: an entitlement to the corpus of some fund on the death of some person (the *life tenant*).

remainderman: the holder of a remainder interest (qv).

rematerialise: to turn uncertificated security holdings recorded electronically as book entries back into holdings represented by scrip certificates.

renounceable rights issue: a new issue of shares, made pro rata to existing shareholders, the entitlements to which can be traded. Non-renounceable rights cannot be traded in this way. See also theoretical value of rights.

rent: the periodical payment by a tenant or lessee to a landlord or owner for the use of a property.

rentier: a person whose income comes from interest, dividends and rent (not just rent).

renunciation: the act of transferring title when selling rights to an issue.

renunciations closing date: the last day on which rights trading takes place, except where a shortened timetable is used. It is the same day as the applications close date.

repayment of capital: the cash return of all or part of a company's issued capital to its shareholders.

replacement cost: the cost which would be incurred in making a fresh purchase of an identical article.

reply: the formal closing speech in a debate, made by the mover of a motion and which summarises the arguments for and against the proposition.

repo rate: is the interest rate for secured overnight or short term financing involving the sale and repurchase of securities. It is basically the rate at which RBI lends to commercials banks for meeting the short-term deficits.

rescission: a motion to remove a resolution from the books of an organisation, either later in the meeting which adopted it or at a subsequent meeting.

reseal: to certify that probate granted in one State is also granted in another.

Reserve Bank of India (RBI): India's central bank. It implements government monetary policy and manages the note issue.

reserve price: the lowest price which the vendor at an auction is willing to accept.

reserves (companies): a type of capital. In popular parlance the term means "surplus cash" and refers to an asset. In company accounts, on the other hand, it refers to a bookkeeping item on the other side of the balance sheet, namely, that part of the shareholders' funds which is not "share capital". Various labels - usually self-explanatory - are commonly applied to the several components of reserves, but the main distinction which should be made is between:

- capital items, which are not available for dividend declarations - for example, asset revaluation or share premium reserves, and
- revenue items, which are available for dividend declarations - for example, accumulated profits, general reserve.

All reserves belong to the whole body of shareholders and should be distinguished from the *provisions* which are made in respect of specific obligations such as future income tax or long service leave for employees, or which are shown in notes to the accounts as reducing the value of certain assets, for example by way of allowance for doubtful debts.

reserves (mining): the extent of the resource base that will prove economic to a mine.

reservoir: a rock formation potentially capable of containing liquids.

reset securities: securities such as non-cumulative non-redeemable non-voting converting preference shares paying a quarterly or half-yearly fully franked dividend at a defined rate (or its equivalent). The securities are subject to periodical reset dates, with the first one typically being five (or, less frequently, three) years after the date of issue. At each reset date the issuing company can vary upward or downward the rate of dividend applying till the next reset date and the other conditions. Alternatively, it can compulsorily convert the shares to ordinary shares, usually at a price involving a discount of 2.5 or 5 per cent to the market price at the time. The investor also has the right to have the shares converted on this basis.

residuary beneficiary: the person or organisation (often a charity) named in a will as the beneficiary entitled to any assets not otherwise disposed of.

residuary estate: see residue.

residuary legacy: property left to a person (the residuary beneficiary) by another person's will after all other legacies have been paid.

residue: the portion of a deceased person's estate remaining after the payment of liabilities (including debts, taxation, funeral expenses and testamentary expenses), specific legacies and annuities.

resistance level: a range of prices which represent a temporary ceiling or floor.

resistance level: in charting, the price level at which there is a tendency for prices not to rise further.

resolution: a formal determination by an organised meeting.

resource: a concentration of naturally occurring solid, liquid or gaseous materials in or on the earth's crust in such a form that economic extraction of a commodity is currently or potentially feasible.

responsible entity (RE): an organisation which acts as both the manager and the trustee of a managed investment scheme.

restricted securities: shares or options held in escrow (qv).

resuing: a mining method used for extracting very narrow veins of ore. Working space is established in the wall rock on one side of the ore and the ore is then broken separately. The wall-rock waste is used as stope fill.

retained earnings: the balance in the profit and loss account, profits which have not been distributed to shareholders but which are being retained for use in the operations of a business. Also known as accumulated profits, undistributed profits, unappropriated profits or plough-back. They form part of the shareholders' funds.

retention period (tax): the number of years for which records need to be kept in order to satisfy the requirements of the tax legislation.

retirement village: a residential complex which contains flat or unit accommodation specially designed and developed for elderly citizens and which offers appropriate services, thus enabling residents to enjoy an alternative lifestyle which maintains their dignity and independence, on a site which also offers additional facilities in a communal centre.

return: the reward for an investment. It can take the form of interest, dividends, rent, profits or capital gains. Theoretically it is tied to the risk of the investment. Returns can be measured in a number of ways, including the internal rate of return and the geometric mean return.

return on assets (ROA): a measure of the efficiency of a company. It is the ratio obtained by dividing a company's earnings before interest and tax (EBIT) by the gross tangible assets, expressed as a percentage. The calculations are best done using weighted average assets figures for the year.

return on capital employed (ROCE): a measure of the efficiency of a company. It is the ratio obtained by dividing a company's earnings before interest and tax (EBIT) by the gross tangible assets less current liabilities, expressed as a percentage. The calculations are best done using weighted average assets figures for the year.

return on equity (ROE): a measure of the efficiency of a company. It is the ratio obtained by dividing a company's profit (net of preference dividends, if any) by the shareholders' funds (net of preference capital and intangible assets, if any), expressed as a percentage. The calculations are best done using weighted average shareholders' funds for the year. The profit after tax is often used for this exercise, but using profit before tax gives more meaningful year-by-year comparisons if the rate of company tax changes.

revaluation (balance sheets): the process of placing a new value on an asset, to reflect inflation or changed circumstances. The revaluation may be based on directors' or independent valuations.

revalue: increase the value of a unit of one country's currency against a unit of another country's currency (the opposite of devalue).

revenue (revenue from operations): sales; the total amount receivable by a company in the ordinary course of its business for goods and services supplied by it during a financial year, excluding any inter-group transactions. Deducting all expenses including the net increase in the provisions from this figure gives the profit.

revenue items: generally speaking, items of a recurring nature received or paid - for example, interest, rent, wages, other running expenses and depreciation (as well as, in the case of organisations, subscriptions and donations), as distinct from capital items.

revenue reserves: those reserves which arise from the operations of a business and which are thus available for distribution to shareholders as dividends. See also reserves.

reversal formation: in charting, the formation which occurs when the price of a share changes direction and breaks out of an existing formation.

reverse mortgage: a first mortgage loan secured on a residential property typically owned and occupied by an elderly person or couple, on the basis that all interest and charges are accumulated against the property, with the loan being discharged only after the death of the owner (or of the survivor of two joint owners), or when the property is vacated and sold for other reasons, such as permanent entry into a nursing home.

reverse takeover: a merger where a smaller company takes over a larger company. Sometimes this device is used as a means of back door listing.

reversionary interest: an entitlement to the corpus of some fund on the death of some person (the *life tenant*).

reversioner: the holder of a reversionary interest (qv).

review (GST): alterations to rent which involve either an element of negotiation between the parties to a lease or at the very least an application of judgement by one of them - as distinct from rent increases made mechanically in accordance with some formula based on an index or expressed in dollar or percentage terms. The term also embraces rises where the right to impose them in order to reflect the imposition of a GST was specifically reserved in the contract.

rib pillar: a side pillar in a stope.

rig: the derrick, drawworks and attendant surface equipment of a drilling unit.

rigging the market: actions which create a false or misleading market; actions designed to artificially raise or lower the market price of listed securities, futures contracts, etc., and/or to give a false or misleading appearance of active trading, in order to make an unfair profit. See also cornering, pool, wash sales.

right: an entitlement given to existing ordinary shareholders in a company to take up new shares at a specific price and by a specific date. Rights are issued pro rata to existing shareholdings and may be either renounceable or non-renounceable. See also theoretical value of rights.

right of first refusal: a special clause in some leases which gives the lessee the right to buy the property if the lessor ever offers it for sale during the currency of the lease. The purchase price available to the lessee under such a clause is the price which another party is willing to pay, and the lessee usually has a limited period in which to take up this opportunity.

right of reply: the entitlement of the mover of a motion to a second speech, which automatically closes the debate on the motion (other persons not being permitted to make more than one speech per question each).

right of way: the right to pass over land owned by another person - for example, a common driveway. See also easement.

rights trading: the purchase and sale of renounceable rights. Rights trading generally takes place between the ex rights date (shortly before the actual books closing date for entitlements) and the applications closing date (or another stipulated date shortly before that date).

rigid trust: a trust under which the deed spells out the specific beneficiaries and their precise entitlements.

ripping: break of a mine roof to increase headroom.

rise: a vertical or an inclined opening above the back of a level.

risk: the uncertainty that the actual return from an investment will vary from the expected return. It is made up of systemic and non-systemic risk. The latter can be reduced but not eliminated by diversification. Modern prospectuses usually set out a long list of risk factors, some serious and others trivial, and some affecting the share concerned and others the market as a whole. Some risks can be insured against, at a price, by hedging techniques.

risk and return: the maxim linking risk and reward, namely, the higher the risk, the higher the expected return and vice versa.

risk capital: equity funds, as distinct from debt funds.

risk free rate: the hypothetical interest rate on a riskless class of asset. As there is no totally risk free asset it is usually taken to be the rate on government paper of a term equal to that under consideration.

risk-weighted assets (RWA) (banking): assets (both on- and off-balance sheet) classified by category, with the amounts included in each category being multiplied by a defined risk weighting. The resulting weighted values are then added together to produce the total risk weighted assets.

RITC: abbreviation for reduced input tax credit.

RMBS: abbreviation for residential mortgage backed securities.

ROA: abbreviation for return on assets.

road show: a series of presentations to potential institutional investors and stockbrokers, conducted by a company and its underwriter, to arouse interest in an imminent float.

roasting: the treatment of clay ores by heat where such ores are not suited to treatment by conventional crushing.

Robson Rotation: the process of rotating the names of candidates in an election on the ballot papers issued to successive voters, so that the favoured top positions are shared equally among all the candidates.

ROCE: abbreviation for return on capital employed.

rock bolting: a system of bolting the roof of a mine to prevent rock falls at joints. It is usually a preliminary protective measure, followed by permanent supports.

rock burst: the sudden failure of walls or pillars in a mine.

ROE: abbreviation for return on equity.

rollover (loans, etc.): the replacement of a loan or bill at maturity by a further loan or bill by negotiation with the party to whom the money is owed.

rollover (managed funds): the transfer of money owned by a client from one fund manager to another, or between two funds administered by the same fund manager.

rollover (superannuation): the conversion of a lump sum superannuation payment or some other eligible termination payment into an approved income stream or a superannuation fund in order to defer or avoid the tax otherwise levied on such payments.

rollover (takeovers): the acceptance by an investor of shares or other securities on one company for similar securities in another company in a takeover situation, with the investor electing to defer crystallisation of any capital gain - see scrip for scrip.

ROM: abbreviation for run of mine.

Romalpa clause: a condition in a contract (sometimes called a "retention of title" clause) under which a buyer gets physical possession of goods but with the seller retaining ownership until the goods have been paid for in full.

room and pillar mining: a system of mining wherein the coal or ore is mined in rooms separated by narrow ribs or pillars.

rotary drilling: a drilling method in which a hole is drilled by a rotating bit to which downward force is applied. The bit is fastened to and rotated by the drill stem, which also provides a passageway through which the drilling fluid is circulated. Additional joints of drill pipe are added as drilling progresses.

roulette clause: a clause in a joint venture agreement allowing one party (the "instigator") to give notice to the other party requiring that party either to sell its stake in the investment to the instigator at a certain price and on certain terms, or alternatively to purchase the instigator's stake at that same price and on those same terms.

round robin (money): a series of cheques from A to B, from B to C, from C to A, and so on, leaving all of them in the same net position as before.

round robin (resolutions): a document (or a series of like documents) signed by the members of an organisation or its committee, or by the members of a board of trustees, or by the shareholders in a company or the unit holders in a unit trust, and having the same effect as a resolution of a meeting. (The term originally referred to a petition signed in a circular form, so that the name of no particular person appeared first, thus reducing the danger of victimisation against the perceived organisers of a protest movement.)

round trip: the two legs of a transaction which involves a reversal, such as the acquisition of an option or a futures contract and its subsequent disposal before the delivery date.

royalties: payments made to the owner of a patent or a copyright for the use of this intellectual property; or payments made to the owner of land or to a government in respect to minerals or oil being obtained. Royalties in the private sector can be assigned to third parties. Mineral and oil royalties are usually based on a percentage of production or the value of production. Overriding royalties are calculated on the gross value of production without the deduction of any expenses.

RSE: abbreviation for registrable superannuation entity.

rts: abbreviation for rights.

RUB: symbol for the Russian rouble.

rule against perpetuities: a rule of law voiding any disposition which purports to postpone the vesting of property beyond a certain period.

rule of 78: a method of calculating interest earned, and unearned income, at any point in the life of a loan which is repayable by level instalments of capital and interest. It is an approximate method only. The effect is to distort repayments as early repayments mainly cover the interest costs. The figure 78 represents the sum of the numbers from 1 to 12.

rules of debate: the permanent rules for the regulation of the business and proceedings at the meetings of an organisation.

rules of order: the permanent rules for the regulation of the business and proceedings at the meetings of an organisation.

run: a spirited rise in the price of one stock.

run on a bank (or on some other financial institution): a panic rush by anxious customers to withdraw their money and the formation of queues outside its premises. Runs are more likely in the case of organisations which "borrow short and lend long", as by definition these will never have sufficient cash reserves to meet unexpected demands.

Panic is sometimes started accidentally - for example, by some ill-chosen words in the media. Rumours may also be propagated for malicious reasons. However, at the time the separation of fact from fiction by investors is not feasible.

Furthermore, denials of problems in such circumstances cannot ever be relied upon, as such denials would invariably be made for obvious commercial reasons, whether justified by the facts of the particular situation or not. This warning applies equally to denials by the organisation concerned, to denials by friendly competitors, to denials by industry associations and even to denials by government spokespersons. Of course, such statements may suffice to stop a run.

Runs can also be infectious. As money is frozen in some organisation, runs are likely to affect its competitors. Partly this is because of psychological factors, but the more significant reason is that as customers lose liquidity because one of their normal cash sources is not available they need to access alternative sources.

rutile: a mineral, a principal ore of titanium. Found in mineral sands.

RWA (banking): abbreviation for risk-weighted assets.

S&P: abbreviation for Standard and Poor's.

SA: abbreviation for Socit Anonyme.

safe harbor statement: forward-looking information, such as financial projections based on certain assumptions - as distinct from historical facts - which a company supplies to investors and analysts.

sage of Omaha: Warren Buffett, successful billionaire investor, CEO of Berkshire Hathaway and author of popular books on investment.

salary sacrifice: an arrangement under which an employer at the request of an employee reduces that employee's salary in exchange for making a corresponding contribution to a superannuation fund for that employee. This gives the employee a tax advantage at no cost to the employer.

sale and leaseback: a method of realising cash but retaining the use of a property or other fixed asset by selling it to an investor and simultaneously leasing it from the new owner.

sales: the total amount receivable by a company in the ordinary course of its business for goods and services supplied by it during a financial year, excluding any inter-group transactions. Deducting all expenses including the net increase in the provisions from this figure gives the profit.

salting: the introduction of metal or mineral into a deposit or samples, usually done with the intent to defraud.

sample: a selected portion of ore taken for assay.

sandstone: a sedimentary rock composed predominantly of quartz.

SAR: symbol for the Saudi riyal.

Sarbanes-Oxley Act of 2002 **(SOX):** Important legislation governing corporate governance in the United States, enacted in the light of recent major accounting frauds in that country. It seeks to protect investors by improving the accuracy of the information supplied to the market by listed companies. In essence the Act says, unsurprisingly, that boards of directors should behave properly. The Act requires enhanced financial disclosures and also deals with issues such as auditor independence and conflicts of interest by security analysts.

SATO: abbreviation for Senior Australians Tax Offset.

saucer: in charting, share price movements which when charted resemble a saucer.

savoy clause: a special provision in certain large contracts. Some listed companies which are involved in 50/50 joint ventures have contracts involving a savoy clause. Such a provision means that one party to the joint venture can at any time nominate a price to the other party, which must then (at its option) either buy the first party's interest in the joint venture from the first party at that price or sell its own interest in the joint venture to the first party at that price.

SBD: symbol for the Solomon Islands dollar.

scale back: a condition in a takeover which offers investors a choice of receiving the consideration either in securities or in cash, but with the proviso that if the total amount of securities or cash (as the case may be) chosen exceeds a defined maximum (known as the "cap") then the amount of the chosen alternative allotted to each of the investors concerned will be reduced on a pro rata basis, with the balance being satisfied by an allotment of the other alternative sufficient to make up the total of the relevant consideration.

scams: see Nigerian scam, Enronitis, pump and dump.

scarp: an escarpment or steep slope along the margin of a plateau or terrace.

scheelite: calcium tungstate, the principal ore of tungsten.

scheme of arrangement: a legal arrangement between companies and their shareholders or creditors to vary the rights of the parties, subject to the consent of a court. Some schemes are used to effect compromises between debtors and creditors. Others are used to effect capital repayments or other reconstructions. Schemes affecting several companies can be used to effect mergers; these can be de facto takeovers.

schist: a type of rock characterised by its flaky texture.

scintillation counter: an instrument used for detecting and measuring radioactivity.

scintillometer: an instrument used for detecting and measuring radioactivity.

scrapers: machines that rip the surface layer.

scrip: certificates of shares or stock units in a company; these are no longer in general use.

scrip covered option: a call option which is written and covered by the ownership of the underlying security rather than by cash.

scrip dividend: in the days of par values, a bonus issue that was made in lieu of a cash dividend.

scrip for scrip: the exchange of shares or other securities on one company for similar securities in another company in a takeover situation.

scrip issue: a bonus issue; in the days of par values, so-called free shares issued to shareholders in proportion to their holdings, either in addition to or in place of dividends - effectively a share split. Did not affect the proportion of a company held or the underlying value of the parcel. For capital gains tax purposes the cost base per post bonus share is the total cost base of the original parcel divided by the new total number of shares.

scrutineer: a person who examines votes in an election and makes certain that the counting has been done accurately.

SDIA: abbreviation for Securities & Derivatives Industry Association.

seam: a stratum of coal.

search engine: a computer programme and an associated database maintained on a special Internet site which in combination enable any Internet user to make keyword searches for desired information. The database performs a similar function to a library catalogue and is in effect a very large index of web pages derived from the electronic inspection of a great number of individual sites according to rules which are similar in character but different in detail for each search engine.

seat: entitlement to membership of a stock exchange.

SEATS: abbreviation for Stock Exchange Automated Trading System. It is a computer network enabling stockbrokers to trade via computer terminals.

SEBI: abbreviation for Securities and Exchange Board of India.

SEC: abbreviation for Securities and Exchange Commission (United States).

second mortgage: a charge on land by way of a mortgage which ranks after a first mortgage but ahead of other mortgages.

second rank industrials: industrial shares that are not regarded as blue chip stock but nevertheless are regarded as financially sound companies.

secondary enrichment: the enrichment of a vein by minerals which have been taken into solution from one part of the vein or adjacent rocks and redeposited in another part.

secondary industry: manufacturing. Compare primary, tertiary industries.

secondary market: the market for securities that have already been issued - in particular the stock exchange.

secondary recovery: the recovery of crude oil from an underground reservoir by means of injecting gas, steam, air or water into the reservoir after it has been largely depleted, thereby driving additional oil to the producing wells and effecting increased recovery.

secondary trend: see trend.

seconder: the person who formally supports a motion proposed by its mover.

secret ballot: the voting on a question before the chair or at an election in writing, in a way which allows accurate figures to be ascertained, but without the names of those voting in any particular way becoming available.

secretary: a person charged with the administrative aspects of running a company or an organisation, including the arrangements for its meetings and the recording of its minutes.

secured loan: a loan that is guaranteed by a charge over all or some of the borrower's assets. Secured debt ranks before unsecured debt in the event of a liquidation.

Securities and Exchange Board of India: is a body set up by the government of India to regulate the securities market of India.

securitisation: the process of an institutional investor for a fee putting a parcel of assorted properties or mortgage loans or similar assets into a single vehicle, aliquot parts of which can then be sold off to separate investors. The institution thus turns an illiquid asset into a liquid one, while the purchasers each get an investment with much less risk than a single property or a single mortgage loan or whatever, and which at the same time is an investment of a size which suits each investor's needs.

security (law): a legal document such as a mortgage which records the charging of some asset as a surety for the repayment of a loan.

security (stock exchange): a type of investment. The term is frequently used as a loose label for investments such as shares, debentures, notes, bonds and options which are traded on the stock exchange; however, the word by itself does not imply that the investment is necessarily "secure" in the sense of being "safe" or that there is any guarantee or any charge over assets (as in the case of a "secured loan").

sediment: solid material, mineral or organic, that has been moved from its site of origin by water, air or ice and deposited above or below water, later to form sedimentary rock.

sedimentary basin: a geologically depressed area with thick sediments in the interior and thin sediments to the edges. The most likely area to find hydrocarbon accumulations.

sedimentary rocks: rocks formed by the accumulation of sediments.

segment reporting: profit, assets, turnover and other figures for conglomerate companies as broken down into components for different divisions or industries or countries.

seismic survey: a geophysical method of prospecting, utilising the knowledge of the speed and reflection of sound waves in rock.

seismograph: a device that detects vibrations in the earth, used in prospecting for probable oil-bearing structures. Vibrations are created by discharging explosives in shallow boreholes or by striking the surface with a heavy blow. The type and velocity of the vibrations (as recorded by the seismograph) indicate the general characteristics of the section of earth through which the vibrations pass.

Sensex: BSE Sensitive Index (Sensex) is a value-weighted index of the 30 largest stocks on the Bombay Stock Exchange.

SEK: symbol for the Swedish krona.

self-assessment: Under this most tax returns are not examined in detail by assessors before assessments are issued, great reliance being placed on the information supplied by each taxpayer. The system is reinforced by measures such as random audits, computerised checks comparing figures with industry norms and cross-matching with other data available to the Income Tax Department. Significant penalties for dishonesty and carelessness apply.

self-funded retiree: a person of pension age who by virtue of the means test is not in receipt of a social security or similar pension.

sellers' market: the state of a market when demand outstrips supply and sellers rather than buyers can dictate prices.

semi-logarithmic graph: a graph where the vertical scale is calibrated in logarithmic values. Most chartists use semi-log graphs. These allow exponential growth to be represented by a sloping straight line.

SEP: abbreviation for stock election plan.

seriatim: one after another in order.

series of options: all contracts of the same class (see class of options) having the same expiration date and an identical exercise price.

server: in relation to the World Wide Web, a (usually large) dedicated computer connected to the Internet which on request provides web pages or files to a (usually small) computer (the "client") associated with a user.

service agreement: an agreement between an employee and a company setting out the terms of employment.

settled sum: the initial amount contributed by the settlor of a trust, together with any subsequent sums accepted by the trustee under the deed of settlement (a concept similar in character to the subscribed capital in the case of a company).

settlement (in relation to a trust): the foundation of a trust by the execution of a trust deed and the vesting of property in a trustee.

settlement (property): the exchange of the documents of title for money on finalising a purchase or sale of land or on the grant or discharge of a mortgage.

settlement (stock exchange): the payment for shares or other securities bought or sold on the stock exchange in exchange for the transfer of those securities out of the name of the vendor into the name of the purchaser.

settlor: the person who legally creates a trust by executing (signing) the trust deed and by feeding in the initial assets of the trust fund (often only a nominal amount of cash sufficient to satisfy a legal fiction).

several: involving two or more persons separately, individually, as distinct from joint.

SGC: abbreviation for superannuation guarantee charge.

SGD: symbol for the Singapore dollar.

SGX: abbreviation for Singapore Stock Exchange.

shadow compliance: substantial compliance, on a voluntary basis, with a regulatory scheme by an organisation which has a statutory exemption from compulsory compliance.

shadow director: a person who has not been elected as a director of a company but who holds influence such that the directors of the company customarily act in accordance with his or her instructions or wishes. Shadow directors expose themselves to the same liabilities as real directors under the corporations legislation.

shadow ledger: a record kept by a bank or non-bank lender showing the liability of a borrower under a loan agreement when the loan is in default. However, under normal accounting standards the lender also has to keep a separate (real) ledger which reflects any commercial view that some or all of the debt owing will not be repaid and that no further interest will be received. This is necessary in order to produce an accurate picture of the asset in the balance sheet and also in order to allow legitimate tax deductions for bad debts to be claimed. The entries in the real ledger naturally do not extinguish the contractual liability of the borrower, including all interest continuing to accrue on the debt. Shadow ledgers are also used in a similar way when defaults under leases occur.

shaft: a vertical or inclined excavation for the purpose of opening and servicing a mine.

shake out: a dramatic drop in share prices over a short time.

shale: a laminated sediment in which the constituent particles are mainly of the clay grade.

shale oil: see oil shale.

shandy rates: local government rates imposed partly on the site value and partly on the net annual value of a property.

share: one of the parts into which a company's share capital is divided, entitling each holder, as a part owner of the enterprise, to a proportion of the profits (after all expenses, interest on the liabilities and income tax) and to a proportion of the net assets after satisfying the creditors in the event of a winding up. The shareholders collectively control the company and elect a board of directors to act on their behalf. All the shares in any one class of shares rank equally. Most shares are either ordinary or preference:

Ordinary shares form the bulk of a company's capital. All companies listed on the stock exchange have to have ordinary shares. In the event of liquidation, these rank after everything else. They may be fully-paid or contributing.

Preference shares, where a company has them, provide a fixed rate of return and have priority over the ordinary shares in regard to dividend payments and to the company's assets in the event of a winding up, but they rank after all the company's liabilities. They can take various forms - for example, with or without cumulative dividend entitlements; with or without participating or partial participating rights. They can be redeemable or irredeemable; convertible or non-convertible; voting or non-voting.

A company can also have deferred shares.

share buyback: the purchase by a company of its own shares.

share certificate: the physical document recording ownership of shares.

share index: a measure of share prices. See also Dow Jones Industrial Average.

share investment plan (SIP): a dividend election plan.

share issue: the creation of new shares by a company and their allotment for cash or in exchange for assets (or, in the case of bonus shares, without consideration) or the bulk offer of existing shares by their holders to new investors. Offers of new shares by companies already listed are usually made to their existing shareholders as a proportionate rights issue, but some are made to outsiders by way of placement. New cash issues normally require a prospectus. See also right.

share premium: in the days of par values, the excess of a share price over the face value of the share. The opposite of share discount.

share price index futures (SPI): a futures and options contract based on Australias benck mark share market index SPI 200.

share qualification (for directors): the minimum number of shares (or their market value) that a person must own in order to be eligible for appointment to a company's board of directors.

If the directors own reasonable parcels of shares in the company then there is a greater chance that their interests will parallel those of other shareholders than if they do not. Correspondingly, small parcels demonstrate a lack of faith in the company.

However, the absence of large holdings by well-qualified but not necessarily wealthy individual directors should not automatically be held against them. At the other extreme, a very substantial holding by a super-rich director would not necessarily signify all that much, as even the total loss of the entire investment in the company would probably make little difference to that person's standard of living.

share raid: see raid.

share raider: see raider.

share register: a company's record of its shareholders and their holdings. It may be maintained by the company or by an agent.

share registrar: the organisation that maintains a company's share register.

share split: the subdivision of a company's shares into a larger number of shares, each with a correspondingly lower market value. The total value of any investor's holdings is not affected by the split. Sometimes splits are made to increase the marketability of a security. The opposite of consolidation.

share swap: a strategic exchange of shares between two companies as a defensive move against an unwanted takeover bid for either. The term is also used for takeovers involving a consideration expressed in shares.

share trader: see trader.

shareholders' funds: the funds subscribed by shareholders and any accumulated profits or capital gains or amounts resulting from a revaluation of assets. They represent the ownership stake in the company held collectively by its shareholders, be they ordinary shareholders, preference shareholders or minority shareholders in subsidiary companies.

shareholders' interest: the ratio which shows the proportion of funds attributable to shareholders. It is calculated by dividing the shareholders' funds by the total assets.

shares of no par value (NPV): shares without a nominal or face value.

shark repellent: a restrictive clause inserted into a company's constitution or alternatively some corporate move primarily made in an endeavour to deter unwanted takeover bids. Such provisions usually help to keep the market price of the company's shares down, by reducing buying pressure both from potential bidders and from investors acquiring shares in the expectation of some bid. Devices include large scale expansion moves and the issue to existing shareholders, ahead of an actual bid, of securities with special privileges which come into play when a hostile bid is made - all of which are actions designed to make the total cost of acquisition higher.

shearing: formation of fracture whereby the portion on one side of the fracture slides past the portion on the other side.

shelf: an underwater plateau surrounding an island or continent at relatively little depth.

shelf company: a company set up with its own constitution but which has never traded. It can be bought and used immediately.

shelf registration: the lodging with the Securities and Exchange Commission in the United States of prospectus type information in respect of a new issue of securities which is not imminent. Such documents can be lodged up to two years in advance, providing great flexibility for a company to raise funds quickly when they are needed and/or when it considers market conditions to be favorable.

shell: a company the shares of which are listed on the stock exchange but the activities of which are minimal, with the assets being mainly cash. Shells are often used as vehicles for back door listings.

shoot: that part of vein bearing values of ore grade.

short position (futures market): a contract promising to deliver. Because futures trading is a zero sum game, for every contract to buy (a long position) there must be a corresponding contract to sell (a short position).

short position (share market): the status arising when shares which are not owned have been disposed of - see short selling. Contrast *long position*.

short selling: the practice of selling shares which are not owned by the seller. The sale is made in anticipation of a fall in the share price, following which the position would be covered by then acquiring the securities and crystallising a profit. If the shares rise instead enormous losses can be made. There are special rules governing short selling, which was formerly illegal.

short term: in accounting, involving a period of twelve months or less; in regard to investments, probably involving a horizon of ranging from one day (or even less) to several months, up to about three to five years.

short term money market: the market where financial institutions specialise in borrowing and lending large sums of money for short periods. It can be the official market, where authorised dealers have the backing of the Reserve Bank of Australia, or the unofficial or inter-company market.

short term paper: a security at call or with a term to maturity of about 12 months or less.

short ton: see tonne.

shortfall: see underwriter.

shortfall facility (rights issues): a facility which allows shareholders to subscribe for any shares which were not taken up by other shareholders in a proportinate rights issue.

shotgun clause: a clause in a joint venture agreement allowing one party (the "instigator") to give notice to the other party requiring that party either to sell its stake in the investment to the instigator at a certain price and on certain terms, or alternatively to purchase the instigator's stake at that same price and on those same terms.

shovel: a machine used in open-cut mining to lift ore into a truck or relocate it elsewhere.

show: an indication of oil or gas encountered in drilling.

show of hands: the voting on a question before the chair by the raising of hands when called upon to do so, to indicate "aye" or "no".

shrinkage stoping: a mining method in which holes are drilled into the roof of the stope and blasted till the stope is full of broken ore.

SI: abbreviation for systeme internationale (the metric System).

SIA: abbreviation for Securities Institute of Australia.

sideways movements: price and yield movements within a narrow range, in a market which is in neither a bull nor a bear phase.

significant item: an item of revenue or expense from a company's ordinary activities that is of such a size, nature or incidence that its separate disclosure in the notes to the financial statements is necessary in order to explain properly the financial performance of the company.

silica: an oxide of silicon.

silicon: the second most common element on earth. Used as a ferro alloy and in glass production. Chemical symbol: Si.

sill: a sheet of igneous rock formed by the crystallisation of magma which has forced its way between the layers of pre-existing rocks. It is generally horizontal.

sill and crown pillars: horizontal pillars above and below the stoping area.

silver: a precious metal normally found in a natural state, usually together with other metals such as lead, zinc, copper, tin or gold. Principal use is in the photographic industry. Chemical symbol: Ag.

simple interest: interest calculated on the original capital only but not on the accumulation of past interest amounts, in contradistinction from compound interest; simple interest is a very misleading and inappropriate way of measuring the return on an investment.

simple majority: the greater part of; that is, more than half.

simplified tax system (STS): a procedure optionally available to small businesses to reduce their compliance burden under the tax legislation and to give them the benefit of certain tax concessions.

sine die: without stipulating a day.

sine qua non: an indispensable condition.

sinter: the heat treatment of fines to produce larger pieces of ore for blast furnace feed.

SIP: abbreviation for share investment plan.

site: in relation to the World Wide Web, one or more interrelated pages (usually written in HTML) put there by the one organisation. See also home page.

site cover: the area of land on which a building is erected divided by the total area of the land concerned - for example, 0.65.

site value (SV): the notional value of land as though it had no buildings erected on it (cf. improved value).

sitting tenant: a tenant already in occupation of a property.

SKI: abbreviation for the jocular expression "spending your kids' inheritance".

slag: the waste from smelting.

sleeping partner: the partner in a business partnership who supplies all or most of the capital while another partner actively manages the business on a day-to-day basis.

sliding: the situation where prices on the stock exchange are falling slightly on light turnover.

sliding scale: voting right entitlements where the voting power is relatively less influential the larger the holding. Also, a device often used to ration shares in floats which have been oversubscribed.

sluicing: washing earth through boxes to separate out heavy minerals, such as tin or gold, from waste.

slump: a sustained, prolonged drop in share prices.

slurry: a thin, watery mixture of cement and water that is pumped into a well to harden; after hardening, it supports the casing and provides a seal in the wellbore to prevent migration of underground fluids. Slurry also refers to a mixture of ore and water that is created as a means of transporting the ore by pumping it through pipes.

small cap: refers to stocks with a relatively small market capitalization.

SME: abbreviation for a small to medium enterprise.

snapshot date: the record date in a company's share register that defines eligibility to vote at a company's meeting.

SoA: abbreviation for statement of advice.

SoAA: abbreviation for statement of additional advice.

social capital: the intangible network of relationships that make things happen in a community and enhance productivity, in part by virtue of the educational, social and cultural advantages that some persons possess.

Socit Anonyme (SA). a limited liability company (French).

soft dollars: non-cash benefits given to intermediaries for selling financial products, and especially for exceeding a sales target.

Such perks are usually not disclosed to the purchasers of the products concerned, who are thus unable to judge the bias inherent in any recommendations. Typical benefits include free computer equipment and trips to conferences held at exotic locations.

solvency: the state of a company which is able to meet all its liabilities as they fall due.

solvency margin (general insurance): the excess of assets over liabilities. Assets of a certain type are not eligible in such calculations.

sotto voce: in an undertone, as an aside.

source and application of funds statement: a statement which details where a company's cash has been derived and what it has been used for in a period.

source bed: a layer of sedimentary rock in which hydrocarbons have been generated.

sovereign risk: that portion of the risk involved in investing in a foreign country that relates to actions of its government - nationalisations, expropriations, exchange controls, devaluations, legislation discriminating against foreigners, revolutions, wars, and so on.

sovereign wealth fund: a government investment vehicle which is often funded primarily by foreign exchange assets. These are managed separately from the official reserves of a central bank or other monetary authority. Such funds are long term investors seeking good investment returns.

SOX: abbreviation for the United States *Sarbanes-Oxley Act of 2002.*

S&P CNX Nifty 50: is an index of well-diversified 50 stock index at NSE. It is used for a variety of purposes such as benchmarking fund portfolios, index based derivatives and index funds.

spec: abbreviation for speculative issue.

special dividend: a dividend so labelled by a company's board of directors in order to indicate to the market that it is a one-off distribution and that it will not be replicated on a regular basis.

special resolution: in relation to a company, a resolution that has been passed by at least 75 per cent of the votes cast by members entitled to vote on the resolution.

special sale: the sale of a large parcel.

specie: see in specie.

specific bequest: a bequest which is a gift of an identified item of property.

specific gravity: density. A substance's degree of consistence measured by the proportion of mass to volume.

specific trust: a trust under which the deed spells out the specific beneficiaries and their precise entitlements.

specimen: a piece of rock or mineral that is hopefully representative of the deposit from which it was derived.

spectrometer: a device for detecting and analysing Gamma Radiation.

speculation: the strategy of trading in relatively more risky stocks in anticipation of a higher profit. Futures contracts can also be used for speculating; persons who have no involvement in a physical commodity as either buyers or sellers can trade in its futures as a convenient way of benefiting from expected price movements. Contrast hedging.

speculative issue: securities that are more risky than normal shares. The term usually refers to exploration stocks.

sphalerite: zinc sulphide, the principal ore of zinc.

SPI: abbreviation for the share price index futures contract.

spin-off: the flotation of an affiliated company in which shareholders of the sponsoring company receive entitlements.

split capital investment funds: managed investments with two classes of units. Typically the holders of the capital units receive no income but on termination become entitled to the bulk of the capital growth on the total capital, while the holders of the income units receive all the income earned on the total capital each year and on termination become entitled to only the balance of the capital growth on the total capital.

split loan (1): a loan with a portion subject to a variable interest rate and the rest subject to a fixed interest rate. This allows borrowers to spread the risk involved in trying to predict future changes to interest rate levels. It also means that the variable rate portion of the loan can readily be used for desired variations to the amount of outstanding principal (up or down) without penalty.

split loan (2): a loan with a portion classed as being for domestic purposes and the rest classed as being for business or investment purposes. As interest on the domestic portion is not deductible for income tax purposes borrowers will usually direct that all repayments should go to that portion of the loan until such time as it is totally extinguished. In the meantime the outstanding balance of the non-domestic portion of the loan increases, thus also increasing the tax deductions available for interest on that portion.

spot market: a market involving immediate delivery and payment, in contrast to a market involving forward delivery and settlement at a later date. Prices on spot and forward markets are frequently different.

spot price: the market price at which buyers and sellers are prepared to trade for a single consignment. See also producer's price.

spread (investments): the holding of a diversified portfolio in order to manage risk better. To illustrate, if an investor has, say, 10 investments of approximately equal size and one of them goes bad then that investor has lost 10 per cent of the money laid out - an unfortunate outcome, but not the disaster which would have occurred if *all* of that money had been put into that one investment. Similarly, in terms of income, if 9 of the 10 do well, returning, say, an average of 10 per cent per annum, then the non-receipt of income from the tenth would still produce a reasonable 9 per cent return on the entire portfolio. This principle applies equally whether one is considering, for example, shares - with some companies not paying a dividend - or income-producing real estate - with some individual property being empty and thus not generating any rent. Of course, diversification can be taken too far: one failure in 20 might mean a 5 per cent loss; one failure in 100 is only marginally better at a 1 per cent loss. Spread is possible in various ways, for example: by class of investment (bank deposits, bonds, shares, property, and so on), by company within each class, by industry (food, steel, textiles, and so on), by currency or by region. See also index fund.

spread (options): the simultaneous purchase and sale of options in the same company with different expiry months and/or different exercise prices. There are several different sorts of spreads: calendar or time spreads, where the options are of the same exercise price but involving different expiry months; price spreads, where the options expire at the same time but with different exercise prices; and diagonal spreads which are a combination of calendar and price spreads.

spud: to move the drill stem up and down in the hole over a short distance without rotating.

spud in: to begin drilling; to start the hole.

SRAA: abbreviation for Securities Registrars' Association of Australia.

SRI: abbreviation for socially responsible investment.

SRI: abbreviation for sustainable and responsible investment.

SRN: abbreviation for securityholder reference number.

SRO: abbreviation for self regulating organisation.

SSAT: abbreviation for Social Security Appeals Tribunal.

stable population: a population with an unchanging rate of growth and an unchanging age composition, because age-specific birth and death rates have remained constant over a sufficient period of time.

stag: an investor who subscribes to a new flotation with the intention of selling the shares immediately upon the commencement of quotation, hopefully at a profit.

stagflation: the phenomenon of simultaneous stagnation and inflation, slow economic growth accompanied by rising prices.

stake a well: to locate precisely on the surface of the ground the point at which a well is to be drilled. After exploration techniques have revealed the possibility of the existence of a subsurface hydrocarbon-bearing formation, a certified and registered land surveyor drives a stake into the ground to mark the spot where the well is to be drilled.

stakeholder: while the directors of a company have legal, moral and professional obligations to run the enterprise for the benefit of all shareholders they also have ethical obligations to other stakeholders: employees, creditors, suppliers, customers, ultimate consumers and the community at large (for example, in relation to the environment or to paying a proper share of taxation).

stale: orders given to a stockbroker and still unexecuted after about a month to six weeks.

stale bull: a share trader/investor who has become disenchanted.

stamp duty: a state government fee levied inter alia on every transaction to buy or sell shares or to buy property.

Standard and Poor's: a corporate credit rating agency. See also rating agencies. The company has also joined with the NSE to produce the S&P/CNX Indices.

standard deviation: in statistics, the measure of the dispersion of a set of scores.

standby credit facility: an undertaking by a lending institution to supply funds when called upon by the borrower.

standing orders: the permanent rules for the regulation of the business and proceedings at the meetings of an organisation.

stapled securities: two or more legally different instruments which under their terms of issue are coupled together for certain purposes. In particular, they cannot be transferred separately either on the stock exchange or off-market. These structures are usually adopted because they are tax-effective both for the organisations concerned and for their investors.

Examples of such stapled securities include ordinary shares and units in an associated unit trust; ordinary shares and unsecured notes; ordinary shares and convertible preference shares; ordinary shares and options; unpaid preference shares and unsecured notes. A "parcel" consisting of one share and one or more units or notes or options is traded on the stock exchange as though it were a single security.

It is also effectively treated as a single asset for capital gains tax purposes, although conceptually the components are regarded as separate assets. However, for ordinary income tax purposes the dividends on the share components are generally treated as dividends in the financial year in which they are received, while any trust distributions (as in the case of trusts generally) are treated as trust distributions in the financial year to which they relate.

statement of financial performance: see profit and loss account.

statement of financial position: see balance sheet.

status quo: the existing condition.

statute barred: see statute of limitation.

statute law: Acts of Parliament.

statute of limitation: the law which prescribes the period within which a legal action to enforce a right must be taken, after which any such action will be regarded as statute barred. For example, in the case of simple contracts (those not under seal) the period ends six years after the cause of action arose.

statutory income (income tax): amounts of income which are included in assessable income by virtue of specific provisions in the income tax legislation, even though they are not income according to ordinary concepts.

statutory liquidity ratio: refers to the amount that the commercial banks must maintain in the form of cash, or gold or govt. approved securities before providing credit to the customers. Statutory Liquidity Ratio is determined and maintained by the Reserve Bank of India in order to control the expansion of bank credit.

STC: abbreviation for Superannuation Complaints Tribunal.

STCA: abbreviation for subject to council approval.

STCT: abbreviation for Small Taxation Claims Tribunal.

steal a property: to seek to acquire real estate for substantially less than its current value.

steam flood: see secondary recovery.

step out well: a well drilled near an existing discovery.

stock (balance sheets): finished goods, work in progress and raw materials. Also known as inventory. For tax purposes trading stock can be valued, at the option of the taxpayer, at cost or at market selling value or at its replacement price.

stock election plan (SEP): a dividend election plan.

stock exchange: an organised secondary market for securities.

stock turnover ratio: the number of times in a year that a company's trading stock is sold. It is calculated by dividing the cost of goods sold by the inventory. The ratio may also be converted into the number of days that stock is held by dividing 365 by the stock turnover ratio.

stock unit: see share. An obsolete term.

stockbroker: a member of a stock exchange who as agent effects buying and selling orders for clients.

stockpile: ore accumulated at the surface.

stocks (stock exchange): (1) shares or (2) (especially in the expression "stocks and shares") fixed interest securities (according to context).

stop loss order: an order given to a stockbroker to sell securities once they have fallen to a certain level. The order is given with the desire to limit any losses that may occur in a shake out or slump.

stope: an excavation in an underground mine from which ore is being or has been extracted.

straddle: an options trading strategy that allows the trader to realise a profit if there is either a rise or a fall in the price of an underlying security. It involves simultaneously buying and selling an equal number of put and call options in the same underlying security with the same exercise price and expiration date.

strata: beds or layers of rocks. Plural of stratum.

strata title: a title to land which has been subdivided vertically as well as horizontally. See also body corporate.

stratification: the natural layering or lamination characteristic of sediments and sedimentary rocks.

stratigraphic trap: a petroleum trap that occurs when the top of the reservoir bed is terminated by other beds or by a change of porosity or permeability within the reservoir.

stratum: a bed or layer of sedimentary rock.

straw vote: an informal and non-binding vote in which those voting indicate their preferred positions on each of the three or more alternatives put to a meeting consecutively (each person voting "aye" only once).

street name: securities registered in the name of a broker on behalf of a client, with a view to facilitating subsequent transactions.

strict liability: a liability imposed by statute even where no negligence is involved.

strike: the direction, that is, the course or bearing, of a vein or rock formation measured on a level surface. The strike is at right angles to the dip.

strike price: the price at which an underlying security may be purchased or sold on the exercise of an option or warrant. Also called striking price. See also writer.

strip: to remove overburden, barren rock and anything else between the miner and the deposit.

stripping: the process of removing a metal from a solvent in which it is dissolved.

structural trap: a trap caused by an anticline or a fault.

structured settlement: compensation for personal injury whereby all or part of the compensation is paid in the form of periodic instalments rather than by way of lump sum, often with these being funded by the purchase of an annuity. Such settlements match the financial needs of injured persons by providing them with similar payments to those which they could obtain on an after tax basis from an expertly managed investment portfolio, but with much better protection against the risks of longevity, inflation, capital losses and poor returns.

STS: abbreviation for Simplified Tax System.

studio (property): a small apartment with a living space, a kitchenette and a bathroom, but with no separate bedroom.

sub judice: before a court.

sub rosa: in confidence.

sub-prime loans: loans to persons without a good credit record and/or on the basis of inadequate information as to their assets, liabilities and income. Because of the greater risk to the lender such loans bear a higher interest rate than conventional loans.

sub-sea completion: the completion of a well with production being piped along the ocean floor to a nearby platform. Only used on marginal fields where there is a nearby platform.

sub-underwriter: see underwriter.

subdivision: the apportionment of a large block of land into smaller blocks which can be owned separately.

sublease: see head lease.

submission: a document commenting on social issues or seeking some political objective, such as might be made to a government or to an official inquiry, especially a document setting out relevant facts, opinions, arguments, analyses, statistical data and/or recommendations for action, or soliciting funding for some worthwhile purpose.

subordinated loan: unsecured debt that ranks behind other unsecured debt.

subrogation: the right of an insurer to recover in place of the insured from a third party who was wholly or partially responsible for a claim met by the insurer.

subsidiary: a company which is more than 50% owned by another company (in terms of either ordinary share capital or voting power) or where that other company controls the composition of the board.

substantial shareholder: a shareholder controlling over five per cent of the voting power of a company.

substantive motion: a motion ordering that something be done, or authorising some past or proposed action, or expressing the opinion of a meeting in regard to some subject, or otherwise dealing with the general activities of an organisation (as distinct from a procedural motion).

substituted year: see financial year.

succession duty: a tax levied on that part of the net assets of a deceased estate which passes to a particular beneficiary

sucker rally: the phenomenon during a protracted period of steadily declining share prices of these prices suddenly climbing higher for a short time, only to fall to even lower levels soon afterwards.

sui generis: of its own kind.

suitor: a company wishing to gain control of another, either by raid or takeover.

sulphide: a compound of sulphur and another element.

sulphide zone: that part of a mineralised deposit in which the primary minerals (often sulphides) have not been altered. Found below the oxidised zone.

sum insured: the amount of money which a life insurance company undertakes to pay on death or maturity or the maximum amount of cover under a general insurance policy.

summation method: a method of valuing property which has regard to the value of the land free of buildings and the separate value of the buildings allowing for depreciation.

sun king: Rupert Murdoch, newspaper proprietor of note, chairman and CEO of News Corporation Inc.

sunrise industry: a new and emerging industry - for example, high technology.

superannuation: the provision of benefits for employees and/or self-employed persons and their dependants, in the form of a pension or lump sum benefits at retirement, or at earlier death or disablement.

superannuation bonds: investment bonds issued by a life insurance company in its superannuation section. These are subject to the usual restrictions applying to other superannuation products which are subject to the concessional tax regime for superannuation.

superannuation guarantee charge (SGC): a compulsory levy imposed by Commonwealth legislation on payrolls and designed to fund a minimum level of retirement benefits for all employees.

supplies (GST): goods and services *sold* or the amounts *receivable* for them.

support level: in charting, the price level at which there is a tendency for prices not to fall further.

surface anomaly: an anomaly on the surface.

surplus: a life insurance company's excess of funds over the actuarial value of its liabilities to its policyholders.

surrender value: an amount payable by a life insurance company to one of its policyholders who surrenders or cancels a life policy. Broadly speaking, the surrender value is equal to the premiums paid, plus interest, less the cost of cover and the marketing and administration expenses, after allowing for tax. Some investors are willing to purchase existing life policies for greater sums than those offered by the issuing life company - see traded policies.

suspended: the state when trading in a company's shares is temporarily halted by the stock exchange pending advice from the company. Suspension may be at the request of the company pending an announcement or it may be imposed by the stock exchange when it feels that the market is not fully informed or if reports have not been lodged by the due date.

SV: abbreviation for site value.

swap: an interest rate and/or currency exchange transaction involving two counterparties.

sweet gas: gas that has no sulphur, as distinct from sour gas, which has sulphur.

sweet spot: the best "value for money" when similar items are available in a range of different sizes or other characteristics at varying prices; the optimum combination of characteristics and qualities.

sweetener: an inducement added to a new issue in order to encourage investors to take it up - for example, "free" options offered to subscribers for shares, or the opportunity to subscribe to shares at a discount offered to subscribers for a fixed interest security.

SWF: abbreviation for sovereign wealth fund.

SWIFT: abbreviation for the Society for Worldwide Interbank Financial Telecommunication.

swing: the general upward or downward movement in the market.

switching (managed funds): the transfer of money owned by a client from one fund manager to another, or between two funds administered by the same fund manager.

switching (stock exchange): the act of selling one security and moving into another. It embraces situations such as selling shares to buy rights or notes in the same company or switching from long dated to short dated government paper.

syncline: a fold in strata in the form of an inverted arch. Opposite of anticline.

synthetic instrument: a derivative, a financial instrument or product that derives its value from the price of another more basic instrument or product - for example, an option, a swap or a futures contract.

systemic risk: that element of risk which cannot be removed by diversification and which arises from political events and other forces which affect the whole market rather than a particular stock. It is also known as non-diversifiable risk, market risk and systematic risk. Beta is a measure of the systemic risk.

t: symbol for tonne (metric ton).

T-note: a treasury note, a short term government security.

T+3: a stock exchange rule requiring both broker/broker and broker/client settlements for most stock exchange transactions to take place on the third business day after the date of a transaction. There are penalties on both brokers and clients who miss the deadlines. This rule enables the bulk "netting" of transactions between brokers each day, thus reducing the paperwork which previously applied when individual buying and selling orders needed to be matched.

TAA: abbreviation for tactical asset allocation.

tabling: a technical device to allow a meeting to discuss a paper which is not otherwise open for discussion.

tabling motion: the procedural motion: "That the question lie on the table."

tactical asset allocation (TAA): an active management portfolio strategy that rebalances the percentage of assets held in various categories in order to take advantage of market pricing anomalies or favourable trends.

tag and drag clause: a clause in a joint venture agreement which gives one partner the right to "tag along" on a sales deal which has been negotiated by the other partner. It also gives one partner the ability to "drag along" the other partner on a sales deal, effectively ensuring the sale of 100 per cent of the enterprise.

tailings: material rejected from a mill once most of the metal has been removed. Changes in technology and metal prices make it possible to economically retreat tailings.

tailings dam: an artificial pond for the storage of the mining residue.

takeover: an offer to all the shareholders of a company to buy all or part of their shareholdings for a specified consideration (or for a choice between two or more alternative considerations). The consideration may be cash; or shares, options or loan securities in the bidding company or a related company; or some combination of these. Takeovers can be of two sorts: an off-market bid or an on-market bid. Off-market bids involve the bidder (the offeror) sending a *bidder's statement* to the target company concerned, setting out details of the bid and how it will be financed, and so on. Directors of the target company (the offeree) have to respond with a *target's statement* which sets out their recommendation to the shareholders. The offer documents including these statements are then sent to all shareholders. The offer may be conditional upon minimum acceptances or other constraints. If these conditions are not met then the bidder can either let the offer lapse or can declare the offer unconditional and accept those shares offered. If, as a result of a takeover bid, acceptance for over 90 per cent of the shares subject to a bid are received from more than 75 per cent of the shareholders then the offeror can compulsorily acquire the balance for the same consideration as previously offered. In an on-market bid the offeror must stand in the market at a fixed price for a fixed time. This also involves bidder's and target's statements. Both off-market and on-market bids can take place simultaneously. See also scheme of arrangement.

takeover defence: tactics adopted to defend a company from an unwanted takeover. Common defences are: share splits, capital repayments, white knights, the seeking of government intervention, and the disclosure of additional information.

takeovers code: This legislation provides a very detailed and somewhat complex set of rules which have to be observed in takeover situations. The main purpose of these rules is to ensure that all shareholders in the offeree company are treated equally and fairly, that they are given sufficient relevant information to enable them to make an intelligent decision as to whether or not to accept any offer and adequate time in which to make a decision or get independent advice.

taker: the buyer of an option contract.

tantalite: the principal ore of tantalum.

tantalum: a primary metal used for plating and medical purposes because of its high resistance to corrosion. Chemical symbol: Ta.

TAP: abbreviation for term allocated pension.

target company: the company which is the subject of a takeover offer.

target's statement: see takeovers.

targeted shares: a distinct series of ordinary shares which participates in the profits of only a defined division of a company rather than in those of the entire enterprise.

tariff: a system of duties imposed on imports, either to raise revenue or as a protective device.

tax avoidance: the lawful minimising of one's tax liabilities. Contrast tax evasion.

tax deduction: an amount which may be subtracted from assessable income before income tax is calculated.

tax effect accounting: a method of accounting which seeks to match the tax charge to the accounting profit for the period concerned. Any difference between the income tax actually payable and the income tax expense charged in the accounts which is due to timing differences is shown in the balance sheet as a deferred tax liability or as an asset labelled future tax benefit, as the case may be. This asset can, however, be recognised only where the recovery of the tax benefit is assured beyond reasonable doubt.

tax evasion: the deliberate failure to pay one's proper tax by breaching the law. Contrast tax avoidance.

tax haven: a country that enables individuals and businesses to earn profits involving a zero or relatively low tax liability. Some countries deliberately set out cater for the worldwide demand for opportunities to engage in tax avoidance.

tax invoice (GST): an invoice or receipt showing certain details set out in the legislation and which is used for GST purposes. Such a document can, of course, also be used for ordinary business purposes.

tax loss: the extent to which a taxpayer's assessable income is less than the allowable deductions in any financial year. A loss incurred in a prior financial year is deductible from the assessable income in later years. Tax losses can now be carried forward indefinitely. Tax losses are not transferable except between wholly-owned group companies.

tax offset: see tax rebate.

tax rebate: an amount which is subtracted from the income tax which would otherwise be payable by a taxpayer; however, except in the case of franking rebates, rebates cannot lead to a negative amount of tax and unused rebates cannot be carried forward. The official term for this currently is tax offset.

taxable activity (GST): any supply of goods or services for a payment, whether in cash or kind.

taxable income: a taxpayer's assessable income less the allowable deductions.

taxable supplies (GST): supplies made by a registered entity in the course of an enterprise, but excluding GST-free supplies and input taxed supplies.

TCC: abbreviation for tax concession charity.

TCR: abbreviation for tangible common ratio (banks).

technical analysis: the process of estimating expected future share prices by reference to historical movements of prices and turnover. Also known as charting. Contrast fundamental analysis.

technical reaction: a reversal in the direction of share price movements. Generally follows a period of sustained buying or selling.

technician: a proponent of technical analysis. Commonly known as a chartist.

teleconference: a discussion between people linked by telephone.

telegraphic transfers: electronic payments of cleared funds that are credited directly to a nominated bank account almost anywhere in the world. The term is still used, although it refers to a technology which has been abandoned.

tellers: persons appointed by the chairman of a meeting to count those voting for or against a motion.

tenancy-in-common: the ownership of an asset by two or more persons collectively in such a way that on the death of one the ownership of a designated proportion of the property (not necessarily an equal share) passes to that person's heirs, as distinct from a joint tenancy. A tenant-in-common is one of the co-owners and not a "tenant" in the sense of "lessee".

tenement: area held under a mining lease, Authority to Prospect or other title to minerals.

tenor: the period of time after which a bill of exchange is payable.

term deposit: a deposit with a bank or similar organisation for a fixed period at a fixed interest rate.

term insurance: a policy under which the benefit is payable only if the life insured dies before a specified age or date.

terra nullius: uninhabited land.

terrace: a step-like structure in an open pit mine.

tertiary industry: the services sector. Compare primary, secondary industries.

Tertiary Period: a period 2 to 65 million years ago.

testament: a will; a formal document governing the disposition of property owned by a person, to take effect on that person's death.

testamentary trust: a trust set up by will.

testator: the person making a will.

testatrix: (feminine of "testator".)

TFN: abbreviation for tax file number.

TFN amount: income tax deducted at source from unfranked dividends, interest, and so on, earned by taxpayers who have not supplied a tax file number to the paying institution; it is treated as an advance payment of tax.

THB: symbol for the Thai baht.

theoretical value of rights: the value which rights would have on the market if the market were perfect and if there were no other changes in market conditions apart from the rights issue. It is calculated, for an issue involving one new share for each *n* old shares held, by adding *n* times the closing cum rights market price per share to the application price per share and dividing the total by *n*+1.

thin capitalisation rules: rules designed to prevent multinational taxpayers exploiting the favourable tax treatment of debt by treating too small a proportion of their total funding as equity.

thin market: a lack of buying or selling volume.

third sector of the economy: the non-profit sector, including charities and activities by volunteers.

Tax Information Network (TIN): is the repository of all tax related information of India. Its function includes modernization of the collection, processing, monitoring and accounting of direct taxes.

tick: the direction in which the price of a share moved on its last stock exchange trade, either up (an up-tick) or down (a down-tick).

tier 1 capital (banking): see minimum capital standards.

tight: referring to rocks of low permeability.

time share: a special form of dividing land into units each of which gives occupation rights for a designated period - for example, a specified week - each year.

time value (options): the market price of an option, less its intrinsic value; the proportion of the value of an option that relates to the time remaining in the life of the option. See also intrinsic value.

times covered: (1) the number of times a company's current earnings after tax cover its current dividend; or (2) the number of times a company's current earnings before tax cover its current interest commitment and any prior charges (according to context).

timing difference: a difference between the pre-tax profit and the taxable income caused by an item which is treated differently in a company's accounts from the way in which it is treated under the taxation legislation and which enters the tax calculation in a different financial year - for cxample, transfers to or from the provision for long service leave. Timing differences, as opposed to permanent differences, are always going to be reversed. They lead to the creation of a future tax benefit or a deferred tax liability.

tin: a primary metal used mainly for plating. Chemical symbol: Sn.

titanium: a primary metal, used in the aerospace industry because of its light weight, strength and resistance to corrosion. Chemical symbol: Ti.

title: the right to ownership of land; or the document (the "certificate of title") which evidences such ownership.

toll smelting: contract smelting.

Tobin tax: a proposed tax on all foreign currency transactions. It was first suggested by Professor James Tobin in 1972. His proposal was for a charge of between 0.1% and 1% on the conversion of one currency into another. It was claimed that this would be too low to discourage long term investment, but that it would nevertheless represent a substantial annual rate on transactions which involved buying and selling a currency within a single day, week or month. The tax was intended to have three main purposes:

- to reduce exchange rate volatility by reducing currency speculation
- to raise revenue for international organisations
- to make national economic policies less vulnerable to external shocks.

However, many commentators believe that such a tax, even if it were feasible, would cause more harm than good, by interfering with currency flows for productive purposes, including hedging in the ordinary course of business, and that it might even trigger off a world recession.

In any case, the proposal is probably impracticable, as even if such a tax were to be imposed in all major financial centres then such transactions would just be carried out in other places. Furthermore, whatever the definition of taxable transaction decided on, equivalent transactions using derivatives not caught by that particular definition could easily be used instead.

tonne: a metric unit of mass, 1000 kg; symbol t. Comparable imperial units are the short ton (2000 lb) and the long ton (2240 lb).

tontine: a fund set up by a number of subscribers on the basis that those surviving each year share the income equally until there is only one survivor left, who then receives the entire capital. Other arrangements involving variations of this theme but specfically benefiting the last survivor can also be described as tontines.

TOP: symbol for the Tongan pa anga.

top down: an equity management style which begins with an assessment of the overall economic environment and then makes a general asset allocation decision regarding various sectors of the financial markets and various industries.

top hat plan: a superannuation plan which is limited to a select group of key employees and which provides better benefits than those available to the rest of the staff.

top twenty: a listing of the twenty largest shareholders of a class of shares.

tops and bottoms: charting formations which occur at the upper or lower range of prices respectively. Formations may have tops and bottoms, i.e., a head and shoulders top is an inverted head and shoulders bottom.

torbanite: a black, kerogen-rich coaly substance.

total shareholder return (TSR): the increase in market value of a share together with its dividend over a year, divided by its market price at the beginning of that year, expressed as a percentage, ignoring both income tax and imputation credits.

tracking stock: a distinct series of ordinary shares which participates in the profits of only a defined division of a company rather than in those of the entire enterprise.

trade creditors: see creditors.

trade debtors: see debtors.

trade deficit: the amount by which the value of a country's imports of goods exceeds the value of that country's exports of goods in a period. See also current account deficit.

traded policies: life insurance policies traded on a secondary market. They are sold by policyholders who desire to get more cash than is available on surrender. They are purchased by arms' length investors as very secure high yielding investments, which may also provide the opportunity to make additional windfall gains in the event of the early death of the life insured.

trader: one who buys and sells regularly.

trading stock (balance sheets): finished goods, work in progress and raw materials. Also known as inventory. For tax purposes trading stock can be valued, at the option of the taxpayer, at cost or at market selling value or at its replacement price.

tranche: a large block of securities.

transfer books: see share register.

transfer form: a legal document through which a seller transfers title to securities to a buyer. No longer required for on-market transactions.

transfer of land: a document notifying the change of ownership of land which is forwarded to the Registrar to allow its registration and the Certificate of Title to be suitably amended.

trap: a closed body of rock that is capable of trapping hydrocarbons.

trauma insurance policy: a policy that pays a lump sum in the event of a diagnosed insurable condition, such as a heart attack, a stroke, cancer, Alzheimer's disease, Parkinson's disease, blindness, quadriplegia or major head injuries.

treasury note: a short term government security.

treasury stock: shares in itself owned by a company. In many countries companies usually have the right to be holders of their own shares and to reissue them later on. Of course, a company can always issue brand new shares if it finds that such a cash raising suits its purposes.

trend: a basic tenet of charting, namely, that prices move in trends - primary, secondary or minor. Primary trends are the broader all over movements of the market over a long period of time. Secondary trends cover intermediate declines and rallies that move contrary to the primary trend. Minor trends are brief fluctuations in price that may or may not move with the primary or secondary trends.

trend channel: in charting, a formation. Chartists believe that share prices move within upper and lower limits which form a channel which, in turn, is in the direction of the trend, i.e., uptrend, downtrend or sideways trend.

triangle: in charting, a formation where the upper and lower boundaries converge.

Triassic Period: a period 195 to 230 million years ago.

trillion: originally a billion was a million million and a trillion was a million million million - a coherent pattern. Unfortunately, a different, quite illogical, usage developed in the United States and France and has now taken over. Under this approach, a billion is 1000 million and a trillion is 1000 billion.

true width: an accurate estimate of the width of a seam, stratum or ore body. It does not reflect the vertical length of material encountered but the thickness, bearing in mind the dip of the deposit.

trust: a relationship, based on confidence, under which property is held by and formally vested in one party, known as the "trustee", as its legal owner, but on behalf of other parties who are entitled to the fruits of that ownership - the "beneficiaries" (or "objects") of the trust.

trust account: a bank account maintained by stockbrokers, estate agents, solicitors and others to keep client funds distinct from their own and protected in the event of their own insolvency. A broker is compelled to maintain with his bankers such a trust account and to pay into that account on the date of receipt all monies received from clients against purchases. The funds must be retained in the account until settlement. Where a broker is instructed by a client to retain monies accumulated from the sale of securities those funds must in the absence of any other arrangement also be held in trust.

trust deed: an instrument "signed, sealed and delivered" which sets up a trust and defines its terms; the rules by which a trust may operate. A debenture trust deed sets out the constraints on a company that must be satisfied in order to raise and maintain debenture borrowings.

trust estate: the net assets belonging to a trust.

trust fund: the assets held in trust from time to time; or the related ledger entries.

trust instrument: a deed "signed, sealed and delivered" which sets up a trust and defines its terms.

trust scheme: the equivalent for trusts of a scheme of arrangement (qv) for companies.

trustee: a person who holds property in trust for another; the person who administers a trust in accordance with its trust deed and with the law (and who very often exercises various discretionary powers).

trustee: a person who holds property in trust for another; the person who administers a trust in accordance with its trust deed and with the law (and who very often exercises various discretionary powers).

trustee investment: securities that meet certain statutory requirements and which may be bought by trustees unless this is specifically prohibited by the trust deed.

trustee security: an investment in which a trustee can legally invest unless the relevant trust instrument specifically prevents it.

TRY: symbol for the Thurkih lira.

TSR: abbreviation for total shareholder return.

TTD: symbol for the Trinidad and Tobago dollar.

tungsten: a primary metal used as a ferro alloy to strengthen steel. Chemical symbol: W.

tunnel: an underground passage open to the surface at both ends.

turnover (GST): taxable supplies and GST-free supplies, but not input taxed supplies or supplies unconnected with the enterprise. For property owners this means that *residential* rents are disregarded, while for stock exchange investors it means that dividends and interest and unit trust distributions are disregarded. Turnover is always measured on a GST-exclusive basis.

turnover (stock exchange): the volume of business transacted in a particular company or in the market as a whole.

turnover (trading companies): the amount of a company's sales during a given period; the total amount received by a company in the ordinary course of its business for goods and services supplied by it during a financial year, excluding any inter-group transactions. Deducting all expenses including the net increase in the provisions from this figure gives the profit.

TVM: abbreviation for tax value method.

TWD: symbol for the Taiwan dollar.

TWI: abbreviation for trade weighted index.

uberrimae fidei: of the utmost good faith.

UCA: abbreviation for uniform capital allowance.

UCCC: abbreviation for Uniform Consumer Credit Code.

UCT: abbreviation for Universal Co-ordinated Time (effectively Greenwich Mean Time, GMT)

UIG: abbreviation for Urgent Issues Group.

UKLA: abbreviation for United Kingdom Listing Authority.

ultra vires: beyond the power.

unappropriated profits: the balance in the profit and loss account, profits which have not been distributed to shareholders but which are being retained for use in the operations of a business. Also known as accumulated profits, undistributed profits, retained earnings or plough-back. They form part of the shareholders' funds.

unbundled policy: a contract which separates the life insurance cover and the savings or investment elements, usually allowing the policyholder to select the desired ratio of cover to investment and to vary this ratio from time to time. Administrative charges may be identified separately. The policy may be either investment account or investment-linked.

uncalled capital: see capital (company accounts).

uncalled premium: see capital (company accounts), premium.

unclaimed money: monies which cannot be paid to their rightful owners and which need to be paid over to the government. The usual cause of the problem is the failure of the owner to advise the relevant organisation of a current address. The amounts concerned can be reclaimed by the rightful owners if they ever turn up. Typically, the assets affected include inactive bank accounts; matured fixed deposits, debentures, notes or life insurance policies; dividend or interest payments; repayments of share capital; liquidators' distributions; the cash consideration in compulsory acquisitions under takeovers.

unconditional: see takeover.

unconformity: a surface that truncates and is overlain by a younger strata.

undeducted contributions: contributions paid to a superannuation fund without any income tax deduction being claimed and which, because of this, do not attract any tax when withdrawn. While within the fund such contributions generate investment income taxed at the relatively low superannuation tax rate.

undeducted purchase price: that portion of the cost of an annuity purchased from a life company which has not attracted a tax deduction or rebate in the hands of the recipient. Annuity payments can be split notionally into a portion representing a return of capital and a portion representing interest. The former, to the extent that it relates to an undeducted purchase price, is not taxable.

under-rent: the amount per annum by which the actual rent received under a property lease and fixed for a lengthy period falls short of the current market rent.

underbidder: the person who makes the second-highest bid at an auction.

undercapitalised: lacking sufficient capital resources to expand. A company in such a situation needs to either increase its debts or increase its share capital.

underlay and underlie: inclined shaft following a lode down dip.

underlet: let at a rental below the current market level.

underlying inflation: inflation as measured by the Consumer Price Index, but with adjustments to eliminate irregular influences and thus better reflect the trend of price changes on an ongoing basis.

underlying security: the shares subject to purchase on the exercise of an option.

underperform: said of a share that decreases in market value more than the market as a whole or that increases in market value less than the market as a whole. Opposite of outperform.

underwriter (stock exchange): an organisation that for a fee guarantees a minimum level of subscriptions to a share or debt issue. If public subscriptions fail to reach this minimum level then the underwriter takes up the shortfall. Underwriters often have sub-underwriters who share the risk. If the underwriting fee for an issue is larger than normal then this factor should serve as a warning to potential investors that subscribing to the issue may lead to losses.

underwriting (insurance): the process by which an insurer determines whether or not and on what basis it will accept an application for insurance.

undistributed profits: the balance in the profit and loss account, profits which have not been distributed to shareholders but which are being retained for use in the operations of a business. Also known as accumulated profits, unappropriated profits, retained earnings or plough-back. They form part of the shareholders' funds.

unfranked dividends: dividends without attaching franking credits under the dividend imputation system.

Uniform Consumer Credit Code (UCCC): a statutory code in Australia under uniform State and Territory legislation governing loans that are predominately for personal, domestic or household use (as distinct from loans for investment purposes).

Uniform Resource Locator (URL): the unique address of a single web page or of some other file on the Internet.

unimproved value: the notional value of land as though it had no buildings erected on it (cf. improved value).

unissued capital: the authorised capital of a company less its issued capital. See also capital (company accounts).

unit trusts: vehicles formed to hold (usually) a wide range of investments. They involve a trust fund which is normally divided into a large number of equal parts called "units", beneficially owned by the various investors who acquire them for cash and who thereby become "unitholders".

Unit trusts can provide small investors with diversification. Unit trusts may be fixed trusts, which have a defined range of investment alternatives, or, more commonly, flexible trusts which have the ability to invest in a wide range of securities. Every trust has a manager who is responsible for the trust's investment strategy and a trustee which holds the trust's assets and distributes the income to unitholders; under recent legislative changes the two roles can now be combined, the responsible entity (RE).

Some unit trusts are listed on the stock exchange and their units can be bought and sold in the same way as shares. Others are unlisted and units can be bought from or sold back to the manager at a price related to their asset backing.

unit-linked policy: a contract with benefits expressed in units, each representing a share in an investment portfolio. The unit price fluctuates with market values and allows for investment income.

unitisation: the combination of adjacent leases for efficient operation.

universal life: a flexible life insurance policy, which combines term insurance and an investment vehicle.

unlisted property trust: a unit trust with the bulk of its assets invested in property and which is not listed on the stock exchange.

unlisted shares: shares in companies that are not available for sale through the stock market.

unofficial short term money market: see short term money market.

unparliamentary language: abusive words which the standing orders deem to be inappropriate during the debate at a meeting.

unrealised capital gain or loss: the difference between the present market value of an asset still held and its original cost. Only realised capital gains attract a capital gains tax liability.

unsecured: a debt security which is not backed by a charge over any assets and which ranks after secured debts in the event of liquidation. However, it ranks before all forms of equity and before any debt subordinated to it. See also debenture.

unsecured creditor: a creditor who is unable to rely on any specific asset owned by a debtor in the case of any failure to pay or any other breach in a loan agreement. In the case of an insolvency all unsecured creditors whether trade creditors or investors rank equally. They rank after secured creditors but ahead of shareholders.

unsecured note: an unsecured fixed interest security.

up-tick: see tick.

uplift factor: a statutory figure formerly used for calculating provisional tax and designed to reflect income growth due to inflation.

upside potential: the perceived likelihood that the price of a stock will rise. See also downside risk.

Uptick Rule: the requirement that a short sale must be made at a price equal to or higher than the previous sale price of the relevant share.

uranium: a primary metal used in the nuclear industry. Can be reprocessed and upgraded to plutonium, a more efficient source of energy. Chemical symbol: U.

uranium oxide: the principal ore of uranium.

URL: abbreviation for Uniform Resource Locator.

USD: symbol for the United States dollar.

use and enjoyment: a clause in a will giving a beneficiary the right to use and enjoy an asset such as a residence for life or for some other period but without ever owning that asset, which remains under the control of a trustee; a sort of life interest.

vacant possession: property not occupied by a tenant or subject to a lease.

valuation (property): a written report by a registered valuer setting out his estimate of the market value of a property. See also capitalisation method and summation method.

valuation (stock): the value placed on stock in a company's balance sheet. For tax purposes trading stock can be valued, at the option of the taxpayer, at cost or at market selling value or at its replacement price.

value added: the market price of goods sold less the cost of materials and services purchased to produce those goods.

value added tax (VAT): a tax based upon the value added to products and services.

value investor: an investor who typically seeks to acquire assets priced below their intrinsic worth, especially where these provide a high immediate return, even if there is little prospect of capital growth beyond inflation. Contrast growth investor.

vanilla: plain, without embellishment; a financial product without any bells or whistles.

variable costing: see direct costing.

variable costs: costs which vary with the level of output.

variable rate loan: a loan with the interest rate made subject to periodical changes (up or down) in line with market changes or according to some formula.

VAT: abbreviation for value added tax.

VEB: symbol for the Venezuelan bolivar.

vein: a form of mineralisation essentially similar to a lode, having a more or less regular development in length, width and depth.

veinlet: very narrow vein, with limited length and depth, usually found in groups.

vendor: the seller of any property.

vendor shares: shares issued by a company as consideration for the acquisition of property from associated parties, usually at the time of a float. There are restrictions on trading such securities immediately after a public issue. Also called founder shares.

vendor terms: the sale of a property on the basis that the purchaser pays only part of the price on settlement, the balance being treated as a loan from the vendor for an agreed period, secured by the property, and often at a concessional interest rate, as an inducement to enter into the deal.

venture capital: investment in more risky industrial companies, often those engaged in high technology.

venture capital: money invested in an enterprise offering the expectation of above-average growth and a high rate of return, but also presenting a high degree of risk. Often a major project engaged in the high technology sector and/or seeking to exploit new patents is involved, with investors teaming up with an entrepreneur to provide start-up funds to an unlisted company.

venture fund: a managed fund specialising in taking equity positions in venture capital situations, usually on a portfolio basis in order to minimise risk and often also providing management know-how to the companies in receipt of the investment funds.

verbatim: exactly as spoken.

vertical integration: the acquisition by a company of other companies which are the source of its raw materials and/or the outlets for its finished products. Captive markets can produce greater stability as well as greater profits.

vertical monopoly: a trading situation where the entire production and distribution process for a product is owned by the one organisation.

vesting (superannuation): the conferring on employees of an irreversible right to superannuation benefits being paid for by their employers, this right becoming available on the cessation of employment.

vibrating table: machine used to concentrate heavy minerals.

virtual bank: a bank licensed as such under the banking legislation but without any physical branches. Such a bank requires all transactions with it to be made electronically. This can usually be done either by touch tone telephone or over the Internet. Instead of being made over the counter all deposits and withdrawals have to be made by means of transfers from and to accounts maintained by customers with normal banks. Cheque facilities are not available. This means that the expense rate of a virtual bank is relatively low, a factor reflected in its fee basis. This feature also allows a virtual bank to pay higher than normal interest rates on call and other deposits, but with the same degree of security as any other comparable institution which holds a banking licence.

viscosity: the measure of the ease with which oils flow.

vital statistics: demographic data on births, deaths, marriages and divorces.

voices: the voting on a question before the chair by saying "aye" or "no".

volatility: the ease with which a substance vaporises.

volcanics: rocks produced at or near the surface by the action of a volcano.

voluntary liquidation: see liquidation.

vote of thanks: a motion which formally acknowledges the appreciation of those present at a meeting to a person for some past service.

vug: a small cavity within an ore deposit.

vulture fund: a fund that specialises in buying securities at bargain prices in distressed situations - for example, bonds that are in or near default and shares of companies that are in or near bankruptcy.

VUV: symbol for the Vanuatu vatu.

w: abbreviation for warrants. Figures after the letter indicate the calendar year of expiry.

WACC: abbreviation for weighted average cost of capital. See cost of capital.

wage cost index: a measure of the movement in the wage and salary cost of a fixed basket of jobs over time.

Wall Street: the street in which the New York Stock Exchange is located. The term is used as a synonym for that exchange.

warehousing: the practice of buying and holding shares by one company on behalf of another.

warrants: derivatives which are effectively long dated call or put options created by a bank or some other *warrant issuer* over the ordinary shares of a listed company or some such. Each series of warrants has a clearly defined *exercise price* and *expiry date* (making all warrants in that series completely interchangeable). Warrants over shares would normally be *deliverable,* meaning that settlement involves the transfer of the underlying security. Warrants over currencies, commodities or indices need to be *cash settled.*

warranty: an assurance of quality on an item sold. Breach of warranty allows a buyer to claim damages but the contract of sale is not invalidated.

wash: a bed of alluvial gravels, etc., containing metals or minerals.

wash sales: purchases and sales of shares where there is no change to their beneficial ownership.

waste: barren rock or material that is too low grade to be economic.

waste to ore ratio: see overburden to ore ratio.

wasting asset: an asset which diminishes in value with use or over time.

water drive: the pressure of water on a reservoir, which forces the flow of hydrocarbons.

water table: the upper surface of a zone of water saturation.

watering the capital: issues of new shares made other than on a pro rata basis to existing shareholders and particularly placements offered to outsiders at a price which is less than either the market value or the net tangible asset backing of equivalent existing shares. These have the effect of diluting the equity of the current investors in the company and for this reason are often regarded as immoral.

WCI: abbreviation for wage cost index.

wealth effect: a phenomenon that results in spending by individuals going up at a faster rate than their after tax incomes in times when economic conditions are favourable. People tend to spend money when they think that they can afford to do so. This is a function of their total actual or perceived net asset position - it is not just a function of the money sitting in their wallets or in a bank account. If their shares and their real estate have appreciated then mentally they feel justified in spending the profits even if they exist only on paper and are not held in a liquid form. People also have regard to the balances they hold in their superannuation funds. When they need cash they borrow - and lenders are only too happy to co-operate, especially if they can get security over such assets. Unfortunately, all this also works in reverse. In a slump, asset values fall and people start spending less - thus accentuating the slump. Not only do incomes fall, but also the proportion of incomes being spent goes down as well. Tax refunds, for example, which might have led to spending on consumption items during a boom are instead used to reduce a home mortgage loan or credit card debt.

wealth tax: a tax levied on a taxpayer's assets less liabilities, usually above a threshold.

weathering: the group of processes, for example, action of air, rain, water, etc., whereby rocks on exposure to the weather change in character, decay, and finally crumble into soil.

web log (or blog): a web site created by a single individual as a form of public diary. Unlike a wiki, it does not allow other users to change the contents, although they can add their own comments.

wedge: a chart formation in which the price fluctuations are confined within converging straight lines. It differs from a triangle in that both boundary lines slope either up or down.

weighted average: see mean.

well completion: the activities and methods necessary to prepare a well for the production of oil and gas; the method by which a flow line for hydrocarbons is established between the reservoir and the surface.

well logging: the recording of information about subsurface geological formations. Logging methods include records kept by the driller, mud and cuttings analyses, core analysis, drill-stem tests, and electric and radioactivity procedures.

well stimulation: any of several operations used to increase the production of a well. See also acidising, formation fracturing.

wellhead: the equipment installed at the surface of the wellbore. A wellhead includes such equipment as the casinghead, tubing head, and Christmas tree.

wet: a supporter of some degree of government regulation of the economy, including protectionism and social welfare spending; an opponent of hard-line economic rationalism. Opposite of a dry.

wet gas: natural gas that contains oil vapours.

wet mining: mining methods that involve the use of water to separate the ore from the gangue. The principal methods are dredging, panning, sluicing and hydraulic mining. Usually used on alluvial deposits of metals with high specific gravity.

whisper numbers: unofficial forecasts of corporate earnings.

white knight: a person or company willing to acquire (on the market or by placement) a significant stake in the offeree company in a hostile takeover situation - a stake which, it is hoped, will be sufficiently large to deter or block the unwelcome bidder. In practice, such support has often proved to be a mixed blessing. While it may succeed in frustrating the original bid, at a later stage the white knight may become a bidder himself. Alternatively, such a holding may become the springboard for some other bidder to whom it passes in due course.

white label product or service: a product or service produced by one company (the producer) that other companies (the marketers) then rebrand to make it appear as if they had made it.

white paper: an authoritative report, especially a parliamentary paper enunciating government policy. Contrast green paper.

whole of life policy: a policy under which the sum insured, plus any bonuses, is paid only on the death (or total and permanent disability, if applicable) of the life insured.

widows' and orphans' stock: a share regarded as a particularly safe investment.

wiki: a collaborative web site that users can easily modify and hopefully improve by editing entries, usually without restriction. Compare web log.

wildcat: a well drilled in an area where no oil or gas has been discovered. With present day exploration methods and equipment, about one wildcat out of every six proves to be productive although not necessarily profitable.

will: a formal document governing the disposition of property owned by a person, to take effect on that person's death.

will trust: a trust set up by will.

winding up: the operation of ceasing a company's business by a liquidator - the conversion of the company's assets into cash and the payment of that cash to creditors and, if there is any surplus after that, to shareholders. Most liquidations are compulsory and relate to insolvent situations. However, a liquidation can also be voluntary and merely represent a reorganisation of a group structure. Defunct companies with no assets or liabilities can be struck off without being formally liquidated.

window dressing: the practice of taking financial actions immediately prior to a balance date in order to give a company balance sheet a more favourable appearance. Some of the more common practices are running down stock in the month prior to the balance date or borrowing money just prior to the balance date. Often these transactions are reversed immediately after the balance date.

winze: a vertical or inclined opening similar to a shaft, except that it starts inside the mine.

wirebar copper: a final form of refined copper that has been shaped into a form convenient for drawing.

with bonuses policy: a policy with the right to share in a life insurance company's surplus.

with profits policy: a policy with the right to share in a life insurance company's surplus.

withdrawal of motion: the removal of a motion from consideration by a meeting before it has been voted on.

withholding tax: a flat rate of income tax deducted at source from dividends, interest or royalties earned by residents of one country from a source in another country.

wolframite: iron manganese tungstate, an ore of tungsten.

working capital: a measure of the short run solvency of a company. It is the excess of current assets over current liabilities.

working capital ratio: a measure of liquidity, the current assets divided by the current liabilities. Also known as the current ratio. Contrast liquid assets ratio.

working interest: a term applied to a joint venture interest where one or more parties are required to contribute to the operating expenses. Opposite of free carried interest.

World Wide Web (WWW or "web"): the Internet information retrieval system which originated from the CERN high energy physics laboratories in Geneva, Switzerland. The information on WWW pages is usually represented using the HyperText Markup Language (HTML) (see above), enabling computer users everywhere, when connected to the Internet, to obtain ready access to other web documents. A special program, known as a "browser" (see above), is employed by users for this purpose.

wrap account: a service which for a fee consolidates the records relating to all of a client's portfolio investments - listed shares and managed funds. Statements summarising transactions, tax return data (including capital gains) and valuations can be obtained periodically or on demand - by mail, by fax, through keypad telephones or over the Internet. Clients can deal with a broker of their choice. See also master fund.

writ of mandamus: an order issued by a court requiring a person (for example, the chairman of a meeting) to carry out that person's duties in accordance with the law.

write-down: the accounting process of reducing the book value of an asset to reflect lost value. The term is also used in reference to capital reductions.

write-off: the accounting process of reducing the book value of an asset to reflect lost value. The term is also used in reference to capital reductions.

writer: a person who provides newly created options to an original purchaser (or *taker*) for a consideration (price) arrived at by market forces and called the *premium*. Synthetic options have been created for a number of listed companies the shares of which are very actively traded on the stock exchange. They involve two standardised contract terms, namely a fixed *exercise price* (also called the *striking price*) and a fixed *expiry date* (also called the *expiration date* or the *maturity date*). They also involve a *standard quantity* (such as the 1000 shares of the underlying company).

WST: symbol for the Western Samoan tala.

WTO: abbreviation for World Trade Organization (previously the General Agreement on Tariffs and Trade (GATT)).

xc: stock exchange quotation symbol for ex return of capital.

XCD: symbol for the East Caribbean dollar.

xd: stock exchange quotation symbol for ex dividend (qv).

xe: stock exchange quotation symbol for ex entitlement.

xi: stock exchange quotation symbol for ex interest.

XPF: symbol for the French Pacific franc.

xq: stock exchange quotation symbol for ex off-market buy-back.

xr: stock exchange quotation symbol for ex rights.

xz: stock exchange quotation symbol for ex priority.

year on year: a company's results for one year compared with the results for the previous year.

yellowcake: the end product of mining, milling and concentrating uranium oxide.

yield (investments generally): the return from an investment relative to the cost of the investment, expressed as a percentage per annum. In some contexts "yield" refers to the compound interest rate of return per annum over a period, in other words, it is the net rate of interest at which the sum invested equals the present value of all income payments plus the present value of all capital payments. This is also know as the internal rate of return.

yield (mining): recovery, as distinct from grade.

yield (property): the return from an investment in property. The gross yield is obtained by dividing the rent per annum by the price and multiplying by 100. The net yield is obtained by dividing the rent less the outgoings apart from interest per annum by the price and multiplying by 100.

yield (shares): the dividend return from an investment in shares. It is calculated by dividing a company's dividends per share (in cents per share) by the current market price of the share (also expressed in cents) and multiplying by 100. It should, however, be noted that dividing a historical dividend figure by a current market price can be misleading. The apparent annual return from ordinary shares as measured by the dividend yield is not at all comparable with the return from fixed interest investments, as the true return from shares includes a capital growth element.

yield curve: a graphical representation of the varying interest yields to redemption available on fixed interest securities at any particular time. The duration to maturity is shown on the horizontal axis and the redemption yield is shown on the vertical axis. Normally the shorter dated securities have a lower yield than the longer dated securities. From time to time this pattern is reversed; this is known as an inverse yield curve and indicates the market's belief that rates will fall in the medium term.

yield to redemption: the actual return obtainable from a redeemable fixed interest investment allowing for both the remaining interest payments and the difference between the purchase price (which may or may not be at par) and the redemption or maturity value. It is the internal rate of return on the cash flow from the investment. In contrast, the flat yield - in other words, the coupon divided by the market price - does not give a useful indication of the worth of a fixed interest security.

YoY: abbreviation for year on year.

ZAR: symbol for the South African rand.

zero coupon stock: a fixed interest security which does not make periodical interest payments. It is issued at a deep discount to its redemption or maturity price (usually styled par). Investors get their return from the difference between the discounted price and the redemption price.

zero population growth: a population in equilibrium, with a growth rate of zero, achieved when births plus immigration exactly equal deaths plus emigration.

zero rated: see GST-free.

zero sum game: a situation where for every winner there is a corresponding loser and for every rupee gained by one player there is a rupee lost by another player. Examples include the two parties to option deals or futures contracts.

zinc: a primary metal the low corrosion properties of which make it ideal for diecasting and galvanising. Chemical symbol: Zn.

zircon: a mineral, the principal ore of zirconium.

zirconium: a primary metal used in the nuclear industry for linings. Chemical symbol: Zi.

zone: an area or region which is distinct from the surrounding rock either because of a difference in the type of structure of rocks, or because of mineralisation.

zone of oxidation: the upper part of a mineral deposit that has become oxidised.

zoning: the control of land use under planning legislation. Separate areas or "zones" can be designated as residential, business, office, light industrial, general industrial, offensive industrial, special use, and so on. Land in each zone can then be used only for purposes specified as appropriate for that particular zone.

APPENDIX A

Some Internet Links of Interest to Investors

finmin.nic.in: This is the Ministry of Finance, Government of India's official website. The ministry of finance governs the entire fiscal system of the Government of India. It regulates all the issues pertaining to economy and finance for developmental programmes of the country.

rbi.org.in: This is the official website of Reserve Bank of India (RBI), the central bank of India. RBI regulates the issue of Bank Notes with a view to secure monetary stability and to operate the currency and credit system of the country.

sebi.gov.in: This website belongs to the Securities and Exchange Board of India (SEBI). This statutory body was set up by the government of India to promote the development of the securities market in India.

irdaindia.org: This website belongs to Insurance Regulatory and Development Authority (IRDA). This body was established by Parliament to regulate and protect the interests of the policyholders, and to ensure orderly growth of the life and non-life insurance industry in India.

bseindia.com: This website belongs to Bombay Stock Exchange (BSE). Located in Mumbai, BSE is the oldest stock exchange in Asia and has the greatest number of listed companies in the world, with 4800 listed as of August 2009.

nseindia.com: This website belongs to the National Stock Exchange of India (NSE). Set up by the leading financial institutions at the behest of the Government of India, NSE operates in debt market, capital market and in derivatives.

fedai.org.in: This website belongs to the association of banks dealing in foreign exchange in India. Its frames rules governing the conduct of inter-bank foreign exchange business among banks and interacts with RBI for reforms and development of forex market.

ccilindia.com: This site belongs to Clearing Corporation of India Limited (CCIL). Established with the initiative of Reserve bank of India, this body was set up for providing exclusive clearing and settlement for transactions in money, government securities and foreign exchange.

APPENDIX B

Selected Currency Symbols

Symbol	Currency
AED	United Arab Emirates dirham
ATS	Austrian schilling
AUD	Australian dollar
BDT	Bangladeshi taka
BEF	Belgian franc
BHD	Bahraini dinar
BND	Brunei dollar
BRL	Brazilian real
CAD	Canadian dollar
CHF	Swiss franc
CNY	Chinese renminbi
COP	Colombian peso
CYP	Cyprus pound
DEM	German mark
DKK	Danish krone
ESP	Spanish peseta
EUR	Euro
FIM	Finnish markka
FJD	Fijian dollar
FRF	French franc
GBP	British pound
GRD	Greek drachma
HKD	Hong Kong dollar
IDR	Indonesian rupiah

IEP Irish punt
INR Indian rupee
IQD Iraqi dinar
IRR Iranian rial
ISK Icelandic krona
ITL Italian lira
JPY Japanese yen
KRW Korean won
KWD Kuwaiti dinar
LKR Sri Lankan rupee
MTL Maltese lira
MXN Mexican peso
MYR Malaysian ringgit
NLG Dutch guilder
NOK Norwegian krone
NPR Nepali rupee
NZD New Zealand dollar
OMR Omani rial
PGK Papua New Guinea kina
PHP Phillipines peso
PKR Pakistani rupee
PTE Portuguese escudo
QAR Qatari riyal
SAR Saudi riyal
SBD Solomon Islands dollar
SEK Swedish krona
SGD Singapore dollar
THB Thai baht
TOP Tongan pa anga
TRY Turkish lira
TTD Trinidad and Tobago dollar
TWD Taiwan dollar
USD United States dollar
VEB Venezuelan bolivar
VUV Vanuatu vatu
WST Western Samoan tala
XCD East Caribbean dollar
XPF French Pacific franc
ZAR South African rand

Source: ISO 4217 - Currency Codes

Tailpiece

THE OTHER SIDE OF THE COIN: DO INVESTORS USE METAPHORS?

Financial journalists use colourful metaphors all the time - for example, share prices don't just go up or down - they either "skyrocket" or "go into a tailspin". Takeover offers are made "with much fanfare".

New chief executives "take the helm". Companies are either "in the black" or "in the red". Some groups make profits or losses large enough to be referred to as "telephone numbers".

Investors are perhaps more conscious of some other terms, as when they "burn their fingers" (lose money by foolish speculation) or when they are asked to "throw good money after bad" (waste further money in a vain attempt to recover their losses).

Little wonder that some of them prefer to "turn in their chips" (convert their assets into cash) after discovering that all investments are not "money for jam" (gains easily earned) and that some of their securities are no longer "above the water" (in excess of their cost price).

Brokers will know clients who try to "fly a kite" (issue uncovered cheques in the hope of covering them before clearance).

COMMERCE

Many expressions from the world of commerce have come into wider usage - for instance:

- "to be A1 at Lloyds" (to be in perfect order)
- "to give someone a blank cheque" (to give a person unlimited authority)
- "the other side of the coin" (the arguments for the opposite point of view)
- "to show dividends" (to be successful)
- "to be below par" (to be less than the desired standard)
- "a Rolls Royce solution" (a high quality but excessively expensive way of doing something)
- "it does not add up" (this does not make sense).

Political allusions to spending taxpayers' funds occur in expressions such as "to pork barrel" and "to engage in pump priming".

MONEY

The actual word "money" used in its literal sense is found in the partly-figurative phrases "to see the colour of someone's money", "to have money burning a hole in one's pocket", "putting one's money where one's mouth is", "money down the drain" and "the money is rolling in".

When a purely figurative expression for "money" is desired, words such as "pocket", "purse" or "penny" are often used, as in "to have deep pockets", "to line one's pocket", "to button up one's purse" and "to cost a pretty penny".

Sometimes colors are used in conjunction with the word "dollar" to convey particular ideas - for example:

- "pink dollars" (the profits generated from marketing goods and services to the homosexual community)
- "blue dollars" (the profits generated from the sale of soft pornography)

- "gray dollars" (the profits generated from marketing goods and services to older persons).

MINING AND OIL

The price of gold does not always "go through the roof". However, investment in the mining and oil industry has led to a number of useful everyday metaphors, such as:

- "to pan out" (to succeed)
- "to stake a claim" (to indicate one's desire to obtain something)
- "to strike pay dirt" (to become successful)
- "a goldmine" (a source of much wealth or of many facts)
- "to get the good oil" (to receive useful, reliable and timely information).

DECIMAL CURRENCY

Strange things happened when Australia's sterling currency was decimalised in 1966. Phrases such as "in for a penny, in for a pound", "the penny dropped", "a ha'p'orth of tar", "penny pinching" and the ungrammatical "he doesn't have two pennies to rub together" remained unchanged.

On the other hand, "to throw in one's six pennies' worth" became "to throw in one's two cents' worth", while "to have two bob each way" was converted to the version "to have fifty cents each way" - hardly close decimal equivalents.

Similarly, expressions involving imperial distances or weights do not always get metricated - for example:

- "to drain every ounce out of something"
- "to go the extra mile"
- "a yardstick"
- "a milestone"
- "not to give an inch"
- "to stand out a mile"

- "to get mileage out of some matter" and
- "to inch forward".

Of course, everyone with even 28.3 grams of common sense realises that exact conversions would not be appropriate in all circumstances.

- (Note: The above essay has drawn on material in the author's popular book, *Renton's Metaphors*.)